THE ESSAYS
of
MARK
VAN
DOREN
(1924–1972)

Mark Van Doren giving a reading in New York City the summer before his death. One of the last public photographs taken. Photographer Daniel McPartlin. *Courtesy of the Department of Parks and Recreation, New York City.*

THE ESSAYS
of
MARK
VAN
DOREN
(1924–1972)

Selected, with an Introduction,
by
WILLIAM CLAIRE

Contributions in American Studies, Number 47

GREENWOOD PRESS
WESTPORT, CONNECTICUT • LONDON, ENGLAND

Library of Congress Cataloging in Publication Data

Van Doren, Mark, 1894-1972.
  The essays of Mark Van Doren (1924-1972)

  (Contributions in American studies ; no. 47
ISSN 0084-9227)
  "A checklist of principal prose works by Mark Van
Doren": p.
  "A bibliographic checklist of selected introductions,
prefaces, and miscellaneous books edited, or with prose
contributions by Mark Van Doren": p.
  Includes index.
  I. Claire, William F.
PS3543.A557A16   1980   809   79-8411
ISBN 0-313-22098-0

Library of Congress Catalog Card Number: 79-8411
ISBN: 0-313-22098-0
ISSN: 0084-9227

First published in 1980

Greenwood Press
A division of Congressional Information Service, Inc.
88 Post Road West, Westport, Connecticut 06881

Printed in the United States of America

10 9 8 7 6 5 4 3 2 1

Copyright Acknowledgments

publishers. "Let the Movies Be Natural" is reprinted from *The American Scholar* Volume 6, No. 4, copyright © 1937 by the United Chapters of Phi Beta Kappa. By permission of the publishers.

American Academy of Arts and Letters: "John Berryman" was first published in the "Proceedings of the American Academy of Arts and Letters and the National Institute of Arts and Letters," Second Series, Number 23.

Encyclopaedia Britannica, Inc., for selections from "Great Books of the Twentieth Century in Literature" which first appeared in *The Great Ideas Today,* 1969. Reprinted by permission of Encyclopaedia Britannica, Inc.

"August 1914" reprinted with permission. © 1973 The Saturday Evening Post Company.

New Directions, Inc.: The Introduction by Mark Van Doren to *Selected Poems of Thomas Merton.* Copyright © 1959 by New Directions Publishing Corporation. Reprinted by permission of New Directions Publishing Corporation.

Several essays and reviews were collected originally in *The Private Reader,* first published by Henry Holt & Company, 1942, and © 1942 by Mark Van Doren, and *The Happy Critic,* published by Hill & Wang, 1961, and copyright © 1961 by Mark Van Doren.

The essay "How Praise A World" was first set and bound by Jene Lyon, in Santa Fe, New Mexico, at his Lightning Tree Press.

Mortimer Adler, for permission to quote from his essay on Mark Van Doren that originally appeared in *Voyages,* Vol. 5, (Nos. 1-4), Washington, D.C., 1973.

Various acknowledgments of first appearances are included in the three sections in notes by the editor, with the following exceptions: "The Possible Importance of Poetry" was first read at the University of Michigan, as the Hopwood Lecture, 1951; the "Artist and

FOR ALL MARK'S STUDENTS—
PAST,
PRESENT,
FUTURE.

CONTENTS

How Praise A World? A Mark Van Doren Miscellany

ACKNOWLEDGMENTS

First and foremost, I want to acknowledge the assistance of the Van Doren family. From the very beginning, Dorothy Van Doren has done everything imaginable to answer my questions and make available material that I might otherwise have missed. Both Charles, at the outset, and John Van Doren, in some crucial later stages, have been similarly helpful.

Many other individuals offered advice and encouragement. I think of Roger Hecht, who always encourages me and Robert Zmuda, Astere Claeyssens, a scholar with extraordinary editorial judgment and knowledge about Mark Van Doren, Robert Walker, and Doris Grumbach, among others. Four former students of Mark Van Doren's, who while not direct participants in this volume, have been continually in my thoughts on this and all previous Van Doren studies. They are Robert Lax, Daniel Hoffman, John Tagliabue, and the late Thomas Merton. And I cannot forget that Patricia Westlein convinced me, many years ago, to do what I was reticent to do—keep in personal touch with my favorite teacher.

The manuscript could not have been completed without the early assistance of Lorraine Middleton and others. In the final days, S. Tobie Hewitt came to my rescue with especially generous help and enthusiastic spirit. And, for a few blissful days in autumn at the MacDowell Colony, I was able to think about this project and the introduction without interruptions.

Finally, I have been conscious that these are Mark Van Doren's essays. Rereading them has been a source of continuing joy and delight.

WILLIAM CLAIRE
Spring 1979
Washington, D.C.

INTRODUCTION

Mark Van Doren's distinguished career as a poet, fiction writer, and playwright was inseparably bound with his role as a teacher of literature and man of letters. His reputation was established first as a critic and scholar, editor and anthologist, although in the last thirty years of his life he did not consider himself a formal critic. There was, however, a continuing demand for his critical views in a variety of public forums.

In the early 1920s and 1930s, Mark Van Doren's name became synonomous in the public mind with intelligent, humane criticism while at the same time being celebrated in academia both here and abroad with the publication, at an early age, of full-scale books on Thoreau, Dryden, and Edwin Arlington Robinson, all written within ten years of his graduate studies at the University of Illinois and Columbia.

A prolific contributor to academic and scholarly journals all of his life, a literary editor of *The Nation* from 1924 to 1928, a critic whose later books on Hawthorne, Shakespeare, and others reaffirmed his reputation as a scholar, together with such books as *The Noble Voice: A Study of Ten Great Poems* and his extremely influential *Liberal Education,* Mark Van Doren not only lived the life of the mind but managed to write an astonishing number of books of his own and to assist in many others.

While the card files of the Library of Congress list over 100 titles that he was associated with, either as principal writer, editor, or contributor, Mark Van Doren's books of essays are out of print, and the majority of essays in this collection appear in now difficult-to-obtain editions. The purpose of this volume is to provide a representative selection of his essays under one cover and to demonstrate the range of his literary scholarship, his particular style, his views of criticism, and his opinion of writers ranging from Shakespeare to Solzhenitsyn.

Mark Van Doren's critical approach was consistent with his belief in an ancient and now abandoned notion that a poet made statements and gave opinions as a professional on the theory that a civilized audience existed to hear them. The principal themes of his prose, enveloped as they were in his creative endeavors, were the relationships of comedy and tragedy, which he found constantly reoccurring in literature. His rapture for learning, his love for the great books, and a seeming ability to read and absorb more than most mortal beings and then make intuitive judgments symbolized his career as a critic and man of letters.

The questions he asked often seemed deceptively simple on the surface:

What is a given poem about? What happens in it? What exists in it? If too little of the world is in it, why is that? If all of the world is there, by what miracle has this been done? Is tragedy or comedy at work, and what is the difference between those two, and what resemblance? Are the facts of life accounted for in the unique way that poetry accounts for them, and is this poem something therefore that any man should read? Does its author know more, not less, than most men know? Such seem to me the greatest questions, though they are not regularly asked by criticism. . . .[1]

He was constantly seeking, with a simultaneous swiftness and lightness of mind—a modern Socratic juggler of paradox—for possible answers to immemorial questions posed by literature. He frequently admitted that ultimate solutions were not likely to be found, but said that the "best men are those who, knowing this, still listen for the truth. It is as old as Creation, as new as the infant who first saw light this morning.''[2]

As a critic, Van Doren resisted obfuscation, though he discussed the most formidable subjects. He seemed naturally equipped, out of a lifetime of humanistic learning, to clarify his positions with a contemporary sureness of manner that, while deeply imbued in Western civilization and scholarship, seemed to suggest an ideal Eastern wisdom. For many readers and students through the years he did become, clearly against his wishes, a kind of Buddha figure whose passionate intelligence presumed a generous response from all people of learning and discernment. Without any trace of condescension, he had a rare capacity to deal with any subject as though it were the only subject that mattered. His was the ultimate seriousness of an enlightened mind at play and one that was, simultaneously, centered on its subject matter.

One of his former students, Mortimer Adler, has captured the quality of his critical approach, noting,

his exploration of an idea was always within its boundaries. When an idea captured his mind, he surrendered himself completely to the vision it offered him. Penetrating a great idea's outer envelope, he moved quickly from its surface to its center in order to grasp the transforming view that it gave him of everything upon which it threw light. His mind, once it became enraptured of an idea and while the idea lasted, experienced the same pleasures, almost sensuous in quality, that his senses delighted in when they explored some natural object. Sense and intellect were so united in him, and so fused by his sense of powers, that the concrete individuality of something lovingly apprehended by sense quickly acquired the universality of an idea; and, correspondingly, the abstract universality of an idea that fascinated him soon turned into something so concrete and individual that he could talk about it as if he were in contact with it through all his senses.[3]

Mark Van Doren's earliest and most important personal influences were his brother Carl Van Doren, who preceded him at both the University of Illinois and Columbia, their literature teacher at Illinois, Stuart Sherman, and his lifelong friend, Joseph Wood Krutch, with whom he traveled to England and France in 1919 and 1920. Van Doren has attested to these influences in a variety of public places. Speaking at the University of Illinois thirty-six years after he completed his studies there, Van Doren called Sherman "the finest teacher I ever had anywhere."[4] What he said about Sherman is worth recalling for the light it sheds on Van Doren, and for its almost uncanny similarity to public testimony frequently given to Van Doren himself as a teacher.

The prime determinant behind Sherman's role as teacher revolved, Van Doren noted, around

one reason in the end: the man was the subject, the subject was the man. Whatever he taught—Shakespeare, Matthew Arnold, Emerson, Carlyle— seemed to be of the deepest personal interest to him: an interest so natural in its depth, so convincing in its force, that I could think it only a sort of accident that he was teaching me what he knew. He knew it anyway. It was his pleasure to do so; indeed it was his very life, which I had the good luck to be living with him. The whole nature of man stated itself in every sentence he spoke; he could not have concealed himself had he tried, and he was not trying. Not that it was himself he labored to deliver; it was, of course, his subject, but somehow his subject always arrived by way of him.[5]

Van Doren's first full-length critical study on Thoreau was presented first as his master's thesis, at the University of Illinois, and then published by Houghton Mifflin, in 1916. Considered a remarkable achievement for an M.A. student, the book was re-printed fifty years later. A leading contemporary Thoreau scholar, Carl Hovde, classified it as "distinguished by his characteristic power—attention to the moral life of literary matters" and as a book that "bound together" Thoreau's life "not only as a man and moralist but as a craftsman and thinker." The book became, as Hovde observed, "one of the earliest modern studies of Thoreau."[6]

His doctoral thesis on John Dryden was published by Harcourt, Brace & Howe (1920) shortly after completion of his Columbia studies. As a young scholar at the outset of his career, about to establish a lasting relationship with Columbia, he could not have anticipated the attention the Dryden book would receive. A lauda-tory review, in the *Times Literary Supplement,* was a principal factor in its success. The unsigned reviewer said, among other things, "The consideration is so thorough, the matter so compact, the appreciation is so just, temperate and enthusiastic and . . . the suggestion of acutely placed facts leads our thought so far—that it is a book which every practitioner of verse should study."[7]

The reviewer, unknown at the time since the *Times Literary Supplement* did not publish signed reviews, was T. S. Eliot, and his observations on Van Doren as critic had much to do with keeping the Dryden book in print here and in England and on many college campuses where it would become an important adjunct to future Dryden scholarship. Some forty years after its first publication, Van Doren, in introducing a Midland Book edition of *John Dryden* for the University of Indiana Press, noted minor revisions in an earlier version (1964) but none in a 1960 paperback,[8] even though aware that in the preceding four decades innumerable critical studies about Dryden had appeared. With characteristic brevity Van Doren said,

I might have presented their conclusions in modification or support of my own views. But I prefer to let the essay stand as I left it; it was altered very little, and I do not wish at this late date to write what in effect would be another book. Also, I dislike arguments and discussions in public with other critics.[9]

By this time, Van Doren's attitude toward formal criticism had taken a dramatic turn. He objected strongly to the New Criticism theories of literary analysis that were raging in academic circles. While he admired and his poetry was praised by John Crowe Ransom and others, Van Doren's approach to criticism was informal compared to the analytic tendencies of the New Critics. He had been writing books of criticism for many years by the time of the New Criticism movement and had more than earned his reputation with several critical books, all widely praised, and with hundreds of reviews, essays, introductions, and prefaces. All this prolific output, or at least the major works, was accomplished as a natural extension of his teaching and his voluminous reading. He had too many genuine critical accomplishments, and because of primary interest in his poetry, for which he received the Pulitzer Prize for his *Collected Poems* (1939), did not feel intellectually stimulated by hair-splitting dialogues on critical theories and methods.

Nonetheless, while working steadily through the years on his poetry, he still wrote prose with amazing alacrity and grace. There is ample evidence that he was possessed with "an extraordinary self-discipline" as Charles W. Everett, his next-door office colleague at Columbia, once remarked.[10] During the presentation of his papers to Columbia in 1960 (some 20,000 pages of text, including his *Dryden* that Jacques Barzun called "a masterpiece of dissertation . . . which redeems thousands of its fallen sisters"[11]), Everett gave some indications of his manner of working. Referring to his card index notes for the Hawthorne book, Everett said they were

almost as interesting as the book itself. They consist of about a thousand 3 x 5 paper slips written in pencil and listed under about fifty heads: politics, boredom, the Peabodys, Melville, the lonely room, Italy, etc. The range of reading they cover is of course enormous, but in each case what is put down is so striking, so genuinely illustrative of a point in artistry or in character, that a less skillful writer would have in some way made a place for it in the book. The power of decision involved in discarding nine out of ten as not essential to the point Van Doren wished to make is central to understanding how a good book is written.[12]

There is also evidence, alluded to by Van Doren himself, that, once his research on a critical topic was completed, the final draft was composed directly on a typewriter with ease and little rewriting.

Much of his prose output from the late 1920s through his retirement from teaching in the late 1950s, stemmed from his celebrated courses at Columbia College which have been credited with launching innumerable careers. It is clear from his public statements that his students deepened his own insights into literature. He was also one of the earliest teachers associated with the great books programs identified with Robert Hutchins at the University of Chicago and at St. John's, the only other institution Van Doren was closely associated with, mainly through visits as a member of the board of governors and by his close friendships with Scott Buchanan and others. Many students have paid public homage to Van Doren's style and influence as a teacher. These include Lionel Trilling, Jacques Barzun, John Berryman, Louis Simpson, Jack Kerouac, Allen Ginsberg, Louis Zukofsky, Donald Keene, Daniel Hoffman,

Richard Howard, Thomas Merton, Robert Lax, and John Tagliabue (to name a baker's dozen), representing every conceivable spectrum of a literary life. There is perhaps an archetypal Van Doren student, the kind he had in mind when he acknowledged their assistance in his widely praised book on *Shakespeare* (1935). These students might be represented by remarks of the late Trappist monk, Thomas Merton, who vividly described the changes that came over him when he left Cambridge (England) for Columbia and came into a Van Doren class. Writing in his celebrated spiritual autobiography, *The Seven Storey Mountain,* Merton says, "I thought to myself, who is this excellent man Van Doren, who having been employed to teach literature, teaches just that: talks about writing and about books and poems and plays; does not go off on a tangent about the biographies of the poets and the novelists; does not read into their poems a lot of subjective messages which were never there? Who is this man who really loves what he has to teach?"[13]

The same qualities of Van Doren the teacher were evident in Van Doren the essayist when, a quarter-century after the Thoreau book, in 1942, he brought together his first prose collection, *The Private Reader,* a book that would create controversy and establish forevermore, in Van Doren's mind at least, his position with regard to formal criticism. In gathering pieces from the principal literary journals of the time (besides *The Nation*) such as *The Kenyon Review,* the *Virginia Quarterly Review,* and *The American Scholar,* as well as more widely circulating publications such as *The Saturday Review,* the *American Mercury,* and *Scribner's Magazine,* Van Doren, considering the irony of a random collection of critical pieces done over a long period of time, announced surprisingly that he had ceased to consider himself a "professional or public critic." He added that "partly in the normal course of things I am done with the desire, but partly also because I have come to certain conclusions about contemporary criticism, a house in which I no longer feel at home, even—or especially—in its finest rooms."[14]

The responses to *The Private Reader* included wide praise and some pain from professional critics whom Van Doren felt were arresting "the lyric in flight."[15] Alfred Kazin captured some of the characteristics of Van Doren's mind in referring to it as both ardent and tidy, never aloof, living on its own track, "a mind generous and often piercing in its intuitions, but very careful never to over-reach, to say too much; ambitious only to stop on the necessary point made, the observation perfectly seen."[16]

Another critic, Stanley Edgar Hyman, later made a rare frontal attack on Van Doren when he condemned, in *The Armed Vision* (1948), his "approach to criticism, consistent with his St. John's College approach to education" as "being opposed to the inroads of any modern knowledge whatsoever." In commenting specifically about the preface to *The Private Reader,* he called it the "most complete and eloquent attack on modern criticism with which I am familiar." Among other things, he accused Van Doren of "obscurantism," and a "tone of bitter elegy, beginning on the theme of exile ('contemporary criticism, a house in which I no longer feel at home') rising to a wail of keening ('our literary age is sick') and ending on the imagery of self extinction. . . ."[17]

If Van Doren, reading anything like the Hyman attack, showed concern, there is no indication. Given the nature of the Hyman work, with its sweeping dismissal of many leading figures in American literature, Van Doren might have felt content with the company. By the time the Hyman book appeared, the highly regarded CBS broadcasts "Invitation to Learning" were in their second year, under Van Doren's leading presence. Broadcast weekly on a coast-to-coast network, their themes were similar to those espoused in *Liberal Education,* with the individual books discussed ranging from the *Oresteia* of Aeschylus to Malthus's *Essay on Population.* In what was widely regarded as perhaps the most literate program ever presented on network radio, Van Doren talked in CBS studios about particular books with guests such as Irwin Edman, Bertrand Russell, André Maurois, Katherine Anne Porter, Julian Huxley, Huntington Cairns, and others. The dialogues in book form can be read today with the same freshness, wit, and understanding as when delivered by some of the most astute thinkers of the twentieth century under the "difficulty," as Van Doren observed, of "being courteous, mind to mind."[18]

The preface to *The Private Reader* begins the first section of this volume, and readers may judge for themselves if Stanley Edgar Hyman's view was justified. The book included general articles on the nature of poetry and literature and more lengthy studies of

Walt Whitman, Robert Frost, Elizabeth Madox Roberts, and others. Other portions of the book contain book reviews written between 1921 and 1938. A few are included here; on Virginia Woolf, Delmore Schwartz, and the letters of John Jay Chapman. And finally, there is a section on films, which Van Doren also reviewed for *The Nation.* While a longer essay, "Let the Movies Be Natural," in this collection may seem dated, since it was written almost forty-five years ago, it is included here as an example of Van Doren's prose style, for the reader's enjoyment, and because of its intrinsic merit.

Despite Van Doren's announcement in *The Private Reader* of his unease with public critical pronouncement, there was a continuing demand for his opinions and lectures. The later 1940s would see the publication of not only new poetry but also critical works such as *The Noble Voice, A Study of Ten Great Poems* (1946), and *Nathaniel Hawthorne* (1949), which Malcolm Cowley hailed as "the best of the critical books about Hawthorne since Henry James wrote the first of them in 1879."[19]

A few years after his retirement from Columbia, Van Doren brought out his second and final book of criticism, *The Happy Critic.* Referring to *The Private Reader,* he admitted his announcement that he was done with criticism premature but he preferred to think not; that his emphasis in *The Happy Critic* was "upon the root rather than the branch, the general rather than the particular truth, if truth at all."[20] He reiterated a view expressed earlier and identified with T. S. Eliot, that there is such a thing as a "normal critic, or as I would say, the happy critic, [who believes] the purpose of literature is to amuse."[21]

The recurring twin themes, for Van Doren, were comedy and tragedy. He says of them:

They are a pair, of course; the most famous pair in either literature or life. Together they yield the largest subject that anyone I think could discuss, for the division between them goes down to the very bottom of things, at least as men see things and report them.

Recalling that he had lectured on these themes for twelve years, he said he never thought he had exhausted the subject, let alone fairly begun it. Nor is it a subject that can be treated systematically, with definitions available at the finish. Tragedy and comedy can no more be defined than life and death can, or love and truth. For one thing, they are different and yet the same. They are twin ways of dealing with human error: the only concern of story when it is serious. One works with darkness and the other with light, one with deeds and the other with the contemplation of deeds; but those opposites are close together, and sometimes they change places.[22]

The essays in *The Happy Critic* give indication of some of Van Doren's public paths during the 1950s and early 1960s. First there were lectures in different parts of the country such as the Hopwood Lecture at the University of Michigan, the Library of Congress lecture series, where Van Doren, besides poetry readings and the production of his first play, "The Last Days of Lincoln," was twice selected to present major addresses on Walt Whitman and Carl Sandburg. Other appearances included the Johns Hopkins Poetry Festival, where the lecture on Thomas Hardy was given, and Bryn Mawr College, where he first delivered his remarkable talk, also included here, on Thomas Mann. He also gave the Blashfield Address at the American Academy of Arts and Letters, where Van Doren served, among other offices, as chancellor, and appeared at Emory University in Atlanta for three lectures on Don Quixote. A visit to Europe with his wife Dorothy resulted in articles for *The Reporter,* and still others appeared in *The Nation, The American Scholar,* and the *Sewanee Review.*

This book represents a tight selection from Van Doren's two books of criticism and also includes several pieces not previously collected and others left unpublished at his death. It consists of three sections beginning with general essays—Van Doren speaking as poet-critic, summarizing his concerns with the role and function of both poetry and criticism and with subjects such as the uses of translations, the importance of poetry in the contemporary world, and other basic convictions that establish his humanistic approach to literature. It begins with *The Private Reader* preface and ends with *The Happy Critic,* and demonstrates a consistent approach to his notion of criticism.

The second section covers the amazing variety of writers of interest to Van Doren. Three writers he was interested in are not included, Wordsworth, Hawthorne, and Emerson. This may seem like a shocking oversight, but in all three cases, books such as the Viking Modern Library introductions to Emerson and Wordsworth are still widely available. The same omissions exist on other writers Van Doren wrote and talked about all of his life: Homer, Dante, Chaucer, and Cervantes. In this case, students of literature can find his views in *The Noble Voice* and subsequent reprints, and in other volumes.

The final section contains general essays that represent a kind of arbitrary summing up, and I think it is appropriate that the last essay end with a poem, *"How Praise A World,"* written near the end of his life. The intention of this volume is that sufficient "private readers" will once again reacquaint themselves with familiar Mark Van Doren essays or themes and a whole host of new readers will discover the pleasures and insights of his passionate and finely attuned mind. By bringing together these essays at this time and by providing a basic checklist of other Van Doren prose works, it is hoped that readers will appreciate, a word Van Doren would accept, the works of literature under discussion, and make discoveries of their own.

The purpose of this volume then, is to provide a representative selection of his prose writings and to show how literary scholarship and creative intuition combined uniquely in him to develop a critical approach which—while its public manifestation changed in time— constituted a holistic approach to life and learning, his love of literature and ideas.

For background information on the development of Van Doren's additional critical interests, a primary source is *The Autobiography of Mark Van Doren* (1958), which covers his life from his rural Illinois beginnings through his retirement from Columbia, after thirty-nine years of teaching. No one interested in the literature of this century could fail to be impressed by this most readable work. First published by Harcourt, Brace, the volume has been reprinted by Greenwood Press.

In conclusion, one further observation might be made. Throughout his long and varied career, Van Doren was constantly compared to a variety of other writers. As a poet the list was endless and included, in no order, Robert Graves, Thomas Hardy, Robert Herrick, Robinson, Frost, Dickinson, to name just a few; as a critic and man of letters, Dryden, Samuel Johnson, T. S. Eliot, and others. But as Allen Tate once observed in a lengthy review of his poetry in which that fine critic alluded to a variety of possible comparisons with others, "all of them adding up to Mark Van Doren, who is not like anybody else."[23] This will be clear to any reader of these essays, whose feelings may be ultimately analogous to the conclusion Van Doren reached on his great friend Don Quixote, and on Cervantes, who gave him life. "Perhaps," he says, "it is the life we should honor, looking at it plainly and looking then at one another; and grinning as we do."[24]

Mark Van Doren's corporeal body may have vanished, but there is a growing coterie of readers who believe that his body of work, poetry and prose, will be examined continually by future generations of writers, readers, and students. They will ask again, as many have in the past, how a man who, as the Nobel Laureate St. John Perse said, "attaching himself so closely to his human environment and his human hour, could be at the same moment more himself and more universal, more immediate and more timeless?"[25]

Notes

1. Mark Van Doren, *The Noble Voice* (New York: Holt, 1946), p. xiii.

2. Mark Van Doren, "Introduction" in *Adventures of the Mind,* eds. R. Thruelsen and J. Kolber (New York: Knopf, 1959), p. vii.

3. Mortimer Adler, in *Voyages,* ed. William Claire, vol. 5, nos. 1-4 (Washington, D.C., 1973), pp. 45-46.

4. Mark Van Doren, "The University of Illinois in Retrospect," Fiftieth Anniversary Lecture Series, University of Illinois, Graduate College (Urbana, 1958).

5. Ibid., p. 6.

6. Personal letter from Carl Hovde to the editor, July 18, 1976.

7. T. S. Eliot, *Selected Essays* (New York: Harcourt, Brace, 1936).

8. Mark Van Doren, *John Dryden,* Note to Midland Book Edition (Bloomington: Indiana University Press, 1960), p. x.

9. Ibid., p. x.

10. *Columbia Library Columns,* vol. 9, no. 2 (New York: Friends of the Columbia Libraries, 1960), p. 18.

11. Jacques Barzun, "The Significance of Literary Papers," Ibid.,p. 15.

12. Charles W. Everett, "Mark Van Doren at Work," Ibid., p. 20.

13. Thomas Merton. *The Seven Storey Mountain* (New York: Harcourt, Brace, 1948).

14. Mark Van Doren, *The Private Reader* (New York: Holt, 1942), p. x.

15. Ibid., p. xiv.

16. Alfred Kazin, *New York Herald Tribune* 22 February 1942, p. 5.

17. Stanley Edgar Hyman, *The Armed Vision* (New York: Knopf, 1948).

18. Mark Van Doren, "Introduction," in *The New Invitation to Learning,* by Huntington Cairns (New York: Random House, 1942).

19. Malcolm Cowley, as quoted on cover of *Nathaniel Hawthorne,* Compass Books Edition (New York: Viking, 1957).

20. Mark Van Doren, *The Happy Critic* (New York: Hill & Wang, 1961).

21. Ibid., Preface, p. viii.

22. Ibid., p. ix.

23. Allen Tate, *New York Herald Tribune,* Book Week, 29 September 1963.

24. Mark Van Doren, *Don Quixote's Profession* (New York: Columbia University Press, 1958).

25. St. John Perse, Association of Alumni, Columbia College, Hamilton Dinner, transl. Maurice Valency (New York: The Association of the Alumni of Columbia University, 1959).

PART 1

THE OTHER HARMONY:
A CRITIC'S RESPONSIBILITY
AND DELIGHT

INTRODUCTION TO PART 1

The essay that begins this volume was written in 1942, at the height of the emphasis on New Criticism. It represents Van Doren's first major statement of his critical credo. The section ends with a kind of final summation with his notions of a "Happy Critic," written in 1961, after his retirement from Columbia.

The few disparate essays between these two are general, although a careful reader will draw conclusions from them that relate to his critical approach. They demonstrate, at different times and for different purposes, the critic's responsibility and delight as practiced by Mark Van Doren.

1

FROM THE PREFACE TO
THE PRIVATE READER

The good critic is both rare and common. The common sort is never heard from, for he is that private reader to whom the writer writes, he is that nameless stranger, wise, humorous, and sensitive, who understands everything; his is the perfect mind which perceives that the truth of a written thing is most apparent while it is being read, and that this truth, though simple to the point of delight, is also multiple beyond the power of commentary. He is a legend in whom the writer must believe, but he is more than a legend; he is any man who reads well. The rare sort reads as well, and as privately; then publishes a record of his reading. But if he is truly a rare one he does not expect too much of the record. He does not count on its being complete, either for the thing he has just read or for literature as the whole thing which I shall henceforth call poetry. He does not assume that criticism, cooled into words, can define poetry any more than poetry, having found even its best form, can be adequate to life. He is bold, or he would not have spoken at all; but he has the modesty, the healthy fear, of one who explores difficult places.

He has also the wit of one who is free to see that he may be out of place altogether, or if he belongs where he is, that his stay should be short. The rare good critic knows above all things how to be brief. This is because he has other concerns than literature alone, and

larger ones, though he may not speak of them; he may only imply
them in the air he has of not being overwhelmed by the duty of the
moment, which indeed in his hand seems less a duty than a pleasure.
The rare good poet wears the same manner with respect to his work,
concerning which we can assume that it was only one way, perhaps
accidentally arrived at, by which in any case he would have said
what he had to say, been what he was to be. The critic can afford
more often than he does to leave some space between him and his
subject; to move in easy, rapid circles around it; and to dart in with
judgments only when they offer themselves to him naturally, as it
were on the fly. He is more likely then to say things which we shall
remember—most critics never do that—and to leave his game as
much alive in the end as it was before he stalked it. He can afford to
keep his head up and his eyes on everything around him; to remember, in brief, that criticism is an art at which luck and love assist.
The last thing he can afford to do is to move in on poetry like a
beater, crouched and tensed, to seize it at the center. For it may not
be there when he arrives; it may be running rings around him as he
creeps; and anyhow, tension is not the tool. The relaxed man may
learn more, even if it is only that when the animal charges the best
thing is to step out of its way, throwing a glance over a shoulder
and saying what one sees.

All of which is fanciful, but the current notion of the critic, judging by the endless articles which accumulate in the quarterlies, is
fantastic. The encirclement which poetry is undergoing there is as
dreadful to behold as it is humorless to hear. The environment for
art which this criticism would provide is sand, not sense: deserts of
ingenuity and plateaus of learning, but almost never the clear figure
of a man who approaches and sees, and with a decent suddenness
says what he sees. The effort, it would seem, is not to liberate poetry
into a current of true and fresh ideas such as Matthew Arnold once
asked for but to crowd in upon it, capture it with definitions, and
immobilize it. Poetry already struggles as if bound, as if breathing
were hard. And this may mean that Arnold's ideas have lost their
freshness. But it may mean too that Arnold was wrong in the emphasis
he placed upon ideas as a condition for poetry, just as he was wrong
in assuming that he or anyone could know the relation between
Shakespeare's art and the thinking of his time. We do not know

that much about poetry, and we never shall. Yet the contemporary critic, more Arnold's grandson than he chooses to admit, goes on heaping dunes of ideas about the figure of poetry in the dry hope that she will then revive. The notion that she had drooped for reasons other than her own was Arnold's too. So there she sits, teased night and day to listen while the possibility of her existence is debated. No wonder she still droops, if she does.

Criticism was never more academic than it is now. But it is not about the rules and the proprieties that we are lectured. It is about the processes and the symbols; criticism, obsessed with a desire to be scientific toward poetry, limits itself to questions of psychology and language. How does it feel to think like a poet, and how does he shuffle the counters of speech? The questions are inherited from Coleridge and Wordsworth, who inherited them from Dryden and Hobbes. "What is poetry?", said Coleridge, "is so nearly the same question with What is a poet? that the answer to the one is involved in the solution of the other." The place to look was in "the poet's own mind," which for Coleridge had become the special wonder of the world. As if it were more wonderful than the mind of man as such, and as if poets must be more or less than men in order to be at all. What the mind thinks is a better question than how it does it, if only because the second question, being unanswerable, begets doubts that thinking is ever done. Contemporary criticism never doubts, however, that this is the place to hover and halt; and it has already halted so long that in the perfection of its rest there is some taint of rottenness. Our literary age is sick with a distempered appetite for the latest news of itself. Its writing is about writing; the heroes of its novels are writers; the death of James Joyce moved many who will never read "Finnegan's Wake" to lament the loss of "one who after all was so pure a writer." So pure that he cannot be read by them. But that does not matter, for is he not the most special case to date of the special mind which poets by definition must possess?

The tragedy of Joyce is a footnote to the comedy of his time, whose thoughts run so laughably in the one groove of language. The obsession with this single element among several in the art of composition is at least as old as Coleridge, who for all his promise that he would substitute poetic thoughts for poetic diction did but commit his successors in criticism to a serial, self-perpetuating revolution of the word. The series grows tiresome, begins to seem temporary; for even if it is tolerably old it cannot claim to be ancient. Language occupies a corner in Aristotle's "Poetics," but only a corner. The foreground is filled with action, character, design; with understanding and discovery; with life itself, of which poetry is a report. And if it be objected that Aristotle limited his discussion to poetry as story, the answer is that he did not therein limit poetry. He released it for the exercise of its largest function, which is to show humanity in motion. Even lyric poetry does that when it is alive: as it never again will be if criticism can help it.

Criticism is doing all it can to arrest the lyric in its flight. Rhythm, gesture, sound box and vocal cord: it disciplines itself to be blind and deaf toward these, which it despises as the mere essentials of an art. The incidentals, the dictionary meanings, are what it loves, and little heed is paid to whether they are truly there in the poem or not. The poem is a bird that threatens to escape the net of analysis; so the net grows ever wider, and tougher with inwoven semantic threads. It will fail of its purpose, but meanwhile it yawns everywhere through criticism and depresses its victim. It can make nothing of first lines like those in Shakespeare's sonnets and songs, or of Defoe's best prose. Such things, being undiscussable, are passed over as unimportant. And indeed their only importance is that they startle us into recognition of the mystery which smiles through language whenever it succeeds. Criticism now is not greatly interested in success, just as it is nervous in the presence of genius. It prefers the poem whose author can be seen sweating at his job of extending or intensifying an image to the point of systematic dullness, to the end of an admirable aridity. Criticism, itself a puritan for work, can praise only the laborious, can respect poetry only when it groans to overreach itself and become discussable. A sensible acquaintance of mine once remarked of the semantic brethren that they missed only one meaning: some people write better than others. But they are not bothered with better and worse, they have not left themselves free to make judgments. Criticism as they practice it is at best a faulty science. It is not an art.

The art of reviewing, what is it? First it is the art of reading without prejudice, without demand, without thought of the reader's self. This is one of love's arts, for it is nothing less than a skill in surrender, a readiness to understand. Afterward comes memory of what has been experienced, and the describer's art which sets that memory down as precisely as possible, honoring its uniqueness. Then and only then come measurement, comparison, judgment, and perspective. It will be gathered that there are few perfect reviews. The fact is that there are none, and I hasten to insist that mine have every imaginable defect. Save, I hope, one. They were written with relish and without omniscience, in the plain lamplight of my affection for literature whenever and in whatever measure it succeeds. What success is I still refuse to define, since it must be clear by now that for me no mesh is subtle enough to check it where it moves. My only ambition as a critic is henceforth to be one of those nameless strangers with whom writers dream that they communicate. Poetry itself can do with silence for a while.

2

THE POSSIBLE
IMPORTANCE OF POETRY

Poetry desires to be interesting; or it should. By tradition it has a right to this desire, for there have been times when nothing was more interesting than poetry. If this is not such a time, the reason may be simply that we have lost our desire; or if not so, that we have lost touch with tradition. The present fact would seem to be that people do not consider poetry either interesting or important— two words for the same thing, and the people are the judge. So have they always been, in spite of every appeal to something beyond or above or beneath them. There is no appeal. It is to people that poetry must be interesting.

When they do not find it so, the fault conceivably is theirs: they have forgotten how to read. It is they, and not the poets, who have lost touch with tradition. But it is dangerous for poets at any time to make such a charge. In our time it is a plausible charge, for we can suspect, and indeed we are often told, that universal literacy has depressed literature. When the only aim is that everybody should be able to read something, no matter what, and when mass production of printed words has become the business of cynics who despise the very audience by which they profit, the outlook for distinguished thoughts and feelings would appear on the face of it to be poor. The contemporary poet, however, cannot afford to rest here. His job is what the job of poets has always been: to think and feel as deeply as he can, and to assume the existence of persons who will be glad that he has done so. And he had better assume that these are more than a few—ideally, he had better assume that they are all of us. He had better not count the number, at least beforehand; for if he does, he will end by limiting himself. "I am always made uneasy," Emerson wrote in his Journal, "when the conversation turns in my presence upon popular ignorance and the duty of adapting our public harangues and writings to the mind of the people. 'Tis all pedantry and ignorance. The people know as much and reason as well as we do. None so quick as they to discern brilliant genius or solid parts. And I observe that all those who use this cant most, are such as do not rise above mediocrity of understanding. . . . Remember that the hunger of people for truth is immense. The reason why they yawn is because you have it not."

Whenever poetry has been good it has had good subject matter—good for anybody, and it has not agonized about numbers. Today, I think, we do not hear enough about the subject matter of poetry. Criticism tends to ignore the question altogether. Poets are damned or praised for their way with language, as if language were the aim and end of all their art. Language is a lovely thing, and only human beings have it; but they have it, presumably, for something better still, and the greatest poets are those who have best understood this. There is no lord of language like Shakespeare; he could and did do everything with it; but what finally moves us as we read him or watch his plays is the knowledge he has of us, on a level deeper than words. We adore Shakespeare because he is wise, and because the world of men is given its right value in his works. It was for the same reason that the Greeks all but worshiped Homer, whom they knew by heart even though they knew nothing about the world of which he had written. The truth is, of course, that they did know his most important world, for it was the human world, and as such it was not different from theirs. Again they had in him a lord of language, but they noticed this less than they noticed how well he understood the passions, the ideas, and the absurdities of men. They watched Achilles learning what honor means; they watched Odysseus coming home; and they saw the soul of Hector reflected in the love of those around him—his family, his comrades, and his friends among the gods. By the same token, what is it that in modern times convinces a true reader of Dante that his reputation is deserved? His verbal cunning, and the peculiar fitness of his rhymes, his syntax? These of course; but at last it is the knowledge of the man, and the pity; the power of his feelings, the unwearied work of his thought, and the deep lake of his heart. Without these he would merely be ingenious, as without them Homer would be sound and fury, and Shakespeare an incessant bustling in the scenery.

But those three are the greatest poets, some may say: the very greatest; and what can we learn from them? They are too far removed, they are monsters of perfection, they are studied more than they are read, they are statues whose pedestals only may be approached. Nothing could be more mistaken. Yet it is the custom of our time. We do not believe that we can learn from the greatest things. They are not for us. Which is why so few discussions of poetry today, even among those who ought to know better, even mention the names of Shakespeare, Homer, and Dante; and why the poet is defined in terms that exclude those masters; and why the impression is abroad that it is somehow bad taste for poetry to be interesting to people. Subject matter is itself an embarrassing subject, from which quick refuge is sought in the techniques of rhythm and image, of caesura and ambiguity. Those things all have their fascination, but it is secondary to the further fascination of the art when ultimate demands are made upon it. The ultimate demand is that it be faithful to its ancient trust: that it treat of human truth, and more wisely and movingly than most men treat it even when they know, as ideally all men know, the content of such truth.

Poetry today means lyric poetry; it means the short poem; and that too can be a great thing, but it is not the greatest. It is as great as it can be when its author has wisdom and passion, and when it is clear that if there were an occasion he could convey his understanding in the more complex forms of narrative and drama. The Greeks never forgot that lyric poetry is but a third of poetry itself, and perhaps the least third. The big things are done in narrative and drama, for poetry's chief business is the business of story—of mankind in motion. Philosophy and science give us knowledge of men in the aggregate, or in essence; poetry commits individuals to action and follows them through careers. It conceives beginnings, middles, and ends, and is perhaps the only thing that can conceive them. Nature does not, and neither may philosophy or science; but poetry must. And it is the test of any poet—that is, of any story-teller—whether or not he can finish the story he has started. The beginning is fairly easy, as any young writer knows; even the middle sometimes charts its own course; but the end—for that, alas, experience and penetration are required. And in addition to those, a familiarity with the forms in which all human conduct finally manifests itself, the two forms of tragedy and comedy.

Tragedy and comedy are forms, not statements; or it may be that they are forms of statement. But any statement which they make is as far from platitude as the most sophisticated poet could desire. Poetry today despises platitude, and it is right in that. The pompous homilies, the ''affirmations'' and hymns of self-praise that pass in times like these as the sort of thing we ought to love in preference to the dim poetry we do on the whole have—I for one will take the dim poetry, since at least it is not hollow. But it must be clear that I would rather have something better than either of these. I would rather have story, and I would like to see it well grounded in the tragic and the comic visions which embrace all the knowledge we have yet accumulated concerning man's life.

Man's life is never good enough, and only men can know what this means. It means more than that the world of any given moment is a poor thing for even the best persons in it. Contemporary literature spends too much time, perhaps, and certainly too much effort, in proving by documentation that the twentieth century is not what some people thought it was going to be. What did they think it was going to be? An earthly paradise? Heaven itself? But if they thought this they were children, and poetry is not for children. Neither can it be written by children. It is the product of long seasoning and of bittersweet experience, neither of which things we have any right to expect in the very young. We do not think of Homer as very young; or Dante, or Shakespeare, or Sophocles, or Milton, or Hardy, or Yeats. Or Chaucer—who sounds in every verse he wrote as if he had been born with quizzical old eyes, and perhaps the small beard we cannot think of him without. The great poet knows the world, and how to live in it—also how not to live in it. He is not surprised because it has failed at being Heaven, or because most people in it fall grotesquely short of being angels. He seems to have expected this, and to have been prepared. The current notion of the poet as young, ignorant, helpless, and complaining is more recent than many of us think. Through most of human time the poet has been thought of in terms that suggest the old man of the tribe—the one who has lived longest and seen most, whose voice nevertheless has retained its original sweetness. Even in our day we have been witness to examples of this: Thomas Hardy, beginning to publish poetry at fifty-eight and ceasing only with his death at eighty-eight; William Butler Yeats, turning at middle age into the great poet he was at last to be; Robert Frost, unheard of by the world until he was nearing forty, and proceeding after that to become more himself with every advancing decade. We have these examples, and still we go on thinking of the poet as knowing less than we do—less, not more, which immemorially has been the assumption.

The poet knows how to live in the world and how not to live in it. That is to say, he locates the good life where it actually is—in the mind that can imagine and believe it. The mind of man not only sees worlds but creates them; and the worlds it creates are not here. This does not mean that they are illusory worlds, made up for solace and thin comfort. They are more substantial than the one we move through every day; but they are not here, and they cannot be verified by those who think this is the only world there is. Those who think that are either deceived or disillusioned, and chronically so. The poet is not deceived, for he has sharp eyes. But neither is he disillusioned, for in one very important sense he has never suffered from illusion. He has not thought that Heaven was in cities—or in the country, either, if that is what you think I mean. It is where it is, and only the mind can travel there. Shakespeare must have known contemporary England very well, but his mind traveled elsewhere in search of persons, stories, tragedies, comedies. It traveled to that region where all men's minds are at home, and it brought back news that made this world seem somehow a foreign place, as indeed it must always seem to the uncompromising imagination. It is the only place where we have addresses, but it is not where we chiefly live. Nor need we hate it because this is true. Dante, traveling also into Heaven and Hell, took his memories with him and used them there. Homer, dropping back several centuries in time, found heroes—which was what he wanted, and he knew he should not look for them in his next-door neighbors whom nevertheless he did not despise. They had not disappointed him, because he had never counted on them for more than they could deliver.

Poetry, in other words, takes it for granted that the world is not good enough for its best men. But all it can do with these men is to make them tragic or comic heroes—to show them as defeated by the very world to which they are superior. What if they succeeded? Poetry asks this question, asks it again and again, and at last decides that the answer is for no man to give. The poet is a man too, laughing and crying with other men. He certainly is not God. So he does not know the answer. But he knows the question, which he asks over and over in such a way as to suggest the extreme distinction of man's predicament. Man wants to change the world and cannot do so. The world will punish him if he tries, just as gravity will operate upon his body no matter how light he thinks it is. Hamlet is inconceivably brilliant, but he must die like any other man, and for the commonest reason—he has not survived his crisis. Don Quixote is the greatest gentleman we know, but the world cannot tolerate one who tries to teach it to be other than it is. The world is indeed a tough place. But what man could make it tender? No man, says poetry, no man at all, and sacrifices King Lear on the altar of the unchangeable. He learned, but learned too late. There is no appeal from the ways of the world, which must continue on its own terms or take us all down with it into chaos and confusion. Which does not mean that we should think it a nice thing. It is a terrible thing; or if not terrible, absurd. So tragedy and comedy say—and salvage out of the wreck the best ideas we have, the ideas that certain men could become heroes by expressing, even though they failed.

What if they had succeeded? The question is meaningless; or rather, we cannot imagine what it means, nor does the poet try. What if Socrates had succeeded in making all Athenians think well? What if Jesus had succeeded in making all Jerusalem over into the image of his Father? What if Don Quixote had persuaded all of Spain that knights were more real than merchants and monks? What if Hamlet had cleansed Denmark of its sin? What if Oedipus' finding of the truth had made him free? For one thing we should not now have the books of which these persons are the heroes. Or if

we did have them, we could not believe them. We believe them
because they falsify nothing in their report of the world. Their
report of the human spirit—well, that is another matter. Neither do
they falsify that by minimizing the dangers it must undergo, or by
denying the supreme courage it inspires in those who properly
possess it. The world is what it is, and the human spirit is what it is.
And somehow they live together: ill-sorted companions, but the
only companions there are for poetry to watch disappearing down
the long perspective of life.

The possible importance of poetry is immense at any time. And
why not now? I would make no exception of our time, though
there are those who do. They are the ones who persist in identifying
poetry with short poems, and who even then do not remember how
great a short poem can be—for it can be dramatic too, and somehow narrative; it can imply careers, for ideas and for men. The
short poem is better in those ages when the long poem is better; or,
at the minimum, when it exists. The forms of literature reinforce
one another, as tragedy and comedy do, which are the forms of
thought. When fiction is good, then poetry can be good; and vice
versa. Fiction indeed *is* poetry; or as I have put here, poetry is
story. This is not my idea, as you very well know; it is at least as
old as Aristotle, and it has prevailed whenever poetry has been
important to people.

But when I say fiction do I mean merely narratives or dramas in
verse? Not necessarily. The ancient categories of lyric, epic, and
dramatic poetry were not conceived in terms of verse alone, and it
is fatal for us to suppose so. What we call prose fiction today is in
fact the most interesting poetry we have; Aristotle would think so
if he were alive, and he would be justified by the interest we show.
Our movies, our westerns, our detective tales—he would wonder,
perhaps, why so many of us failed to recognize those things too as
contributions, however bad or good, to the poetry of this age. I
have already spoken of Cervantes as if I thought he was the great
poet of his age, along with Shakespeare his contemporary. That is
exactly how I regard him, and I am not prevented from doing so by
the fact that he wrote his greatest work in prose. He was a versifier
too, but as such he does not interest us; whereas his vast poem
called *Don Quixote* is among the glories of the world. Shakespeare

wrote both verse and prose—sometimes, it would seem, indifferently, as if convenience alone dictated his choice; and his prose, unlike the verse of Cervantes, was itself a great thing, there being no better prose I think in English. But the question does not greatly matter. The vision was the thing in either case: the vision, and the knowledge that backed it up. The wisdom of these men is what makes them poets, as it is the wisdom of Tolstoy and Dostoevsky and Chekhov that makes us think of them, when we are serious, as Russia's poets. Is Dickens not a poet? Consider his passion and his joy as he contemplates humanity and sets it moving. The possible importance of poetry includes the chance that such men as these should continue to appear, and that we should have the generosity to recognize them as belonging to the highest class.

That we do not do so is perhaps the fault of our education, which keeps first things separate from one another. We study literature as if it were a thing by itself, and not only literature but English literature—even American literature, God save the mark. When American literature is good it is *literature,* as English or Greek literature is. And when *literature* is good it is a part of all we know. Not the only part, or even the best part, but certainly a part; and it is well that we should remember this. It is more likely to excel when the society that produces it considers neither it nor science, nor mathematics, nor philosophy, nor theology, nor medicine, nor law, nor mechanics, nor politics, nor economics, nor history, as the central subject matter of its thought. The central subject matter for any great age is life and truth; or perhaps it is justice and mercy. At any rate it is something that all arts and studies serve, and serve, we may suppose, equally. The Greeks were at one and the same time supreme in poetry, in philosophy, in science, and in mathematics. But this was not a coincidence, I suspect. They were great in each of these things because they were great in all the others, and because they thought that each of them testified to a vision which itself was the central thing. Their education, that is to say, was not specialized. All arts for them were finally one art, and the name of it was living well. Nor did they set the fine arts of poetry, painting, music, and sculpture above the practical arts and the intellectual (we should say liberal) arts. There was no hierarchy of importance among them, because there was none of them with which serious men could dispense. The carpenter made a house, the logician made a syllogism, and the poet made a poem. Each was doing what he could and therefore should, and nobody doubted the benefit.

We specialize, with the paradoxical result that no one knows for sure what it is that he is doing. Where there is no connection there can be no comparison. What is the difference, for instance, between the poet and the philosopher, or between the poet and the scientist? We do not state it well, because we do not think of all three men as artists. If they had that much resemblance in our minds, then they might have differences too, and we could measure these. We tend to assume that the differences are absolute; but this means in the end that they are absolutely small; or that the men themselves are. We often talk, as I have said, as if the poet were small. He might grow larger if he knew, or if we knew, what sphere he works in as distinguished from any other man; and if we thought of him as working in that sphere for our benefit; and if we thought of all men in their spheres as working in them for our good—our knowledge, our happiness, and our wisdom.

The poet has his subject matter as well as his skill; and his skill increases as he realizes what his subject matter is. If poetry has made any advances in our time—in, that is to say, the twentieth century—we should wonder what new subject matter it has found. I for one think it has made advances; but I am not in sympathy with those who say that these are merely technical. The concern, the conscious concern, has often been with devices of language and principles of diction. So was it in 1798, when Wordsworth called for poetry to adopt the language that men use. But Wordsworth had something to say in his new language; he needed the language, in fact, so that he *could* say what he thought and felt. The situation is no different now. With the new style of 1912—if that is the year from which we date a certain renaissance—there came new stuff; and I think the stuff explains the style. Wherever we look in that time we discover poets who themselves had discovered, or rediscovered, something worth saying in human speech. Irony returned, and the sense of tragedy; the sense of comedy, too, and even the sense of sin. Edgar Lee Masters dug up the Greek Anthology; Ezra Pound ransacked the older poetries of Europe and Asia; and Edwin Arlington Robinson attempted again the difficult art of story. T. S. Eliot experimented, to be sure, with stanzas and free verse; it is quite important that he did so; but it is still more important that he restored to poetry the stuff of theology, long absent and all but lost.

Robert Frost has rediscovered Job, whose wife says in *A Masque of Reason:*

> Job says there's no such thing as Earth's becoming
> An easier place for man to save his soul in.
> Except as a hard place to save his soul in,
> A trial ground where he can try himself
> And find out whether he is any good,
> It would be meaningless. It might as well
> Be Heaven at once and have it over with.

There we have the accent we desire, and it is inseparable from the subject Frost has found. He found it where it waited for him, as the world waits for any man to recognize it. For any man, and for any poet. For there is nothing more important about a poet than that he is a man. He may not know more at last than all men do, but what he does know he knows well, and perfects himself in the art of expressing. What he knows, and what we know, is that the world is a hard place to live in at any cost, but that the cost is prohibitive only for those who make the mistake of thinking it is Heaven—or, worse yet, that it should have been.

3

POETS AND TRIMMERS

One of the hundred cantos in which *The Divine Comedy* describes a world is devoted with compendious scorn to those lost people who lived without blame and without praise, but were for themselves; who now have no hope of death; report of whom the world permits not to exist; who never had any "good of the intellect"; who from cowardice made the great refusal. Only one canto deals with these trimmers, and not even all of that; but Dante makes it clear how many of them there are—they are the majority of mankind—and how absolutely both he and Virgil despise them. "Regard, and pass." "I should never have believed death had undone so many."

We meet them in the third canto of the hundred, and we are not reminded of them again. The rest of the journey is among those who sinned or who did not sin; who chose between the only two alternatives faced by men, and according to their choice are now being punished or blessed. The trimmers are not even in Hell, as certainly they are not in Purgatory or Heaven. Dante has glanced at them and passed; he has other latitudes to climb, low, middle, and high. The vast world he will traverse dwarfs the very memory of that multitude which never lived, and which includes almost everybody. *The Divine Comedy* is about the relatively few who will live forever, either as sinners or as saints. Hell has its immortality, no less than the scented country beyond the river, in sight of the breathing Rose. There is ample escape from these suffocating regions of death and yet no death.

For the modern poet there is no such escape. He strangulates in a universe populated entirely by trimmers, and therefore, and everywhere, dead. There is no entrance into the earth which can conduct him to where some souls are interestingly damned; there is no mount beyond where in the sweet light he can see others happily punished; and still beyond this mount there is no ladder of arcs which he can ascend and be free of human place or time. He himself is condemned to live his whole life and do his whole work in the midst of a multitude he cannot but loathe.

"Let others complain that the age is wicked," wrote Kierkegaard in 1843; "my complaint is that it is wretched; for it lacks passion. Men's thoughts are thin and flimsy like lace, they are themselves pitiable like the lacemakers. The thoughts of their hearts are too paltry to be sinful. For a worm it might be regarded as a sin to harbor such thoughts, but not for a being made in the image of God. Their lusts are dull and sluggish, their passions sleepy. . . . This is the reason my soul always turns back to the Old Testament and to Shakespeare. I feel that those who speak there are at least human beings: they hate, they love, they murder their enemies, and curse their descendants throughout all generations, they sin."

"The modern world debases," wrote Charles Péguy a generation ago. "Other worlds had other occupations. Other worlds had other ulterior motives and other ulterior intentions. Other worlds had other temporal pastimes, between meals. The modern world debases. Other worlds idealized or materialized, built or demolished, meted out justice or exercised force, other worlds created cities, communities, men, or gods. The modern world debases. This is its speciality. . . . It debases the state; it debases man. It debases love; it debases woman. It debases the race, it debases the child. It debases the nation; it debases the family. It even debases . . . what is perhaps most difficult in the world to debase because this is something which has in itself, as in its texture, a particular kind of dignity, like a singular incapacity for degradation: it debases death."

There, taken quite at random, are attestations from Denmark and France. And attestations to what? That the majority of men are trimmers. Which Dante could take for granted and go on. It is strange that there should be a generation, late in time, for which there is poetic news in the discovery that the world is a waste land. It always was, and the happy times for poets were when the fact was not surprising. It is as if we could be thrown into consternation by the announcement that each of our neighbors had two legs and needed food to live. The one great commonplace of morality, which is that most people are not moral at all—neither good nor bad— has ceased to be available. With it have ceased to be available such things as tragedy, comedy, irony, and the kind of indignation that can be sharp because it is final. The modern poet cannot end his plaint. His disgust grows monotonous. D. H. Lawrence races around the earth in search of a continent in which devils are indigenous, and angels common as air. He never arrives. So he never stops howling that the world is—what it is.

The problem is thought to be social, but it is theological. This does not mean that it is easily solved. Nor does it mean that those are wasting their time who work for the improvement of men's condition. Men are badly off, and simple justice could be farther spread; indeed it had better be, or mutual massacre will remove the race. The reformers are not wasting time. They are wasting eternity. The fraction is fixed: a very small numerator of those who are good or bad enough for poetry to be interested in, a very large denominator of those concerning whose existence poetry has no report to make. Poetry is fiercely moral, as to be sure Baudelaire was when he announced the agony of his *ennui*. But poetry is also, at any rate it was built to be, somehow the conqueror of time. It should pause as Pascal did to note that man's natural life is boredom, that time is endless and terrible; but it should only pause. The rest of the journey is through Hell and Heaven. The modern poet scarcely gets started on the long road, in the great subjects. This is because he shares the common delusion that Hell and Heaven are far away. They are here or nowhere, as Dante's unremitting relevance might prove. But we do not think they are. And in a sense we are right. We have lost the theology which placed them for us, and we have not found another which can place them again.

It may take thousands of years to find such a theology, to cut escape doors out of waste land which can take us into worlds whose footing is solid. When we escape now it is into oxygenless atmospheres and baseless wilds. Thousands of years. And meanwhile, what shall the poet do? A poet cannot make a theology. Blake tried and is incomprehensible, Hardy tried but only gave names to mist. Poets have to share a theology; and with many people. What then can the poet do in a world like ours which thinks that time, future time, will bring all things to clarity? Will see the little justice grow into the great justice? Will invert the fraction? Will sanctify the trimmers? Heaven only knows what he can do. He can refuse to be a fool in the infinite ways that foolishness is possible. But that is not enough for heaven. Or, in the long view, for poetry. Whether there is anything positive he can do is not for this note to determine.

4

THE USES OF TRANSLATION

One piece of pedantry we have with us always—a book is not read well unless it is read in its native tongue. Some go farther and say that only then it is read at all: Homer in English has nothing left of his greatness. And so with Dante. And so, presumably, with Cervantes, Rabelais, Montaigne, Pascal, Voltaire, Rousseau, Stendhal, Balzac, and Proust; so with Tolstoy and Dostoevsky; so with Ibsen; so with Goethe; so with Plutarch; so with Lucretius; so with Plato and Aristotle; so with Herodotus and Thucydides; so with St. Augustine and St. Thomas; so with Machiavelli and Molière. So too, of course, with the Bible. If you cannot read Hebrew you will never know anything about Abraham, and if you are not a master of first-century Greek you will have no notion of what Jesus said.

The list, which could be longer, itself reveals the pedantry. Many a person, speaking thus, forgets in his pride of knowing Greek that he knows no Hebrew; or, if he knows some Russian, that he did as a matter of fact first feel Raskolnikov's force through the English of Constance Garnett; or granting that he reads Russian as Russians do, that he did once, in a moment of inadvertence, enjoy Li Po by way of Ezra Pound. But this is not the biggest mistake he makes. His true crime—the word is scarcely too strong—consists in his ignorance of how the literature of the world has exerted its power.

It has exerted it—in the world—by being translated. Only great writers, to be sure, can be translated without deadly loss; the others having at best a minor, a local virtue, die promptly in foreign air. But it is the great writers that count in the great world; for the great world understands, as none other does, the language of literature. There is the English language, but a few who have used it wrote also in the human tongue, and that tongue—witness Shakespeare—can be comprehended anywhere. Even we who are most vain of our knowledge that Shakespeare wrote English as no one else ever has can also take pleasure in contemplating that the Germans once did, and the Russians now do, consider him their best poet. To insist that he is only ours would be to deny his ultimate distinction. It would be, in fact, to expose our incapacity to see what that distinction is. It would prove that we read him badly even in English, as many classical scholars read Homer badly in Greek. They read him, that is to say, without suspecting his immense, his humorous, his natural, his wise, his temperate, his courageous power.

A recent translation of *Don Quixote* has been recommended as the first such translation to render in English the true meaning of that tremendous masterpiece. Those who say this, and by a certain logic they should add that *Don Quixote* should not have been translated at all, tell us that only now can we know—well, what the whole world has known about Cervantes for three hundred years. Comedy at its deepest and best is not a Spanish thing, it is a human thing, it is an intellectual and emotional thing, and somehow neither Fielding nor Dickens nor the author of *Huckleberry Finn* missed it; not to speak of a million other readers in whose minds the influence of Cervantes will never be traced. The influence of great literature is universal, and in the course of things works through translation. The Romans did not understand all the Greek they turned into Latin, but without the part they did understand they would have had no literature at all. The Elizabethan Age was ushered in by translations of Plutarch, Montaigne, Seneca, Ovid, and many another ancient or foreign writer without access to whom Shakespeare, for instance, would have been poorer. I have never heard it seriously suggested that he should not have tried his hand at *Julius Caesar* and *Antony and Cleopatra* because North's Plutarch was the only Plutarch he could read. Dryden's Virgil and Pope's Homer created an age of English poetry, just as French translations of English books caused 1789, and just as English translations of German books caused Transcendentalism.

I am told that I cannot know what Aristotle is saying in his *Poetics* unless my Greek is perfect, but I must refuse to believe this. I must admit, to be sure, the difficulty of rendering each term precisely as the greatest of literary critics intended it. But another sort of precision in him nobody can miss. It is the precision that guards his mind against the blunder of leaving any important consideration out as he decides what poetry—we would say story—at its fullest is. A complete story, he certainly is saying, will be good in its language, its characters, its scene, its sentiments, its ideas, and its plot—most of all its plot, which is its very soul, and indeed is always the thing an unwise poet manages worst. Modern criticism can praise a novelist or a playwright for one of these virtues alone, and regularly does. To do so is not to ask him for enough, and in the long run is not to get enough. Literature dries up without a living memory of what it is that happens when it uses all its power. Here, finally, is the one use of translation that outmeasures the others. It keeps us open to greatness wherever it may be, and it may be anywhere. As one literature withers another revives it; as one nation of writers forgets its chief business another nation shows it has remembered. Translation keeps literature going in the world. It always has, and it always will unless the pedants have their way. Of course they will not have their way.

5

THE ARTIST AND THE CHANGING WORLD

In times like these the artist thinks of the world. He also thinks of himself; but the world changes faster than he does, and his eye cannot but follow it as far into the future as thought will go. Perhaps the activity should have been chronic with him; perhaps he should not be startled now. The world was always changing; it always will be changing; and who should know this better than the artist? He has to know, too, that the world never changes—the same old place, for better or for worse, simply looks different to its successive inhabitants. It is indeed different, and yet the *it* remains. The work of any artist, when it means enough to matter, means exactly this; and if it is given to few artists to mean so much, it is likewise given to few men to understand the mysteries of permanence and change. Few men of any sort have understood them, and no man has done so perfectly. The problem of the artist, like that of the philosopher, is immemorial and difficult and strange.

Just now the artist is particularly tempted to grow melancholy, forced as by many circumstances he is to remember how much art in the past has died. Whole languages and literatures have disappeared without even an echo to tell us how they sounded or what they said. Millenniums of plastic art have faded out of view, been buried under dust and clay, or crumbled to impalpable powder.

And these are but the changes wrought by time's catastrophes, which in spite of many a poet's boast have silenced powerful rhyme as well as leveled marble and the gilded monuments of princes. The artist of today remembers other catastrophes, historical and human. He remembers that fashions change, that populations desert their teachers and audiences their entertainers. The spirit of an age, the character of a culture, demanded this or that; but then it ceased to do so and demanded this or that; but then it ceased to do so and demanded something else. What had seemed determined was indeed determined, and not to be denied; yet all the while upheavals were preparing—the shores of taste were sinking, or were rising, and the artist who stood securely on them was getting ready, whether he knew it or not, to be submerged or beached; either to go down out of sight and be forgotten, or else to be left high and dry like any other unintelligible, irrelevant thing which only history can explain.

We like to believe that certain artists have been good enough—have been sufficient masters of permanence and change—to save themselves through all of time to come from dangers such as these. It is natural, for instance, to think of Shakespeare, who still outtops our knowledge and seems more fresh with every century he lives. He, if anybody, might be invincible to time and fashion. Yet Tolstoy, one of his great rivals for the privilege of surviving, has doubted that he is. And at this moment we are forced as seldom before to wonder what it would mean to have no such doubt at all. How much knowledge would we need? And knowledge of what things?

We know one thing already: that most of the books in our libraries, like many of the objects in our museums, have long since been dead. And their lifetimes were short; and here is Shakespeare, not to speak of Homer and the Bible, in all but innumerable editions which themselves suggest that no end is in sight. Yet something asks us now to be quite serious in our thought of this. Time ticks loudly in our ears, and change is real. Human history as we know it is still a recent thing. Say ten more thousand years pass; say a million. Our imagination grows geological, grows astronomical, and staggers us. How can we know what things, if any, will last as long as we like to think society will last? There is even the fear that it and the earth are not to last; but forgetting this, again how can we know that changes are not coming which will doom our dearest monuments to extinction—the extinction of oblivion rather than of disappearance, or unintelligibility rather than of death by moisture and dry rot?

In times like these the artist thinks of this. But his talk is of his freedom—his freedom to survive, or else his freedom to go on doing what society has so far tolerated from his hand. The freedom of an artist, like the freedom of any individual, is what he thinks most personally about, since it feels to him like his very life. Yet it is not a simple thing, for all it may seem to be so in the minds of those who say it is only doing what one pleases. The trouble is, time also does what it pleases. Fashion, from which there is no appeal, does what it pleases. Thought marches on; society grows deaf and blind to what once entertained it; history is heartless, and leaves whole armies of artists stranded where they were. They were not free from that, however free each one of them was in his own private fancy. And it is worth remembering in how few ages of the world the artist's fancy has ever told him he was free. Liberty as you and I know it has been limited to a few brief periods of time and a few small areas of earth. We may take it for granted, but history does not.

To us it is a very precious thing, and not merely for the reason that it is the base of our operation as artists. It is no less precious, we assume, to the society of which we are a part; society, we have been taught to say, benefits in proportion as we are free to give it our vision without dictation or interference; society may not like what we do, but it would like still less what it thinks we ought to do; time will tell that we were right. We may not be free from the catastrophes that crush cities and bury civilizations under tidal water and volcanic ash; nor are we exempt from the law that inferior work dies of its own weakness; but our habit is to insist that nothing shall stand in the way of individual inspiration. The only penalty, if this inspiration be wrong or shallow, is the deserved penalty of failure; but meanwhile we shall not have been prevented from trying. The freedom of the artist is like the freedom of the citizen; he too must be left free to say in public what he thinks is true; suppress this right, and society suffers; suppress it long enough, and civilization dies.

For confirmation of this faith we point to the dead civilizations that archeology has unburied. They were perfect of their kind, but the kind was doomed. The perfection was insect, not human—the right kind only if men were other than what they are, namely creatures who live longest together in happiness and strength when they hold on to the doctrine that every individual is somehow king; or rather, that he is both king and subject, with the duty to think and speak as he deems best; for only then will the structure of his community maintain that flexibility and inner well-being which guarantees survival. Archaeologists tell us that the dead cultures of Mesopotamia, Egypt, and Central America were too strictly ordered under priests and kings; that they were bureaucracies of vast refinement which nevertheless broke down when danger came; and that their artists were drones of the hive who likewise died in swarms and now have become, as indeed they always were, indistinguishable from one another. Our own civilization, that of Greece and Rome and modern Europe and America, still flourishes because it has kept the power to criticize and renew itself. It has changed again and again, but it has never become unrecognizable, and with every alteration it has taken on more life. And this is because its artists, like all of its citizens in whatever category, have remained free men. Such a civilization lives dangerously, and reaps glorious rewards.

But even our own history has periods when faith departed, or at least had to be re-examined. Plato's great dialogue of the *Republic* marks such a moment in the career of Athens. Change had reared its head, and war was shaking the foundations that men had supposed to be indestructible. How free could society afford to keep on being at a time when strains were felt in every portion of its superstructure? The *Republic* endeavored among other things to imagine the greatest change of all—one that would prevent change forever, and still leave Athens free from stagnation and Mesopotamian death. Socrates invited his friends to consider how they would proceed to build a state if they had the power and the opportunity to do so, and if they understood that they alone were responsible for its continuing health—really responsible, as no man born into an existing state ever is. Would they, for instance, be indifferent to its art? Would they have art at all; and if they did, would they make no attempt to censor and control it? What if it is true that bad art can enervate and corrupt a people? And if it is true, what should be done about it by such hypothetical authorities as Socrates conceived? The questions are famous, for they push the problem to its conclusion, and so we have never forgotten the *Republic*. We remember it most clearly in times of crisis like our own, when wars and dangers threaten. Meanwhile, we know, the wars of Greece went on and its civilization prepared to die; though it died only in that place, for it lived again, and it still lives in us.

And now we are having to decide again how free we can afford to be as artists and as men. Society has grown nervous. Real or imagined dangers revive the problem Plato saw. The twentieth century is different from the century before, and now in the very middle of it we wonder what is happening. Perhaps no man knows what is happening, or could possibly know; but every day we ask the question, and most days we are apprehensive. For something may be disappearing that we have always taken for granted. We may hope that it is not, but how can we be sure?

What every artist notices is that he lives in a society every member of which has a greater stake than formerly was the case in what we have come to call security. The world is a vast web that twitches incessantly with premonitions of disorder. Demagogues may exaggerate, and predatory persons may tell plain lies for their own advantage; but the people themselves are less carefree than once they were, and less certain, it would seem, that they will lose nothing by indulging the speculations of artists and philosophers. We accuse enemy countries of having murdered freedom, yet borrow from them some of their techniques; or if not that, we permit them to infect us with their doubt. We are not so sure but that some huge danger does after all exist, and that until the sky is clear we had better shut all doors against the storm. And nobody knows whose fault it is that this is so. Something has happened that no individual or party caused. We live with bureaucracy that turns in upon itself and contemplates its own elaboration, its own refinements which recall the delicate balances of those insect cultures long ago.

Public works have become more important than private houses. Education is moving toward the moment when all schools and universities will be administered by the state. Education will be too expensive for individuals to support; or else the state will doubt that individuals should do so. These may be the same thing in the end. The economic symptom is itself, perhaps, a symptom of something else. A thing becomes expensive when we have decided that we cannot afford it; the decision lies far back in our souls, or in the soul of society if society can be said to have one. We seem to think it does. We tax ourselves in the interest of a whole that is more precious than any of its parts. Even if it is not yet a monster, it estimates itself at the expense of individuals. It is the thing that must survive, and it acts as if it thought no man or artist could help it very much. It has its own laws and exacts its own penalties, the chief of which bear such cheerful names as obsolescence and liquidation.

The artist has all of this to think about today. He lives in a different world, and wonders how he should accommodate himself to it, or whether he should try. Perhaps he should take arms against the thing he sees. Perhaps he should labor to prove that freedom as he has known it will, if lost, be not well lost. Other civilizations have suffocated under their own dead weight, but this one of ours must not do so; and the secret of salvation lies in him. So he might say. And he would have to believe what he said. Also, he would have to understand it as he never understood it before. This freedom of which he speaks had better sound like a necessity. Sometimes it has sounded like a luxury which we could afford to indulge because we were rich and because the organization of our common life was comfortably loose; and because there was no great and present danger. Two world wars, and now the possibility of still another, have tightened our hearts more than many of us know and have shrunk the area in which freedom is supposed to play. But perhaps it is supposed to work. Freedom may be even more valuable than anybody has yet said. It may be our universal secret, bound to save us if we press out of it all its possible meaning. The time may have come to do just that—to persuade the people of our world that freedom is their own best good, and that if necessary they should pay for it as much as it will cost.

Its cost is measured by the danger it keeps alive: the danger from speculation and experiment. People may have to be persuaded that this is worth its weight in other gold than that of the familiar market; that the continuance of our culture depends upon its power to survive itself—if not in Greece, then in Rome, and if not in Rome, then in Paris, London, and New York—and that such power is found only in those societies which, while they love the truth, believe it to be always coming, and not here. But they must really love the truth; and the sign of this will be that they love all individuals who sincerely seek it. How sincere then will the artist have to be— how sincere, how humorous, and how profound? And how much more will he have to do in the present crisis than he has been doing in Europe and America over the past hundred years, when his subject matter has for the most part, and rather monotonously as it now appears, been the corruption and decay of modern life? The diagnosis was good, but the patient still waits upon his cure. The artist is not a physician, yet he had better be a thoughtful person. And in the current situation he had better be a person who knows what thought at the most can mean. The truth is not what anybody thinks. It is not even what the best of us think. It is still coming, and it will never be here. Meanwhile, and at any time, how much error can we afford? And how indifferent can we be to the deeper question of how we might live with the truth if we ever found it? These are tough questions, which the artist, like any responsible man, is answering even now as best he may. He is asking his world to gamble on him; and wondering, perhaps, if he is worth the risk.

He will be, it seems easy to say, as soon as his work is beautiful and good enough. Some of us could worry about this more than we do—not merely about our reward, but about what we are doing to deserve it. The artist may have to earn his freedom, with pictures and poems for which the world will gladly pay with some of its security. There could even be a poem for which a people would fight, as now they fight over insults and land. There could be a picture which society would dislocate itself to house and frame. There could be ideas that make ideologies look pale and hollow by comparison. The artist should be as ambitious as all that; should study, in addition to his own capacities, the capacities of his art itself, as if another practiced it and he stood by to see that all of its resources were remembered. We compete with our contemporaries more often than with the masters. What made them masters was that they remembered everything, and somehow put it in. The art of the novel suffers today from its leaving so much out. Most of its practitioners seem never to have read a great story, or any story at all. They have everything but what it takes to make a novel; and they complain of their reward. So, it may be, with other arts and artists. Ambition is a godlike thing, and men will worship it whenever it is supported by performance.

But ambition now might take on still another dimension—not a greater one, for nothing is greater than excellence, yet one that will serve excellence in the end. Society continues to change, and there are those who say it is already the monster we have feared. Whatever in truth it is, the artist ought to be one of the first to understand it, to sympathize with its predicament, and to start making it better at the core. He might even become a philosopher or a politician in order to do this well; but short of that, he can think more deeply and feelingly than he has done about the courage it now takes to be the sort of individual whose dignity matters more than wars and revolutions, more than welfare and the sovereignties of states. Such dignity is given to no one. It has to be created in the mind, by slow and painful stages, amid the total darkness of other men's refusal to make the attempt at all. But once it is created, it proves everything. And once it is created in an artist whose ambition is otherwise unbounded—and whose skill—it becomes the final excellence of which the rest of us had dreamed. It could even change again the changing world.

6

THE HAPPY CRITIC

A good critic, like a good poet, is made as well as born. It is impossible to imagine him without education and experience, or even erudition. He has learned how to do what he does. But he was born, too—born able to learn, and to delight in the exercise of his art. He also is an artist, and as such will never be competent wholly to explain his processes, or to teach others how they may imitate them. It is as hard, or almost as hard, to know how a fine critic arrived at his result as it is to know how a great poem or story took shape in its author's mind. The rest of us had read the work the critic read, just as all of us have lived the life the poet lived; yet we had failed to notice certain things, or to see how they combined with other things to produce the final effect which now, in the critic's words, is clearly before us.

A good critic, then, is born as well as made; and Ben Jonson, whom I paraphrase, would not I think protest the conversion of his terms. I am not so sure about my own contemporaries. Their perpetual discussion of what criticism is rarely pauses for contemplation of the fact, if it is a fact, that good critics are rare and wonderful, and not easily explained. To me it is a fact, and I take pleasure in contemplating it. The method of a given critic, or his knowledge, or his seriousness—these are important things to consider, but the sum of them is a little less important than the presence in him of genius if he has it. If he hasn't it, nothing else that he has will save him in the long run.

Genius in a critic is sense. I do not mean common sense, though that is a great thing; nor do I mean anything negative. Of course the good critic is no kind of fool, and of course he has what all men have in common; but these are not enough. I suppose I mean wisdom—the fullest, the most natural, the freest and happiest sense of what is true. The good critic is free of his knowledge and his method. And he is free of the delusion that he can explain everything in the author he treats, or that he can say once and for all what literature is, has been, should be. His seriousness does not make him dull; rather, it makes him light—not heavy, at any rate. He may not know what literature is, but he does know how it lives and breathes, and how it can make us happy. He himself knows how to be happy in the way that none but serious persons are. Not cheerful, not complacent, not easily pleased; but *when* pleased, capable of joy. We cannot take seriously one who is incapable of joy.

The foregoing must sound strange in this grim time when literature is so seldom enjoyed. By the critics, anyway. It is all work for them and no play, and I have actually encountered laymen—neither writers nor critics—who thought them dull boys. Let us not say that, but let us regret with T. S. Eliot that it has become so difficult in recent decades for anyone to be what he calls a "normal critic." Dryden for Mr. Eliot was such a critic. He practiced the art "before writing about poetry had come to mean philosophizing about it, . . . at a time when neither the fundamental nature of the poetic activity nor the social function of poetry was yet considered the subject matter for literary criticism. . . . In that happy age it did not occur to him to inquire what poetry was *for,* how it affected the nerves of listeners, how it sublimated the wishes of the poet, whom it should satisfy, and all the other questions which really have nothing to do with poetry as poetry; and the poet was not expected to be either a sibyl or a prophet. The purpose of poetry and drama was to *amuse;* but it was to amuse properly; and the larger forms of poetry should have a moral significance; by exhibiting the thoughts and passions of man through lively image and melodious verse, to edify and to refine the reader and auditor."

"I do not know," adds Mr. Eliot, "that we have improved upon this conception of the place and function of poetry." Indeed we have not, but it is depressing to note how few of Mr. Eliot's admirers have been moved by what he says here, and to realize how many of them must have jumped to his implied conclusion that it was easy in Dryden's time to do what Dryden did. No one else was doing it. Thomas Rymer, for instance, was doing the dull things we do, with enormous industry and impressive system; he was applying "the rules" to Shakespeare. He was not without merit, either; but he lacked the genius which in Dryden showed as ease, good nature, wit, and the simple power to see greatness wherever greatness was. Dryden must have seemed to Rymer a careless amateur, without true consistency or a statable plan. Yet he was the first to praise Shakespeare and Chaucer as we praise them now. Judging by the critical equipment he exposed, he should not have known how to do this. But he did know, and that is everything.

Also, he was a master of prose. A good critic must be a good writer, and it is no accident that this is so. I suspect that Rymer was sometimes infuriated by the success of Dryden's essays. It was among other things a literary success; people were ravished by their grace, as people still are. But again this was no accident. Art cannot be praised except by those who have the language; who can say things worthy of their subjects; who can be compendious and memorable; who themselves, though in another mode, are artists too. Rymer, who thought the business of the critic was to instruct the poet against negligence and miscarriage, expressed the fear in 1674 that "some critics are like wasps, that rather annoy the bees than terrify the drones." It did not occur to him that critics can be drones. They can be, even now.

PART 2

FROM SHAKESPEARE
TO SOLZHENITSYN

INTRODUCTION TO PART 2

The title of this part, obviously arbitrary, was irresistible. Van Doren, noted for his studies of classical writers, was one of the first contemporary critics to hail the work of Solzhenitsyn. Of course, the section could have begun with selections about Homer but, as stated in the Introduction, this material is available elsewhere.

It is hoped that the first three essays, the general one on Shakespeare and the two plays, a tragedy and a comedy, will lead readers to rediscover Van Doren's Shakespeare, *now surprisingly out of print. The volume has been used by a generation of students and readers, and consists of a separate essay on each Shakespeare play and one about his poetry.*

The essay on Herrick was written when Mark and Dorothy Van Doren returned from a European trip after his retirement from Columbia. It follows the plays of Shakespeare in this collection because of the vague chronological following of Herrick in English letters. No importance should be placed on the chronology, however; it is merely an editorial device for the arrangement of parts. While Van Doren's poetry demonstrates an interesting chronological development, the general essays included in this section range from his earliest years at The Nation *to the period just prior to his death. But they were not written in any particular order.*

The review of Emily Dickinson is an example of his early writing for The Nation. *A great admirer of her work, Van Doren was considering two volumes:* Further Poems of Emily Dickinson, *a volume withheld from publication by her sister Lavinia and edited by her niece Martha Dickinson Bianchi and Alfred Leete Hampson, and* Unpublished Poems of Emily Dickinson, *also edited by the Bianchi-Hampson team.*

Van Doren wrote frequently about Whitman, going back to a lengthy piece titled "Walt Whitman, Stranger" in the American Mercury *in 1935. The well-known Viking Portable Whitman carries his introduction to the poems and prose. But the piece included here is from a major address given at the Library of Congress in Washington, D.C., on the occasion of a Whitman celebration in 1955. Van Doren was one of three guest speakers along with Gay Wilson Allen and David Daiches.*

Similarly, a public festival, The Johns Hopkins Poetry Festival in 1958, was the occasion for Van Doren's views on Thomas Hardy. The program consisted of readings and lectures by eight American poets: Archibald MacLeish, Marianne Moore, John Crowe Ransom, E. E. Cummings, Robert Frost, R. P. Blackmur, and Mark Van Doren. The lecture part of the festival was sponsored by the Percy Graeme Turnbull Lecture committee.

Three reviews are interspersed with the Thomas Mann essay that was first given at a Bryn Mawr festival honoring Mann. They cover a Nation *essay-review of Mark Twain that follows Whitman, a look at Virginia Woolf's book,* The Years, *which appeared first in the* Southern Review *in 1937, and* In Dreams Begin Responsibilities *by Delmore Schwartz, which first appeared in the* Kenyon Review *in 1939. The Nation review of the Chapman was based on M. A. De Wolfe Howe's* John Jay Chapman and His Letters.

The essay on the poetry of Thomas Merton was given, as acknowledged, by courtesy of J. Laughlin, publisher of New Directions, *the principal publisher of Merton. It appears in the collection of Merton's poetry still available from that firm. In view of its intrinsic merit and the relationship of Van Doren to Merton, it is a natural for this collection. The same is true for the short tribute to Van Doren's friend and former student, John Berryman. While this essay just glances over the work of Berryman, it does "hint" at*

Berryman's development and his particular gifts. He, too, was among Van Doren's closest friends.

The penultimate essay before his brushstroke Great Books of the Western World *was actually a review of* August 1914 *by Alexander Solzhenitsyn that appeared in the revivified* Saturday Evening Post *after Van Doren died. It was not his first review in that publication, which carried many other prominent contributors since its return to publication in a larger format. In the same issue with the review, the* Post *editors mourned Van Doren's death but said "his star is fixed."*

Finally, in this section, while his comments are brief, the Great Books essay seems to me a remarkable sign of Van Doren's wide interests, that he was able to master the principal works of a variety of twentieth-century writers such as the playwrights Ibsen, Shaw, and Chekhov, the poets Yeats, Robinson, T. S. Eliot, James Joyce, Proust, Faulkner, Kafka, Camus, Orwell and, once again, Solzhenitsyn. I have edited this essay to avoid duplication with earlier essays; the full essay is available in the Great Ideas Today *series published by The Encyclopaedia Britannica, Inc.*

7

THE PLAYS OF
WILLIAM SHAKESPEARE

If the plays of Shakespeare had not been easy to write they would
have been impossible. If their solutions had once been problems
they could not have been arrived at in a dozen lifetimes, let alone
one lifetime in which two or three plays were often the output of a
single year. The great and central virtue of Shakespeare was not
achieved by taking thought, for thought cannot create a world. It
can only understand one when one has been created. Shakespeare,
starting with the world no man has made, and never indeed abandon-
ing it, made many worlds within it. Some of them are more interesting
than others, and a few of them are merely sketched; but each of
them tends to be internally consistent, immediately knowable,
and—at the same time that it is familiar—permanently fresh and
strange. He may never have said to himself that this was what he
had done, and if he talked to himself at all there were other excuses
for congratulation. As a poet, considering the term in the narrower,
verbal sense which is its commonest meaning now, he had written
so well that any kind of poetry and any kind of prose can be found
in him at its best. This has its lasting importance, being one of the
reasons that the words he used have become so widely known. But
a reason of deeper importance is the context of those words in the
worlds they helped to make.

How these worlds came into being cannot be plainly said. If it could be, the criticism of Shakespeare would at once reach an end. Criticism grows desperate from time to time and denies their existence. Shakespeare was merely a poet, a word-magician; or merely a carpenter of plays; or merely an Elizabethan; or merely a man who wrote for money. He was all those things and more things like them, but to be satisfied with saying so is to be thrown off the scent of his distinction. At the opposite extreme criticism grows fanatical in the definition of devices by which the miracle of creation was performed; performance assumed, the investigator looks for tricks. The styles of Shakespeare are studied—the styles, for it is true that he had no style, no special way of writing beyond the way of writing well, and that he is not to be imitated except by one who will say things both as clearly and as interestingly as he did. But his success is not a matter of devices; or if so, they are secondary to a larger method which ordered them instinctively to the ends of unity and delight. The unity of any play is not alone a matter of images, though the coherence of its metaphors may be amazing; or of diction and syntax, though the monosyllables of "Julius Caesar" and the involutions of "The Winter's Tale" have much to do with the natures of their respective universes; or of atmosphere, though the difference between the environment of "Lear" and the environment of "Antony and Cleopatra" is so palpable that one may well become lost in the exercise of feeling it; or of character, though Shakespeare's people live forever; or of plot, though he is inimitable at story-telling. Beyond all these, worthy of study and praise as of course they are, there is in any of the successful plays a created or creature life, a unity of being which reveals itself with every step of our progress into its interior.

It is literally true that while we read a play of Shakespeare's we are in it. We may be drawn in swiftly or slowly—in most cases it is swiftly—but once we are there we are enclosed. That is the secret, and it is still a secret, of Shakespeare's power to interest us. He conditions us to a particular world before we are aware that it exists; then he absorbs us in its particulars. We scarcely say to ourselves, this world exists; nor do we pause to note how consistent each thing in it is with every other. Our attention is on the details, which we take in as details should be taken in, one at a time. Meanwhile there is for us no other world. The great world is not forgotten—Shakespeare indeed knows best how to keep us reminded of its greatness—but it is here confined to a single mode of its being. He is not telling the whole truth in any play, nor does he do so in all of them together, nor could he have done so had he written ten thousand. But the piece of truth with which he is occupied at a given moment is for that moment eloquent both of itself and of the remainder. It seems to be all. It is satisfactory and complete. With each new line a play of Shakespeare's lights its own recesses, deepens its original hue, echoes, supports, and authenticates itself. The world is not there, but this part of it is so entirely there that we miss nothing; it is as if existence had decided to measure itself by a new standard. And the secret of that standard is shared with us. Shakespeare, who denies his reader nothing, denies him least of all the excitement of feeling that he is where things are simply and finally alive.

Only a remarkable artist could have done this, and only a remarkable man—a man, moreover, in whom the balance was well-nigh perfect between understanding and observation, between intellect and instinct, between vision and sight. It has long been recognized that his characters, while irreducibly individual, partake of that nature which belongs to all men, and seldom desert the types in whose terms they were conceived. Hamlet is young, melancholy, courteous, brilliant, and moral. Falstaff is old, fat, drunken, untruthful, and witty. None of those traits is new, and it would almost appear that nothing in either man had been invented by Shakespeare. Each, however, has his unique carriage and voice, and will not be mistaken for any other man on earth. He is first of all a member of the human race. After that he is himself, saying things which Shakespeare knows how to envelop in a silence so natural that for the time we hear no other sound than that of his discourse. Yet the act of being himself never takes him beyond the range of our understanding. We hear him with our ears and we see him with our eyes, but he is most valuable to us because we can think about him with all the mind we possess. He is not that monstrous thing, an individual undefined, any more than Shakespeare's worlds are irresponsible constructions, or any more than Shakespeare's poetry is idiot-pure. Sometimes this poetry struts on cumbrous wings when it should go by foot, but seldom is it being written for its own sake, as if poetry were the most precious thing in the world. To Shakespeare it was apparently not that. The world was still more precious—the great one he never forgot, and the little one in which he knew how to imprison its voice and body. What he dealt in was existence, and his dealings were responsible, high-hearted, and humane. The reader who places himself in his hands will not be protected from any experience, but he will be safe from outrage because he will always know his bearings. What is supposed to happen in Shakespeare's plays does happen; and what has happened anywhere cannot be finally hated. Shakespeare loved the world as it is. That is why he understood it so well; and that in turn is why, being the artist he was, he could make it over again into something so rich and clear.

8

HAMLET

It has been said of Hamlet that something in his genius renders him superior to decision and incapable of act, and it has been pointed out that he dominates the busiest of all known plays. Both views are right. His antic disposition has been analyzed as a symptom of abnormality and as a device for seeming mad. Neither theory is without support. He has been called the best of men and the worst of men. One judgment is as just as the other. Opinions have differed as to whether his deepest attention is engaged by the murder of his father, the marriage of his mother, the villainy of his uncle the King, the senility of Polonius, the apparent perfidy of Ophelia, the reliability of Horatio, the meddling of Rosencrantz and Guildenstern, or the manliness of Fortinbras. Any of them will do. Scarcely anything can be said that will be untrue of this brilliant and abounding young man the first crisis in whose life is also, to our loss, the last.

It has been said of the play "Hamlet" that its best scene is the one in which Horatio first sees the ghost, or the one in which he tells Hamlet of it, or the one in which Hamlet himself sees it and swears his friends to secrecy, or the one in which Polonius bids farewell to his son and warns his daughter away from the prince, or the one in which Ophelia reports Hamlet's disorder, or the one in which Polonius explains it to the King and Queen, or the one in which Hamlet, entering with a book, seems to Polonius to support the explanation, or the one in which Hamlet discovers the intentions of Rosencrantz and Guildenstern and discourses to them of his misanthropy, or the one in which he greets the players and conceives a use to which they can be put, or the one in which Ophelia is loosed to him while the King and Polonius listen as spies, or the one in which he addresses the players on the subject of their art, or the one in which the play he has planned breaks down the King's composure, or the one with the recorders, or the one in which Hamlet cannot kill the King because he is praying, or the one in his mother's closet when Polonius is stabbed and the ghost walks again, or the one in which he makes merry over Polonius's supper of worms, or the one in which he watches Fortinbras march against Poland, or the one in which Ophelia sings mad songs and rouses her brother to revenge, or the one in which, while Laertes plots with the King, the Queen reports Ophelia's death, or the one in the graveyard, or the one with Osric, or the one at the end which leaves only Horatio and Fortinbras alive. Any of them will do. For all of the scenes in "Hamlet" are good, and relatively to the play as a whole each one in its turn is best.

The two absolutes are related. Neither the hero nor his play can be taken apart. The joints are invisible. The character of Hamlet would appear to be no character at all because a name cannot be found for it, or—which is the same thing—because too many can be found. Yet no reader or beholder of the play has ever doubted that Hamlet was one man, or doubted that he knew him better than most men. He is so singular in each particular, to paraphrase Florizel's account of Perdita, that all his acts are kings. He is alive to the last syllable, and where there is so much life there is no blank space for labels. So likewise with the tragedy of which he is the heart and brain if not the whole moving body. There is no best scene in "Hamlet" because it is not made up of scenes; it is one situation and one action, and though like any whole it is composed of parts there is no part whose tissue can be separated from the rest without the sound of tearing. "Hamlet" is a highly organized animal, sensitive and thoroughbred, each of whose sinews overlaps another, each of whose tendons tightens some extremity, and all of whose blood-stream is necessary to the unique, quick life which even the quietest movement expresses.

An attempt to enter the play through any scene of the conventional division will leave us still outside it—aware once more of its unspeakable vitality, but rewarded with no other sight than that of divers muscles rippling under skin. The thing has been put together, but either there are no joints or there are so many that the creature is all curves. Take, for instance, the section of the play which is called Act II, Scene ii. The number of its incidents is not the measure of its fullness, nor is the sum total of the things it tells us about Hamlet the final sum of our experience. The linkage of the incidents, the way they glide into one another without our being warned, is more important than their number; and our experience is not confined to the present Hamlet, or to what is happening around him now. The scene twitches remote corners of a dramatic web whose size we for the moment do not see; we gather that the whole play is implicit here, though we cannot be specific as to what is coming.

Rosencrantz and Guildenstern, two old friends of Hamlet, have arrived at court to keep him company; to draw him on to pleasures in the midst of which, as now the King makes clear, he may disclose the nature of his affliction. The King admits no other explanation than a father's death, and lets it be understood, the Queen concurring, that the motive behind this lawful espionage is a desire to cure the prince's condition. As Rosencrantz and Guildenstern are led away to find Hamlet and begin their work, Polonius enters to announce that the ambassadors from Norway have returned and to assure the King and Queen that he has found the cause of Hamlet's lunacy. They are eager to hear the cause, but first they must receive the ambassadors, who bring word that old Norway has forbidden Fortinbras to continue the advance on Denmark which has so much troubled the King; and that Fortinbras, marching now against Poland, requests the right to cross Denmark so that he may gain his objective. The King, promising to consider the request at another time, dismisses the ambassadors and turns to Polonius, who with more art than matter, and with promises of brevity which his amusing tediousness belies, develops the theory that Hamlet is mad because Ophelia has repulsed him. The Queen has believed that her overhasty marriage was the cause, but agrees that Polonius's explanation is very likely. The King asks for better proof, whereupon Polonius remarks that Hamlet is in the habit of walking here in the lobby and that Ophelia can be set in his way while the King and her father watch behind an arras. As the King consents, Hamlet, who may have overheard the conclusion of the dialogue, enters reading a book. Polonius asks the King and Queen to be left alone with him, and argues from the nature of the insults he stays to receive that Hamlet is indeed afflicted with love-melancholy; though Hamlet's only state would appear to be boredom with old fools and anxiety for his own safety—"except my life, my life." As Polonius goes out, bewildered yet all the more convinced that he is right and that a meeting between Hamlet and his daughter must take place, Rosencrantz and Guildenstern pass him and are greeted by Hamlet, who plays a game of wit with them until their guard is down and he can ask them bluntly why they have come to Elsinore. They hesitate and temporize, but he forces them to confess that they have been sent for by the King and Queen. At once he tells them he will make everything clear: he has of late lost all his mirth, so that the earth and the great sky above it are to him but foul and pestilent, and man—the beauty of the world, the paragon of animals, the creature nearest the angels and most like a god—delights not him. He has spoken his best prose for the benefit of two fools upon whom he wishes to make a certain impression. But he has been betrayed into the eloquence of truth, and so he breaks off with the abrupt addition that woman delights him neither, though by their smiling they seem to say so. Their only thought, they assure him, is of the poor entertainment such a prince would be able to offer the players who have just come to Elsinore. He is very much interested in the news that players have come, and as a trumpet announces their approach he summons high spirits to inform Rosencrantz and Guildenstern that the King and Queen are deceived: he is but mad north-north-west. In still higher spirits he jests at Polonius who has entered in advance of the players, and when they enter at last he greets them excitedly, pressing one of them to recite Aeneas's speech about Priam's slaughter. The player complies, but is so overcome by the speech that he weeps and cannot go on. Hamlet, dismissing the rest of the troupe to Polonius's care, holds this one member until he consents to play "The Murder of Gonzago" tomorrow night and to learn some dozen or sixteen lines which will be inserted in the text. Then Hamlet, commanding him to follow Polonius and mock him not, and sending away Rosencrantz and Guildenstern with assurances of their welcome to Elsinore, is left alone for the soliloquy which ends the scene. In a mere dream of passion, a fiction, this player here has wept for Hecuba. What would he do had he the motive and the cue for passion that Hamlet has? Is Hamlet a coward that so far he has done nothing to avenge his father's murder? The question enrages him and he falls to cursing the King. But that is nothing. He must act. He still must be indirect, for the spirit he has seen may have been the devil and not his father. So—now he has it—he will act to gain the knowledge he needs. He will put on a play that will make the King blench if he is guilty. And if he but blench, Hamlet will know his course. The play's the thing.

Such a synopsis is circumstantial and would seem to be complete. But it leaves almost everything out. It does not suggest the quality of Rosencrantz and Guildenstern—the combination in them of the sinister and the commonplace—and it does not begin to explore the processes of Hamlet as he discourses with them, or to explain the full meaning for himself of the great speech about earth and man. It does not record the suspicions we may have as we listen to the King's expressed motive for spying on Hamlet; for we can guess that he is lying, but we do not know just what he fears, nor do we know how deeply the Queen is disturbed. It does not render our still unripened sense of a stern and remote significance in the military movements of Fortinbras, whom we perceive we are not being permitted to forget but whose importance as a symbol is to manifest itself much later. It does not balance Polonius on that subtle point of space which he occupies throughout three acts, moving us to consider him simultaneously as ridiculous and pathetic, consequential and a nuisance, the father of Ophelia and the victim with her of the prince's newborn savagery; it does not indicate that his diagnosis can be credited as correct, and it certainly does not examine the whole question of Hamlet's feeling towards the man who was to have been his father-in-law—"and look you mock him not." It does not register as well as particular; he has thought much about the theater, and it may be that he is more at home with actors than with other people. It does not describe the beautiful courtesy, even if it be tempered by mockery, with which he welcomes Rosencrantz and Guildenstern to Elsinore. It fails, in brief, to follow the in-numerable nerves which connect this part of the play with every other part, and which converge in the vital organ of the closing soliloquy as extensions of the same nerves converge to produce other soliloquies, other organs, in other areas.

No synopsis of "Hamlet," whole or part, can hope to succeed. The play is its own synopsis, and nothing short will do. Neither will anything longer; analysis in this case overruns and outrages art. Shakespeare for once has perfectly translated idea into act. What-ever the idea was, we now have only the play, and it is so clear that it becomes mysterious. For it is nothing but detail. The density of its concreteness is absolute. We do not know why Hamlet does this or that, we only know that he does it, and that we are interested in nothing else while he does it. We can no more understand him than we can doubt him. He is an enigma because he is real. We do not know why he was created or what he means. We simply and amply perceive that he exists.

Hamlet is intellectual, but we do not learn this from his thoughts, for he has none; he does not deliver himself of propositions. Of the many statements he makes there is none which is made for its own sake, and with the sense that it would be true at another time or place. In any situation only the relevant portion of the person speaks; the whole man never does, except in the play as a whole, which can be thought of as his body speaking, or rather his life. He is that unique thing in literature, a credible genius. But the reason is that Shakespeare has kept our view restricted to the surface. Here is an intellectual seen altogether from the outside. We know him as one from the way he behaves, not from the things he says he believes. We may not assume, indeed, that he believes what he says. For one thing he is a soul in agitation, his equilibrium has been lost. This glass of fashion and this mold of form, this noble mind whose harmony was once like that of sweet bells rung in tune, this courtier, soldier, scholar whose disposition has hitherto been generous and free from all contriving, this matchless gentleman who has never been known to overstep the modesty of nature, is not himself save for a few minutes at the end when his calmness comes back like magic and his apology to Laertes can almost avert the catastrophe which every event has prepared. His words elsewhere are wild and whirling; or they are cruel in their kindness; or they are simply cruel. Or they are spoken for a calculated effect—the calculation in most cases being extempore. For Hamlet is immensely sensitive to his environment, and adjusts himself with marvelous quickness to its many changes. His asides are sudden, like needles whose function is to keep both him and us awake to the farthest implications of the danger close at hand. His repartee is pistol-swift, whipped out by one forever abnormally on guard against real or imagined enemies. And his soliloquies are secret mirrors the subdued brilliance of whose shifting planes reflects the predicament that surrounds him, past and future as well as present.

Curiously then we know a man in terms of what he is not; this gentlest of all heroes is never gentle. But it is more complicated than that. Hamlet is an actor. Like any character in whom Shakespeare was greatly interested, he plays a role. He plays indeed many roles, being supreme in tragedy as Falstaff was supreme in comedy. His long interest in the theater has taught him how, but his best tutors now are the pressure of circumstance and the richness of his own nature. Like Falstaff he shows the man he is by playing many men. With the exception of Horatio there is no person in the play for whose benefit he has not conceived and studied a part. He acts with the King and Queen, with Ophelia, with Polonius, with the court at large; taking on and putting off each role as occasion dictates, and at the climax of the tragedy wearing all of them simultaneously. For in the scene of the play within the play he has his audiences for the first time together. Now the fiction of Ophelia's Hamlet must harmonize with that of her father's, of the King's, of the Queen's, and with that of the general public. Only a virtuoso would succeed. But Hamlet, not to speak of Shakespeare, is a virtuoso, and he succeeds. No playwright ever attempted a subtler scene, or ever achieved it with so little show of labor. The only thing we are conscious of is the intentness with which we follow the waves of meaning across Hamlet's face. The whole meaning of the play is in vibration there, even if we cannot put it in words of our own. There is, of course, no slightest reason why we should desire to do so.

As always in Shakespeare, the style of Hamlet is the man. He is made of mercury and so has many styles, yet they are one if only because they ever are telling us of what he is made. His tongue is as flexible as his mind. It knows its way among all words, all tones, all attitudes. And it is superbly trained. The intellect of its owner is apparent in nothing so much as his literary skill. With no notice at all he can say anything, and be master of what he has said. "Well said, old mole! Canst work i' the earth so fast?" "To be honest, as this world goes, is to be one man pick'd out of ten thousand." "You cannot, sir, take from me anything that I will more willingly part withal." "Then is doomsday near." "Denmark's a prison." "O God, I could be bounded in a nutshell and count myself a king of infinite space, were it not that I have bad dreams." "To be, or not to be: that is the question." "Thus conscience does make cowards of us all." "Get thee to a nunnery, go." "I say, we will have no more marriages." "No, good mother, here's metal more attractive." "You would play upon me, you would seem to know my stops, you would pluck out the heart of my mystery." "I will speak daggers to her, but use none." "I must be cruel, only to be kind." "Not where he eats, but where he is eaten." "I see a cherub that sees them." "Where be your gibes now, your gambols, your songs, your flashes of merriment, that were wont to set the table on a roar? Not one now, to mock your own grinning? Quite chop-fallen?" "But I am very sorry, good Horatio, that to Laertes I forgot myself." "But thou wouldst not think how ill all's here about my heart." "If it be now, 't is not to come; if it be not to come, it will be now; if it be not now, yet it will come; the readiness is all." "The rest is silence." The simplicity of such utterances reveals a great man and a princely artist, an artist too much the master of his medium to be proud of what he can do with it, or even to be conscious that it is there. But Hamlet can be elaborate as well as simple, artful as well as quick. His address to the players says something which he wants them to understand, and the thing it says has been said for all time; yet the man who is speaking enjoys his speech, and may be a little proud of the nobility which knows its way so well among the short words and the long ones, the epigrams and the periods.

Speak the speech, I pray you, as I pronounc'd it to you, trippingly on the tongue; but if you mouth it, as many of your players do, I had as lief the town-crier spoke my lines. Nor do not saw the air too much with your hand, thus, but use all gently; for in the very torrent, tempest, and, as I may say, the whirlwind of passion, you must acquire and beget a temperance that may give it smoothness. O, it offends me to the soul to see a robustious periwig-pated fellow tear a passion to tatters, to very rags, to split the ears of the groundlings, who for the most part are capable of nothing but inexplicable dumb-shows and noise. I could have such a fellow whipp'd for o'erdoing Termagant. It out-herods Herod. Pray you, avoid it. . . . Be not too tame neither, but let your own discretion be your tutor. Suit the action to the word, the word to the action; with this special observance, that you o'erstep not the modesty of nature. For anything so overdone is from the purpose of playing, whose end, both at the first and now, was and is, to hold, as 't were, the mirror up to nature; to show virtue her own feature, scorn her own image, and the very age and body of time his form and pressure. Now this over-done, or come tardy off, though it make the unskillful laugh, cannot but make the judicious grieve; the censure of the which one must, in your allowance, o'erweigh a whole theatre of others. O, there be players that I have seen play, and heard others praise, and that highly, not to speak it profanely, that, neither having the accent of Christians nor the gait of Christian, pagan, nor man, have so strutted and bellowed that I have thought some of Nature's journeymen had made men and not made them well, they imitated humanity so abominably.

"Imitated humanity so abominably," "capable of nothing but inexplicable dumb-shows and noise." Only a skilled tongue could say such phrases well, and only a proud tongue would undertake them at all. A man who can talk like that must be aware of everything in the world—except perhaps the disproportion between his discourse and its occasion. And of Shakespeare we are to remember that he never used in his play the speech which for his hero had seemed to call for so long a commentary. But then we shall be confirmed in our belief that the character of Hamlet is the character of an actor, and that the instinct of Shakespeare as a dramatic poet is to pour his fullest gifts into such persons. That Hamlet is histrionic is no less clear than that he is high-strung, cerebral, magnanimous, and sometimes obscene. Richard II had been an amateur of the boards, Jaques had been a sentimentalist spoiling to be a star, and Brutus to his own loss had been no actor at all. Hamlet is so much of a professional that the man in him is indistinguishable from the mime. His life as we have it is so naturally and completely a play that we can almost think of him as his own author, his own director, and his own protagonist. We can even think of him as his own entire cast, he is the plexus of so much humanity, the mirror in which so many other minds are registered.

We see Hamlet in other persons even more clearly than in himself. His relation to each of them is immediate and delicate; his least gesture records itself in them—in their concern, their pity, their love, their anger, or their fear. They cannot be indifferent to him, and this is one reason that we cannot. Nor is vanity in him the cause. He has not willed or desired his eminence. It is not in his nature to dominate humanity, and at last destroy it. Yet he does; this gentleman warps every other life to his own, and scatters death like a universal plague. Not quite universal, either. The world of this tragedy, like that of any other tragedy by Shakespeare, is large; Denmark is a prison and its air is close to breathe, but four times we have heard through darkness the brisk tramp of Fortinbras's feet on the bright ice beyond tragedy's frontiers. Fortinbras is Hamlet's frame. He is not completely drawn until his cannon, his drums, and his colors come on with him at the end to announce that human existence will be what it was before Hamlet lived. But then he is firmly drawn; the story of Hamlet, however morbid, has been confined. Another frame, an inner one, is Hamlet's good friend Horatio, who will live on until he has reported Hamlet and his cause aright to the unsatisfied, until he has healed a hero's wounded name. For just as Hamlet with his last breath remembers the state and thinks to give Fortinbras his dying voice for king, so he remembers that his aim had never been to strew the stage of life with corpses; to deliver Rosencrantz and Guildenstern to an English hangman, to feed Polonius to politic worms, to end Ophelia, dripping with tears and muddy death, into unsanctified ground. Within these two frames the spectacle of Hamlet is forever suspended. A merest glance from us, a chance return to any scene, and the whole movement recommences. Hamlet walks again, alone and yet surrounded: a genius of unfathomable depth who yet is in contact at every point of his clear surface with another life as sensitive to his as a still night is to sound. That honor could too much change him, that scruples too fine could distort him into a dealer of coarse death, was both his tragedy and the world's. The world could not let so destructive a man live longer, but when it sacrificed him it lost the light of its fiercest sun.

9

AS YOU LIKE IT

The airiness of "As You Like It" is as much the work of thought as the reward of feeling. The comedy seems to balance like a bubble on a point of thin space; yet space in its neighborhood has not worn thin, and the bubble is as tough as eternity, it does not break. This, doubtless, is because the sentiments of its author were at the moment in a state of rare equilibrium, and because his nerves were happy in an unconscious health. Also, however, it is because his mind was tuned to its task. "As You Like It" is so charming a comedy that in order to enjoy it we need not think about it at all. But if we do think about it we become aware of intellectual operations noiselessly and expertly performed. We see an idea anatomized until there is nothing left of it save its original mystery. We watch an attitude as it is taken completely apart and put completely together again. And all of this is done without visible effort. Shakespeare's understanding of his subject increases until the subject is exhausted, until there is no more to understand; and still there are no signs of labor or fatigue. Shakespeare has been denied an intellect. But whatever it took to write "As You Like It" was among other things mental, and the exact like of it, as well as the exact degree, has never been seen in literature again.

"As You Like It" is a criticism of the pastoral sentiment, an examination of certain familiar ideas concerning the simple life and the golden age. It is not a satire; its examination is conducted without prejudice. For once in the world a proposition is approached from all of its sides, and from top and bottom. The proposition is perhaps multiple: the country is more natural than the court, shepherds live lives of enviable innocence and simplicity, the vices that devour the heart of civilized man will drop from him as soon as he walks under a greenwood tree, perversion and malice cannot survive in the open air, the shade of beech trees is the only true Academy, one impulse from the vernal wood will teach us more than all the sages can. Yet it is single too, and pastoral literature has monotonously intoned it. Shakespeare relieves the monotony by statement which is also understanding, by criticism which is half laughter and half love—or, since his laughter is what it is, all love. The result is something very curious. When Rosalind has made her last curtsy and the comedy is done, the pastoral sentiment is without a leg to stand on, yet it stands; and not only stands but dances. The idea of the simple life has been smiled off the earth and yet here it is still, smiling back at us from every bough of Arden. The Forest of Arden has been demonstrated not to exist, yet none of its trees has fallen; rather the entire plantation waves forever, and the sun upon it will not cease. The doctrine of the golden age has been as much created as destroyed. We know there is nothing in it, and we know that everything is in it. We perceive how silly it is and why we shall never be able to do without it. We comprehend the long failure of cynicism to undo sentiment. Here there is neither sentiment nor cynicism; there is understanding. An idea is left hanging in free air, without contamination or support. That is the place for ideas, as Shakespeare the comic poet seems to have known without being told.

"Where will the old Duke live?" asks Orlando's villainous brother of the still more villainous wrestler Charles. The unscrupulous bruiser answers in terms that may surprise us by their pettiness:

They say he is already in the forest of Arden, and a many merry men with him; and there they live like the old Robin Hood of England. They say many young gentlemen flock to him every day, and fleet the time carelessly, as they did in the golden world.

That is the text to be annotated, the idea to be analyzed in the comedy to come. But analysis has already taken place, a cross-glance has already been shot by one whose mind will go on to draw lines in every direction athwart the theme. Shakespeare's first operation consists of putting such a speech into such a mouth, and letting it be ground between great molars there, unsympathetically. We get the doctrine, but we get it cooked, as comedy prefers: through the most unlikely medium, and the most unconscious. The first act is for the most part mechanically introductory to what follows; its business is to push everybody off to Arden, and Shakespeare writes it without much interest, since his sole interest is Arden. Rosalind is introduced, and of course it is important that we should find her from the first a gallant and witty girl, as we do. But she too is being saved for the forest. Charles's speech is the one memorable thing we have heard before we plunge into the depths of Arden at the beginning of the second act. But it is distinctly memorable, and it modifies the music which plays for us in the old Duke's mind.

> Now, my co-mates and brothers in exile,
> Hath not old custom made this life more sweet
> Than that of painted pomp? Are not there woods
> More free from peril than the envious court? . . .
> Sweet are the uses of adversity,
> Which, like the toad, ugly and venomous,
> Wears yet a precious jewel in his head;
> And this our life, exempt from public haunt,
> Finds tongues in trees, books in the running brooks,
> Sermons in stones, and good in every thing.

There is the text once more, translated into so quiet and so sweet a style that we may be tempted to believe it is the author speaking. But he was speaking as well in Charles; or rather he speaks in both—in their relation, which is only one of many relations the play will explore. The simple text will receive further statement through four pleasant acts. Good old Adam reminds Orlando of "the antique world" which was so much purer than "the fashion of these times." Shepherds appear named Corin and Silvius, and one of them goes sighing through the forest for love of his Phebe. A member of the Duke's retinue in exile knows how to be philosophical about everything; the humorous sadness of Jaques promises to ripen into wisdom now that ingratitude is forgotten and ambition can be shunned. We look to him for the sermons that so far have remained silent in their stones.

> Give me leave
> To speak my mind, and I will through and through
> Cleanse the foul body of the infected world,
> If they will patiently receive my medicine.

So radical a boast in such emancipated terms, delivered by one who sees through the mummery of manners and considers compliment to be but the encounter of two dog-apes, leads us to expect that in Jaques if in no one else the doctrine of the Duke will yield edifying fruit. Glimpses of a paradisal landscape are not withheld— boughs mossed with age, antique oaks whose roots peep out at brawling brooks, and purlieus of the forest where stand sheepcotes fenced about with olive trees. And Shakespeare by no means stops short of miraculous conversions under the influence of this place. It seems to work. Oliver's transformation tastes sweetly to him, making him the thing he is; he will live and die a shepherd. The base Duke Frederick scarcely sets foot in the forest before an old religious man, harmonious with the wild wood, turns him not only from his hatred for the old Duke but from the world. The text is given every opportunity to state itself, and nowhere does the comedy overtly contradict it.

All the while, however, it is being subtly undermined and sapped of its simplicity. Touchstone shreds it with the needle of his dialectic, with the razor of his parody. Silvius's cry of "Phebe, Phebe, Phebe" reminds him of his country love:

> I remember, when I was in love I broke my sword upon a stone, and bid him take that for coming a-night to Jane Smile; and I remember the kissing of her batlet and the cow's dugs that her pretty chopt hands had milk'd; and I remember the wooing of a peascod instead of her; from whom I took two cods and, giving her them again, said with weeping tears, "Wear these for my sake."

Encountering Corin in the forest and receiving from him the pastoral gospel—that courts are corrupt and manners unnatural—he juggles it till he has proved that courtiers are indistinguishable from shepherds, for tar on the hands of the one class is equivalent to civet on the hands of the other, and both substances are lowly born. When Corin takes refuge in the immemorial claim of the countryman that he lives and lets live, his only pride being to watch his ewes graze and his lambs suck, Touchstone trips him up by translating what he has said into the cynical language of cities:

That is another simple sin in you, to bring the ewes and the rams together, and to offer to get your living by the copulation of cattle; to be bawd to a bell-wether, and to betray a she-lamb of a twelvemonth to a crooked-pated, old, cuckoldy ram, out of all reasonable match.

Rosalind enters reading one of the poems Orlando has written for her on the bark of a tree. It is a bad poem, and she knows it; but Touchstone knows it well enough to have a parody ready. He has no patience with country love, yet because he is where he is he cultivates the one wench available—ill-favored Audrey, whom the gods have not made poetical, and on whom literary puns are lost. He makes one nevertheless, on Ovid and the goats; and presses in at last among the country copulatives to be wedded with his poor virgin. He is without illusion; so much so that he will not claim he can do without it. His dryness touches the pastoral text throughout, and alters it; the detachment of his wit gives everything perspective, including himself. He is intellect afield; contemptuous of what he sees so far from home, but making the thin best of what is there. Not much is there when his withering, somewhat bored glance has circled the horizon.

Nor do we miss the sour look in Jaques's eyes as he roams this paradise. The exiled gentlemen are tyrants to the deer even as their usurpers are to them.

> He pierceth through
> The body of the country, city, court,
> Yea, and of this our life.

The songs which thread the play so prettily are little better than noise to him, and he parodies one of them without mercy. Orlando does not impress him by the innocence and eagerness of his love; he is a young fool who mars trees with verses. The huddle of marriages at the end is "another flood, and these couples are coming to the ark." He is not dry like Touchstone, for there is in him the juice of discontent; but he also takes down the temperature of romance, he sophisticates the pastoral text with grimaces of understanding.

But nothing is more characteristic of the comedy than the fact that its heroine is the most searching critic of its theme. Rosalind's laughter is neither dry nor wry; it is high and clear, it has a silver sound, and the sun dances among its fiery, impalpable particles. Her disguise as a man does not explain the quality of this laughter. There are as many kinds of men as of women, and a different girl would have become a different boy; one, for instance, who moped and sighed and languished in the purlieus of romance. Rosalind has no difficulty with the language of scoffing youth. To such a fellow the poems of Orlando are tedious homilies of love. "I was never so berhym'd since Pythagoras' time, that I was an Irish rat, which I can hardly remember." Her vocabulary is as tart and vernacular as that of Mercutio, Faulconbridge, or Hotspur. The skirts of the forest are for her the "fringe upon a petticoat," love is a madness deserving the dark house and the whip, if Orlando will accept her as his physician she will wash his liver "as clean as a sound sheep's heart," Phebe has no more beauty than without candle may go dark to bed, when lovers lack words they should kiss as orators in the same predicament spit, she will be jealous over Orlando as a Barbary cockpigeon over his hen, her affection hath an unknown bottom like the bay of Portugal, love hath made Silvius a tame snake. Language like this is not learned by putting on man's apparel, nor is there any sign that it goes against Rosalind's grain to jest about incontinence, your neighbor's bed, and the inevitable horns; there is a rank reality in her speech, as in the speech of Shakespeare's best women always. And she would appear to be without any understanding whatever of the rare states to which lovers can be reduced. Her account of Oliver and Celia is that they

no sooner met but they look'd; no sooner look'd but they lov'd; no sooner lov'd but they sigh'd; no sooner sigh'd but they ask'd one another the reason; no sooner knew the reason but they sought the remedy; and in these degrees have they made a pair of stairs to marriage which they will climb incontinent, or else be incontinent before marriage. They are in the very wrath of love and they will together. Clubs cannot part them.

The tone is unsympathetic, logically enough for a young woman whose diatribe against the doctrine of the broken heart has become classic:

The poor world is almost six thousand years old, and in all this time there was not any man died in his own person, videlicet, in a love-cause. Troilus had his brains dash'd out with a Grecian club; yet he did what he could to die before; and he is one of the patterns of love. Leander, he would have liv'd many a fair year though Hero had turn'd nun, if it had not been for a hot mid-summer night; for, good youth, he went but forth to wash him in the Hellespont and being taken with the cramp was drown'd; and the foolish chroniclers of that age found it was—Hero of Sestos. But these are all lies. Men have died from time to time and worms have eaten them, but not for love.

The realism is uproarious, as the prose is artful and the wit is incessant. "You shall never take her without answer," she warns Orlando of the true Rosalind, "unless you take her without her tongue." Her gaiety runs like quicksilver, and is as hard to head off. She is of great value for that reason to her author, who can so easily use her as a commentator on his play when it grows absurd—as, being a pastoral play, it must. He can use her, for instance, to silence Phebe, Silvius, Orlando, and even herself when the four of them have carried too far the liturgy of one another's names. "Pray you," she says, "no more of this; 't is like the howling of Irish wolves against the moon."

All this is true. Yet it is also true that Rosalind loves Orlando without limit, and that she is the happiest of many happy persons in Arden. Her criticism of love and cuckoo-land is unremitting, yet she has not annihilated them. Rather she has preserved them by removing the flaws of this softness. That is the duty of criticism— a simple duty for a girl with sound imagination and a healthy heart. As Arden emerges from the fires of "As You Like It" a perfected symbol of the golden age, so Rosalind steps forth not burned but brightened, a perfected symbol of the romantic heroine. Romance has been tested in her until we know it cannot shatter; laughter has made it sure of itself. There is only one thing sillier than being in love, and that is thinking it is silly to be in love. Rosalind skips through both errors to wisdom.

She, not Jaques, is the philosopher of the play. Hers is the only mind that never rests; his bogs down in the mire of melancholy, in the slough of self-love. He is too fond of believing he is wise to be as wise as he sounds, either in the set speech he makes about man's seven ages or in the insults he considers himself at all times to deliver. His distrust of manners turns out to be the disaffection of a boor. His melancholy, like his wit, is an end in itself, a dyspeptic indulgence, an exercise of vanity that serves none of wisdom's purposes. "Motley's the only wear," he decides, but when he is dressed in it he has no place to go. "I can suck melancholy out of a song as a weasel sucks eggs," he tells Amiens, and the figure is better than he knows. He slithers through Arden, in love with his own sad eyes. "Will you sit down with me?" he asks Orlando, "and we two will rail against our mistress the world, and all our misery." Orlando's answer is priggish, but it is nearer to the meaning of the play. "I will chide no breather in the world but myself, against whom I know most faults." Jaques is a fat and greasy citizen of the world of easy words. He is a fine poet at this stage of Shakespeare's career, but he will degenerate into Thersites and Apemantus. Rosalind it is who knows his weakness best.

Jaques. I have neither the scholar's melancholy, which is emulation; nor the musician's, which is fantastical; nor the courtier's, which is proud; nor the soldier's, which is ambitious; nor the lawyer's, which is politic; nor the lady's, which is nice; nor the lover's, which is all these; but it is a melancholy of mine own, compounded of many simples, extracted from many objects; and indeed the sundry contemplation of my travels, in which my often rumination wraps me in a most humourous sadness—

Rosalind. A traveller! By my faith, you have great reason to be sad. I fear you have sold your own lands to see other men's; then, to have seen much, and to have nothing, is to have rich eyes and poor hands.

Jaques. Yes, I have gained my experience.

Rosalind. And your experience makes you sad. I had rather have a fool to make me merry than experience to make me sad; and to travel for it too!

Jaques has seen much and can say anything, but he has nothing. Experience has made him sad. The more experience Rosalind has the merrier she grows. She too is a traveler, but she has not sold her own lands. She has taken her integrity with her to Arden, tucked under her three-cornered cap. It is proper that the limitations of Jaques should be stated by her, for if in him we have the pastoral sentiment criticized we have in her the only intelligence capable of judging the criticism. She judges with more intelligence—with, for instance, instinct and love—but that again is proper to the comedy of Shakespeare's prime.

10

ROBERT HERRICK REVISITED

It began in Cambridge. The master of one of the oldest colleges, in the midst of a conversation about the changes that have come over England, the universities, and all of the modern world, said suddenly: "Lyric poetry, you know, is now a mere survival." I said I didn't know it, and he went on to still more dismal subjects. But the death of lyric poetry, evidently a grimmer possibility for me than for the master, since he seemed to forget what he had said and could not be drawn back into argument, was something I thought about for days. Then I remembered Herrick, a lyric poet if anyone ever was, and I wished I had cited his case. For the poems of Herrick died, then lived again. His one book, *Hesperides and Noble Numbers* attracted little attention in 1648 when it was published; was ignored for the rest of its century and for all of the one that followed; and was not reprinted until 1810. Since then, of course, it has enjoyed innumerable editions, and so many people know by heart so many of its delicious lines that its bibliography is scarcely to be believed. Yet there it is, sufficient proof that a poet can be reborn.

Doubtless in 1648 this poet whom we think we cannot do without looked like a mere survival of quiet, sweet days before the flood of revolution and civil war. Herrick was classical, was a literary son of Ben Jonson, and through him of Horace. Martial, Ovid, and Catullus; also, he was a Royalist, faithful to King Charles who in another year would lose his head; and worse yet he was a vicar in the Church of England, or he had been until the loss of his living a year ago. Then he had come up from a remote village in Devon to publish in London the work of his life thus far; he was fifty-six, and unemployed. And London, busy with becoming modern, had little interest in a book that should have been published twenty years before. It had no time for lyric poems, no ear for songs that might have been proper in some springtime of the world. Now it was hot summer—even wild autumn, even dead winter—and the gathering of rosebuds was a quaint game for children, not to be revived.

London was wrong then, judging by the remarkable way in which it reversed itself a hundred and sixty-two years later; and so, I told myself, it might be wrong now—or my friend in Cambridge might, not to speak of all those in America who periodically announce the death of deathless things. We shall know the answer in time, I said—perhaps in a good deal of time—but meanwhile, what about a trip to Dean Prior, in Devon, where Herrick had his living, and where he inhabited, by the testimony of at least a dozen peoms, so small a house that the very weather of three hundred years might have worn it away? The church, however, would be there, and the meadows where Herrick walked, and the modest streams beside whose banks he witnessed the brief careers of flowers:

> Fair daffodils, we weep to see
> You haste away so soon.

So on a windy, showery day in late September we drove down. I admitted all the way that such a visit made no special sense. It is never necessary to be in body where a poet was in mind; furthermore, since he was a highly trained artist, Herrick had continued to see in Devon what Horace and Ben Jonson had taught him to see in London and Rome, and what this was we can see for ourselves in his perfect poems, which could have been written anywhere on earth once their creator was free of the earth as only art could free him. Further still, he hated Devon. Or he said he did. For him it was a place of exile, days or weeks away from the streets and courts where he had once been used to drink the heady wines and to catch in flight the winged words of the capital in which he was born. A goldsmith's son and then a student of law, and after that a poet whose pieces got into the best contemporary collections, he had been forced at forty to accept this distant benefice if he was to live at all.

But like Swift, who said he had been sent to Dublin "to die like a rat in a hole," Herrick affected to despise Dean Prior. Perhaps he really did; doubtless no brilliant people were there, and his epigrams describe some dreadfully unattractive habits in certain yeomen of the vicinity. It was a dull place, he said, and loathsome. He was an old bachelor, again like Swift; and like Swift too he was possessed of a wit that would never let him *seem* to be pleased with where he was. I have always supposed that he did like Devon after all, with an affection such as strong men can still have for life when it has lost its strangeness. Nevertheless he might have said: "For God's sake, don't come down. My little house is less than nothing, and the one maid I have is but a country maid—a good girl, but no manners." This would be Prudence Baldwin, whom several of his poems celebrate and whom he must have warmly liked. He wouldn't have expected us, I thought, to take him at his word and stay away.

Also, he had his mistresses. Or he said he did. Julia, Anthea, Perilla, Perenna, Lucia, and the rest—their Latin names can make us wonder if they were more than literary relatives of Horace's Lydia and the Lesbia of Catullus. Not that they were therefore the less real; the liquefaction of Julia's clothes, the sweet disorder in another's dress, the stately hair of still another when she was costumed to his liking are realities for us at any rate, and for all we care the ladies lived.

This man must have had many secrets, not the least of which was that he wrote verses. Who else in Dean Prior knew? The vicar was a huge, ugly man with a hooked nose and a mop of curly black hair that fitted his head like a wrestler's cap. Who then, seeing him every day, would have guessed the delicacy of his musician's touch, the cunning of his mind when he set out to carve the lyrics that will keep their shape forever? His passion was poetry, there can be no doubt of that; and if he loved a dozen girls he loved as many poets quite as fondly, and wore them in his inmost heart where he worshiped them either in the direct way of praise or in the devious way of imitation.

Ah, Ben!
Say how or when
Shall we, thy guests,
Meet at those lyric feasts
Made at the Sun,
The Dog, the Triple Tun?
Where we such clusters had,
As made us nobly wild, not mad;
And yet each verse of thine
Out-did the meat, out-did the frolic wine.

He never forgot his English master who would permit no falseness in the note, no dullness in the file, and who himself, despite his brutal size and his bully manners, had written "Drink to Me only with Thine Eyes."

The richest of Herrick's secrets may have been the art he continued in the desert of Devon to practice as if he were still a free citizen of poetry's entire world, resolving never to falter or to let his craft decay, and finding subjects where no subjects ought to be. For here they were after all, in the purlieus of his exile: brooks, fields, and country wassails, and a rosebush by a rock, along with the high color in Perilla's cheeks, and the importunity of desire, and (alas!) the signs in him of old age when performance was to be outlived; and the meannesses, some of them quite filthy, that he found in his parishioners, whom he railed at in a hundred epigrams—copied, to be sure, out of Martial—now often dropped from chaste editions of his work, to our loss and to his. For nothing human was alien to this man, and he put everything into the book he took to London when he thought his exile was over. It was not over; he was to return when another Charles was king and was to spend twelve more years in Devon before he died at eighty-three—for all we know without again touching pen to paper, though it may be that the poems of his old age were buried with him.

Even before he left, however, he had written *Noble Numbers* as well as the *Hesperides,* and the printer bound both books together. The second, the religious one, is no less happy than the first, and no less wonderful. Perhaps his very deepest secret was the way he could pass in the same hour from pagan fantasy to sober meditation, just as he could entertain at the same instant, or at least with the same mind, the hue of violets and the foulness of some yokel's breath. Like Swift again (Swift's mother, it may be time to say, was born a Herrick) he shrank from dirt—perhaps too far and too fastidiously. Yet no one who has read every word of him will wish him different. We are glad he left no manuscripts behind him when he took the long ride to London. We can only wonder how many of his neighbors knew about the book when he came back, a man of seventy-one, to resume his ways and walks. "There he goes, the poet parson. What is he thinking now?" We can hope that the secret was kept until the end.

Dean Prior, when we found it on that dripping day, had no appearance of a literary shrine. England is rich in these, and can afford to leave the tally incomplete. For me at least it was just as well; I preferred to find my way alone—past the thatched village, then another mile along the Plymouth highway until Herrick's church, grey and unprepossessing, showed up among some wet trees on the left. We entered its yard by a rusty gate and walked between weeds to a door that few strangers ever enter. Inside, the spectacle was neat but poor: no splendor anywhere, and little color except in a modern window above the altar which was to be sure a Herrick window, with his gross likeness in one of its lower corners and some fragments of his verse curling in ribbons across the whole design. I was more touched by a card hung on a pillar, saying in effect that we who had come here because Robert Herrick was once vicar were entreated to pray for the present incumbent and his living people. But I was most touched, as I turned to see what the rear wall was like, by these four lines on a piece of wood that I think the present incumbent must have put there, for it bore no marks of age:

> In this little urn is laid
> Prudence Baldwin, once my maid,
> From whose happy spark here let
> Spring the purple violet.

Not that Herrick himself had ever seen this best of all his epitaphs in place. Prue did not die until 1678, four years after her master, perhaps with her help, was lowered into his grave outside the church. We shall never know why he wrote the lines: whether in pure affection, or to see if he could, or because the subject of them had requested that he do so—even, on some winter evening, dared him to. In any case their art is such that they contain as in a tiny glass the essence of both the vicar and the maid.

A young woman was playing the organ, and when she stopped she informed us that the vicar was away in Exeter for the day. She only practiced there, she said. And where was Herrick's house? Why, just across from the gate we had come in by. She was going there now, and she would take us. I said I had thought it too big, and she laughed. "Oh, other vicars have enlarged it. But Herrick's part *was* little—you can see—I live in that."

It was quite as he had described it, at least as regards dimension. A few boxes of rooms, and out of one door a miniature garden, no longer well kept. Here Herrick had hidden for thirty years, here prayed, here eaten, and here relished versing, as George Herbert puts it. Here he had been tended by Prue: here he was called on by persons of the parish who perhaps had found him strange at first; here, sitting alone, or it may be with some companion who was in on his secret, upon occasion he raised his glass in a toast to those long dead who were his bosom friends, the lyric poets who for him were not dead after all, nor mere survivals either. One of his finest poems is such a toast, bearing the infectious title "To Live Merrily and to Trust to Good Verses."

> Then this immensive cup
> Of Aromatic wine,
> Catullus, I quaff up
> To that terse Muse of thine.

To trust to good verses. That would have been his answer to anyone who asked him how important lyric poetry was in those terrible times. Perhaps all times are terrible, but some are clearly so, and they are the very ones when we should drink to the imperishable line, the music that nothing muffles. If Herrick were here now and we asked him how much chance our poetry had to be remembered in the future, it would be his right to ask in turn: "What poetry have you got?" And he would examine what we showed him with a view to the perfection of its sound and sense.

Perfection, that is to say, if any. For perfection is a rare commodity, as he knew better than most men. It appears but here and there; almost never in whole poems, though that is possible too; more probably in the sudden witty, sweet phrase which labor and good luck have generated between them. It was such phrases, such turns of thought, that made him tremble when he found them, either on the paper before him or in the volumes of his masters. Nothing mattered to him more. And if when he published his own book he admitted many pieces he knew to be imperfect, I fancy it was for a human reason that I like in him as much as I like the best of his poetry: he was fond of the places or the persons they were about. He trusted us, I mean, to find the pure gold on the other pages, as indeed we have. The best-known poems of Herrick are the best. They tend to be the best, too, of their kind in any language.

They are so good, I sometimes think, that criticism is at a loss before them. Criticism now at any rate. For we have fallen out of love with lightness, we are worried by a poet's wit. As critics we prefer the solemn or confused author whose mind it is easy to enter because in despair he has left it open. The better artist conceals his mind, as he wants us to conceal ours, in the service of a third thing, the subject, which stands between us, and which he would convert into a product—a poem in the present case—more interesting than either him or us. In proportion as any poet approaches this goal he is perfect, he is classic. Or to put it bluntly, he is successful.

But criticism shies these days from the spectacle of success. Shakespeare and Mozart, who really finished their thought and left it to be ours if we can take it, are seldom considered in terms of their success. Their blazing triumphs are hardly ever looked at face to face and talked about with the courage that living with masterpieces requires. So Horace, whose select and rare felicity is one of the few things worth a critic's attention, is assumed instead of discussed. And Herrick, his faultless pupil, is passed over for the very reason that in so many poems he was perfect—which is the precise place for criticism to begin. Not that it is easy to go on from there. It is almost as difficult to talk well about a good poem as it is to write one. Yet we can try.

11

NERVES LIKE TOMBS:
ON EMILY DICKINSON

After great pain a formal feeling comes—
The nerves sit ceremonious like tombs;
The stiff Heart questions—was it He that bore?
And yesterday—or centuries before?

The feet mechanical go round
A wooden way
Of ground or air or Ought,
Regardless grown,
A quartz contentment like a stone.

This is the hour of lead
Remembered if outlived
As freezing persons recollect
The snow—
First chill, then stupor, then
The letting go.

This fine poem, though it is not the finest of these new poems by
Emily Dickinson, might be taken as a text for several sermons on
the quality of her art. She is so much the best of women poets, and
comes so near the crown of all poetry whatsoever, that her art,
being in the very nature of the case somewhat mysterious, has been

little talked about, and that little feebly. I shall be feeble about it, but at least I shall recognize that she is an artist, and not discuss her as a New England woman, a cloistered soul, an intense and trembling stoic, or a lover of birds and bees.

She wrote with brains, as all good poets do, and she is to be appreciated in the brain or not at all. Her life was necessary for her poetry, and of course her feelings were; but a still greater importance attaches to that other life which she lived in her quick thoughts. These thoughts, the poems say, were deeper than tears, wilder than weeping, and colder, much colder, than chastity. They were about nothing abstract; they were about her deeds, her visions; yet their existence was so clear and real that they surpass in significance anything she ever did or saw. She was once in love, for instance, and the present volume is supposed to be remarkable because a section of it is devoted to the circumstance, but it is more remarkable in its own right as poetry; her love is vastly less interesting than what she said about it. Expression was her master first and last; if she renounced anything it was in favor of words and for the sake of a unique career in which she should be able to find for almost every perception a phrase at once as precise as ice and as profound as thunder.

> Suspense is hostiler than Death.
> Death, tho' soever broad,
> Is just Death, and cannot increase—
> Suspense does not conclude,
> But perishes to live anew,
> But just anew to die,
> Annihilation plated fresh
> With Immortality.

One should not be deterred by the awkwardness of the first three lines here from going on to the wit of the last two. Wit is the word, I think, which sums Emily Dickinson up; and we must go back through several centuries of usage to find its full content. In the seventeenth century it meant the point at which imagination and idea, passion and understanding, experience and form meet in good poetry; it meant, in short, good poetry. Emily Dickinson has wit in one of the richest combinations that I know, and therefore I call her one of the best poets. One proof of its presence is her ability to conceive the phrase "formal feeling." But proofs are everywhere in pleasantries like this:

> It was not Saint,
> It was too large—
> Nor Snow—it was
> Too small.
> It only held itself
> Aloof
> Like something spiritual;

or in love poems like this:

> I got so I could hear his name
> Without—
> Tremendous gain!—
> That stop-sensation in my soul,
> And thunder in the room.
>
> I got so I could walk across
> That angle in the floor
> Where he turned—so—and I
> Turned—how—
> And all our sinew tore.
>
> I got so I could stir the box
> In which
> His letters grew,
> Without that forcing of the breath
> As staples driven through. . . .

Wit is everywhere in her best work, glowing there as promise that what she felt as pain you shall not feel as pain, that what she was able to say you shall be forced to admire. She has been called a personal poet. She is anything else than that. What we know of her belongs to the universe of poetry; what she was is perfectly hidden away.

   A further value of the present volumes is that they make finally very clear how intense their author's existence was; how intense, indeed, all existence was to her, and how much terror there could be for her merely in the thought that a given individual thing had been created: a bird, a day, herself.

> I am afraid to own a body,
> I am afraid to own a soul;
> Profound, precarious property,
> Possession not optional.

To dismiss such lines as the confession of one who was "afraid of life" is to forget how the imagination of any person with a capacity for abstraction (and was not Emily Dickinson a metaphysical poet?) trembles before the fact of the concrete, the object into which infinities of space and time have been so unaccountably crowded, the delicate thing which somehow endures eternity's pressure against its form. Nothing less than all that is the source of Emily Dickinson's irony, and of her poetry.

12

THE POET: WALT WHITMAN

Nothing about Walt Whitman is better known, or should be better known, than that in 1855 he sent an early copy of *Leaves of Grass* to Emerson in Concord, and received in due course such a letter of thanks as any obscure poet in any age would almost have died to deserve. "I am not blind," said Whitman's master and the master of most writers in that day, "to the worth of the wonderful gift of *Leaves of Grass*. I find it the most extraordinary piece of wit and wisdom that America has yet contributed. I am very happy in reading it, as great power makes us happy. . . . I give you joy of your free and brave thought. I have great joy in it. I find incomparable things, said incomparably well, as they must be. . . . I greet you at the beginning of a great career. . . ."

The criticism of *Leaves of Grass* may be taken as starting here. Emerson was not specific; he cited no lines, no poems; and he said nothing of the subject matter concerning which Whitman had been witty and wise. If he remembered his own first book, *Nature,* published nineteen years before, he may have had in mind these sentences from its Introduction: "We are now so far from the road to truth, that religious teachers dispute and hate each other, and speculative men are esteemed unsound and frivolous. But to a sound judgment, the most abstract truth is the most practical. Whenever a true theory appears, it will be its own evidence. Its test is, that it will explain all phenomena. Now many are thought not only unexplained but inexplicable; as language, sleep, madness, dreams, beasts, sex.''

Our guess can be that Emerson saw in Whitman some sort of religious teacher, or at any rate a speculative man; that he felt in him the force of abstract truth; that he found him struggling with a true theory and with its evidences; that he suspected in this theory the power to explain all phenomena; and that he recognized here the very phenomena whose names he had spoken in 1836: language, sleep, madness, dreams, beasts, sex. For all of the six were important to Whitman, who indeed may have read the passage too, and even perhaps may have got it by heart. They are important phenomena at any time—now, certainly, no less than then—and only the most ambitious poets address themselves to them. We can be sure that Emerson admired Whitman's ambitions; it was why he called him free and brave; and we may be nearly as sure that for him the ambition was enough. For Emerson, that is to say, there was little necessary difference between having great subjects for poems and being a great poet. And it is well to bear such a view in mind, because it is connected with the truth. But it is only connected; it is not the whole truth about poetry, which among other things is an art. Emerson had little patience with the art of poetry: a luxury he could afford, since now and then he was one of the finest of poets himself. If he was not so more often, the reason may have been this very indifference to art which meant that he could take ambition for success, or promise for accomplishment, as perhaps he did in the case of the stranger who had sent him *Leaves of Grass,* and certainly as most critics of that stranger have done throughout the ensuing century.

And still it is difficult to keep the distinction clear. Whitman himself never kept it clear; indeed he did all he could to confuse it. He could never make up his mind as to how he wanted the world to consider him: whether as a poet or as a thinker, as an artist or as a prophet, as a sayer or as a seer. He saw the distinction well enough to be worried by it; he was uneasy about it until he died; but from the first—that is, from the time of the famous preface which Emerson undoubtedly read with the same excitement that it generates today—Whitman thought he must denounce those whose concern was with the art of poetry, or as he put it, with the ''gaggery and gilt." Their concern, he said, was merely with devices to perfect "piano tunes." They were an effeminate crew, dainty and afraid. They did not know what he claimed to know, namely, that a great poet is neither more nor less than "the channel of thoughts and things without increase or diminution, and is the free channel of himself." The thoughts, the things, the poet's self—those are enough, he insisted; we shall not bother with detail, or craft, or criticism.

But criticism cannot be forever kept at bay. Nor at its best is it a trivial thing. It does, to be sure, assume that a poet is an artist, but so does time make this assumption—even more ruthlessly, for it is interested in nothing save success. A successful artist, says time, is one who knows how to do the thing he sets out to do, and knows how to do it so well that nothing, or at any rate the fewest possible things, can touch the result. Time has seen the death of many poets, and may be supposed to think, as criticism clearly does, that something must have been the matter with their work. It was not strong enough, or tough enough, or sure enough, or simply good enough to resist the doubts men finally have that any book should be permitted to survive. Such doubts are sound, because we cannot have too many classics; the best must be indeed the best, beyond our power to deny it. A classic must stand at last alone: without apology, exegesis, or alibi. It must speak for itself to strangers; it must be intelligible, and seem true, after all its special friends are dead. It must have the minimum of weakness, vagueness, vanity, wind. It must be well made at the seams, to stand the long voyage it hopes to make, and to endure the waves either of contempt or of competition. It must have been made, in other words, by one who knew how to make such things, and nothing else about him will matter—who he was, how he looked, or what he thought about other things than the things he treated. Time and criticism ask no further questions, because no further questions are sensible. They are interested in nothing that is not sensible, and neither is any serious man.

Only two poets have weathered time and criticism without any loss whatever: Homer, still great and still popular after two and a half millenniums, and Shakespeare, still great and still popular after three and a half centuries. A few others come close to this distinction, but they have had their ups and downs of fame, their ins and outs of favor, and probably they will continue to do so. It is to Whitman's credit that he was never blind to Homer and Shakespeare; they were his heroes, and in a sense he had no others. In prose, in verse, he spoke of them constantly, either with simple reverence or with that more complicated respect which involves the recognition of rivals. For various reasons he refused to consider himself in competition with his contemporaries; but a sound instinct told him to beware of the great Greek and the great Englishman in whom he himself could find no fault—except, to be sure, that they had written for other times, which he vaguely called "feudal," and therefore were not for these times, which he vaguely called "modern." Even then he was disturbed by their close presence on Broadway and in public and private libraries. For they had survived without loss and were the best-loved poets of these times as well as theirs. Who was more successful on the current stage than Shakespeare, and who but Homer still seemed, as Whitman knew he had always seemed, the very type of poet, the living model whom most if not all other poets merely approximated? Neither one of them, in spite of the fact that he had written for an age long dead, was dead himself. So all that Whitman could do when the rival's mood descended upon him was to reassert the difference he saw between the age of Agamemnon and the age of Jackson, or between the world of Hamlet and the world of Lincoln. This difference could be to him a very solid comfort; for he was the poet of the new world, and as such was beyond the reach of those august giants before the flood. Yet even then he had his nervous moments; the matter remained one that he must discuss; and the models were in his mind whenever he labored, as chronically he did, to enlarge, to reshape, to rearrange, to relabel the one book, *Leaves of Grass,* by which he expected his name to stand.

How long and how securely will it stand? That is the question which criticism at last must pose, and patiently wait for an answer. Thus far the answer has been slow in coming, and it may be that many further years must pass before it can state itself with confidence and clarity. Yet it is already time that we be as serious as we know how to be concerning the stature of Whitman's poetry; that we make of it the strictest demands, that we compare it with the greatest poetry, not the least, and that we pay no more attention than we please to the opinions of it held either by Whitman himself or by any of his numerous champions. For as everybody knows he had his champions; and he still has them—has, that is, critics in name only, persons who take the intention for the deed, the promise for the fulfillment, the ambition to be great for the fact of being great. These may be admirable persons, and indeed they are, but it is not their function to criticize; their function is to promote—a harmless function when recognized for what it is. Fortunately for criticism, they are fewer than they used to be. They are dying out with the times of which Whitman was so proud to be the spokesman. The middle of his century is less and less like the middle of ours. He thought his world was here to stay, but it has not stayed. Already then he is to some extent a period poet; not altogether so, of course, or else he would interest the historian more than he does the critic. And that is not the case. He is a living poet, and as such deserves all that criticism can do to him—or for him, if you please. It can do much for him first and last. It can disembarrass him of irrelevant claims. It can separate the better from the worse among his poems; it can cut away the soft parts, it can leave the firm parts standing; it can say, or attempt to say, just what in him is great by any standard.

It was not for Emerson to apply standards in the angelic letter he sat down to write. If he saw Whitman as a philosophical poet, as pretty certainly he did, it was the philosophy that interested him most. He liked Whitman's ideas, which were not too different from his own, and which in any case were likable because they touched reality. Not only were they good ideas; they were good for the times; they were perhaps older than Whitman thought, but he had made them his own, and he had given them the airing they now needed. So did the times need airing; they would get that too, by virtue of this book. Emerson, rubbing his eyes, saw life in a volume of poems at last, and he did all that should have been expected of him when he said so in the way he did. Certainly he should not have been expected to judge this new philosophical poet 'as a poet,' which is what has finally to be done. Nor does this mean anything so mechanical as judging the philosophy first and the poetry second. The two things are not that separable, assuming them to be separable at all. They are separable only to the extent that we can speak their names one after the other. But they operate at the same time in the same poem. The philosophy causes the poetry, and the poetry causes the philosophy, with the grand result that we feel and believe that we are in the presence of the truth, that the whole world is what the poet says it is, that he has explained, in Emerson's phrase, all phenomena; and not only explained them, but made them present and real, so that other or contrary things seem false or pale by comparison, and so that we who read are robbed, if only for the time being, of the power to imagine any other way of seeing, feeling, and comprehending the world we live in, and are proud to live in, with the poet.

Emerson of course did not have before him the bulky volume we now know as *Leaves of Grass*. Including the preface, there were only 93 pages, though they were large ones, in the book he read, and there were only 12 poems, all without titles. The first of the 12, later to be called "Walt Whitman," and still later "Song of Myself," occupied more than half of the pages. It was and is one of Whitman's masterpieces, if not the chief one; it had the right position in the book, for it said most of what Whitman had to say, at least until 1865, and it said it altogether personally, drawing its authority from Whitman's innermost being insofar as he could be conscious of that being. Emerson needed no more than this magnificent poem, so candid and yet so cryptic, so loose and yet so terse, so flowing and yet so broken, as evidence of the author's wit and wisdom. It still is the key to *Leaves of Grass,* however reluctantly it sometimes turns in the lock. It is not systematic; it is perhaps a series of notes, or better yet a collection of inspired sayings; it is not cluttered with transitions; it does not seek to explain itself; it simply and confidently, if arrogantly too, is what it is, to be taken or left as the reader desires. Emerson took it, and then went on, we may suppose, to take such further masterpieces, minor only by comparison, as "The Sleepers," "I Sing the Body Electric," and "There Was A Child Went Forth."

It was an excellent selection, an exciting selection, from the poems Whitman had been writing since his 30th year or thereabouts: since the day when he cut himself loose from his own past and from what he took to be the past of the human race. We can envy Emerson the experience he had with a lean book that was mostly nerves and muscle. *Leaves of Grass* in its ultimate state is a greater book because it contains further masterpieces then unwritten.

But in one vital respect it is less attractive. It is stuffed with repetitions of statements that once were fresher and did not need to be made again. Its author is afflicted with the modern disease of rewriting: he is always tinkering with his text—sometimes, granted, for the better, but sometimes not so. He cuts and he inserts; he regroups and rearranges; he improvises sections, and provides transitions—dead connective tissue—between them. He composes "Inscriptions" which the reader shall find first, and at the end he keeps saying farewell to this same reader, bidding him take note and remember, assuring him of this or that meaning that he may not have expressed, hanging on for dear life to some image of his book as the rounded, systematic work which in fact it never was or could be, and indeed should never have tried to be. We do not require of a philosophical poet that he be systematic; we require only that he be always keen and convincing. Whitman dulls his final effect by laboring to convince us with something less than the best poetry he could write. For he is full of the notion that *Leaves of Grass* is a scripture, and that he is its editor as well as its maker. He is preserving it for posterity, he is altering it, coaxing it into shape, inserting things in it, taking things out, so that nothing will prevent its survival through the centuries ahead. Hence all the putty and the plastic wood. He is unwilling to let the individual poems stand free as their progenitors did in the original edition. It is as if he thought he had to keep on writing at a book he had not yet written, though in truth he had, for the best of his poems were that book. In his own words he was "garrulous to the very last"; and though we may love him for the admission, we are sorry that it has to be made.

It has to be made because Whitman, strangely enough for one whose first appearance was in the role of the supremely satisfied person—satisfied with himself and with every portion of his world—has come to be a person so tentative, so unsure, that he irritates and tantalizes rather than reassures us. He seems uneasy as to whether he has said what he wanted to say, or whether he knows now what that was. He slips away into hints and approximations, and above all into promises that he will say it yet, or that if he never does, others coming after him will. But so far, he sometimes confesses, his subject has eluded him; it is not in the book at all.

> For it is not for what I have put into it that I have written
>   this book,
> Nor is it by reading it you will acquire it. . . .

The subject, then, is over and above the book, which merely suggests it, or if the subject is himself, he is forced to say:

> Before all my arrogant poems the real Me stands yet
>   untouch'd, untold, altogether unreach'd,
> Withdrawn far, mocking me with mock-congratulatory
>   signs and bows,
> With peals of distant ironical laughter at every word I
>   have written. . . .

The excuse he hopes he has, and keeps insisting he has, is the extreme difficulty of his assignment. Like Dante and Spenser he speaks of his book as a little bark that ventures in huge seas almost certain to overwhelm it. Like Milton he reaches after things unattempted yet in prose or rhyme. He must break new ground, and no wonder it is hard.

He remembers—or perhaps he does not remember—that the artist's business is nevertheless to find his subject and to finish the work which embodies it; to steer the bark into some port at last; to get there and make an end. He remembers—or perhaps he does not remember—that the great poet knows how to write his poems; he does not talk about the difficulty because he is occupied with conquering it; he does not promise to succeed tomorrow, he succeeds today. Homer did not discuss the problem of the epic; he wrote the *Iliad* and the *Odyssey*. Shakespeare did not write, at any rate in public, about whether or not it was possible to write *Hamlet;* he wrote it, and made it seem easy. But Whitman, after his brave start, is forever doubting that he knows where to go or what to do. Which indeed is strange, considering that start. And which is why, for all the fine poems his book contains, it is not the finished thing, the effective scripture, the moving whole he presumably once desired that it should be. Even his retouchings, his nudgings, his inscriptions and farewells, do not accomplish the result. For they are done half-heartedly, as if he knew they would not succeed.

The answer he gave himself, and in many a place gives us, is that *Leaves of Grass* is not a work of art at all. "This is no book," he says. "No one will get at my verses who insists upon viewing them as a literary performance, or attempt at such performance, or as aiming mainly toward art." *Leaves of Grass,* he seems to be saying, is so little like other books that perhaps it should be called something else. And if we ask again why it is that he expends so much effort in perfecting whatever he has between his hands, he says again that it is not a book as other books are books. If it is actually one, it is "a book separate, not link'd with the rest." Nor does it occur to him that this is a handicap rather than a help, since it means that he neither competes nor contributes, and so is lost, as it were, in literary space, with no masters for models, no company as he works. "The words of my book," he says, are "nothing, the drift of it everything." But in the long run, under the scrutiny of time and criticism, it is only the words that will count. The work of any poet is done with words. It is done with drift, too, but we must be the judges of that. And Whitman knew that this was so, or else, he would not have denied it so vehemently. Somewhere in him was the consuming ambition of an artist. Somewhere in him too was the appalling suspicion that he had failed—not absolutely, in view of his masterpieces, but relatively to the vast vision of himself he once had had, and to the vaster vision he had had of the good world whose air he breathed.

He loved this world as a lover loves his mistress—loved all of it, including its alleged imperfections. And it is a fine thing to be able to do this, and to talk about it in the intense, free way we associate with no one more than we do with him. But much of his talk is not intense, not free, and therefore, by his own criterion, not good. *Leaves of Grass* is more often than not relaxed and flabby; it is uncertain of itself; on many of its pages it is, frankly, a bore. And this could be not alone because Whitman paid too little attention to his art; it could be as well because his theory, his thinking, failed at times to be first-rate. A philosophical poet must have examined at some stage the grounds of his thought, and made them as firm as possible. He has to be more than a thinker, but he had better think. He will always have a problem, of course, since that is the fate of philosophers. And Whitman's problem was an immemorial one: if the universe is to be accepted in all of its parts, if every part of it is to be loved and praised, how can one avoid monotony and unreality, how can one say more than the simple word "Yes"? For most men find the world both good and bad; they like some parts of it better than others, even when they don't know why. And this is likely to be true even of men like Whitman who do not want it to be true. For Whitman, as for Lucretius, all things were natural; and at least for Whitman all things were good. How then could he disapprove of anything—for instance, the piano poet, or the fool who corrupts, degrades, and defiles his body? Whitman regularly denounces this poet and this fool, and does so in the face of his insistence at other times that he accepts everything and everyone. But then he realizes what he has done, and makes amends by listing all the objects in the world for which he feels affection. Hence his famous catalogues which no one can read through. Every river makes the grade, every trade and occupation, every city, every valley, every individual, every class, every thought, every mountain, every man. Somehow the review is not impressive; it can even be ludicrous, with its suggestion that if Whitman had not come along to love these things they would have felt neglected. He has a special license to approve of you and me, of democracy and sin, of India and Christ. It is something of a jumble before he has finished.

He embraces too much; he stretches himself thin; he becomes breathless with adoration. He sounds as if he were exaggerating—in art, a fatal weakness. Nor does he sound at these moments like one possessed, and therefore in some degree to be condoned. He makes his catalogues in cold blood; his theory tells him to. So there could be something wrong with the theory, or else with the thinker who holds it. And this could be summed up in his own phrase: "There is no evil." An artist, or at any rate a literary artist, is seriously handicapped if he has no theory of evil; for then his vision of good lacks definition; he does not know why he likes it. It is natural to love the good, but before that it is necessary to know how to recognize it, and to guess what its price is—or better yet, its pricelessness, which experience of evil defines. The vision of good which does not start from a sense of evil will be a watery vision, colorless and shapeless, indistinct and finally depressing. Whitman's vision of the good is at its best a sharp and wonderful thing; at its worst it is unconvincing because it lacks lines to limit it, and consequently lacks form. It is an ample vision, and for that it is to be admired, just as Whitman is to be admired for his all but incredible refusal ever to judge. He is like Christ in this, except that he has no such reason as Christ had, and incidentally no such capacity for anger in the presence of evil. The figure of Christ is always clear and firm: Whitman's figure is wavering, and sometimes it is timid—because he does not know what he thinks. He does not follow his thought even as far as Lucretius followed his; he is by no means so ruthless, so possessed, so on fire. Lucretius, with bad logic, denounced religion; if everything is a part of nature, then religion is too; but religion was in his way and he said so with his whole might. Whitman, who had his own religion, accepted all others too, though most of them were in his way. He was not sure he shouldn't. He was not sure of most things. He did not see his vision to the end.

This may have been why he played as he did with the notion of himself in the role of orator. "A Song of Joys" inevitably gets around to the subject:

> O the orator's joys!
> To inflate the chest, to roll the thunder of the voice out
>   from the ribs and throat,
> To make the people rage, weep, hate, desire, with yourself,
> To lead America—to quell America with a great tongue.

Memorandums survive which show that he studied the techniques of the platform, and hungered for success upon it. And it has been supposed that it was good for his poetry to do so; whereas it was surely bad, since it made his poetry exclamatory, gesticulative, hyperbolic, and loud. The art of oratory as he understood it was the art of saying very little with vast force. Socrates suggested more than once that when understood most deeply it is like any other art: its function is to tell the truth. The arts of oratory and poetry are not enemies of each other when both of them are understood to have this function. But Whitman's ideal orator was all voice, all ribs and throat, all personality; and that has nothing to do with poetry, which does its work with a deadly stillness, marshalling words somewhere behind the scenes and sending them forth when it is time for them to come. The poet makes his words do his work, and hopes that they will seem to be doing only their own. Whitman himself could get good work out of his words, though not in such a passage as this from "Song of the Open Road":

> Forever alive, forever forward,
> Stately, solemn, sad, withdrawn, baffled, mad, turbulent,
>   feeble, dissatisfied,
> Desperate, proud, fond, sick, accepted by men, rejected
>   by men,
> They go! they go! I know that they go, but I know not
>   where they go,
> But I know that they go toward the best—toward something
>   great.

It would be difficult to find in any poet a series of lines more forced and hollow than these. And the reason is that Whitman does not believe what he says; he simply could not, if he is the man who wrote "Song of Myself" or "The Sleepers," in neither of which is anybody going anywhere, least of all forward. "Go" and "forward" sound like cant words, and so they lack the force that the words of poetry should have. The words of poetry can do with stillness for a subject—as when in "The Sleepers," Whitman hovers over all the prone people on earth and gazes down at them raptly, motionlessly, while the night itself stands fixed and watches with him. So in "Song of Myself" he is being what he is, and saying so; he is going nowhere, there is no forward or backward, there is only the present moment, here, with him the solitary figure, "gross, mystical, nude," somewhere near its center, contemplating himself. The great poet does not ask where the world is going or where it should go; he considers what it is in its own quiet essence, year after year and age after age, now no less than then, and there no more than here. The mystic—and Whitman at his best was that—is stricken where he stands, ecstatic over what he sees; and he refrains from moving lest the thing he looks at be startled and depart. Nor is it always easy to comprehend what he murmurs while he gazes. He is not saying it for us merely, though it is also true that he is not talking in his sleep. The obscurity of certain stretches in "Song of Myself," not to speak of "The Sleepers" again, is almost absolutely dense. An example would be the description of the speaker's senses, particularly his sense of touch, which must have been an extraordinary thing, comprehensible perhaps only to psychologists. But this obscurity is preferable to the hollowness of the "forward" passage in "Song of the Open Road." In the first case he was being a prophet, in the second he was trying to sound like one; he was saying what he thought he ought to say about "the progress of the souls of men and women along the grand roads of the universe." In what he called his "native moments" he did not bother with such nonsense. The soul, he knew, goes nowhere. It simply is. And it is Whitman's distinction that he belongs in the company of those who have suddenly seen, felt, heard that this is so.

The experience was mystical, which is to say that its truth did not have to be proved. It was its own evidence, as Emerson said. Whitman remarked in "Song of the Answerer" that "The words of true poems do not merely please." Not merely, no; but our pleasure is one of their aims, and in Whitman's best poems, or if you like, his true poems, the words please instantly, at the same time that they suggest all sorts of things the reader will have to think about before he is through. But they do please; they are natural; they are memorable—they give us the impression that just as they had never been used this way before, so they will never need to be used this way again. Their authority is simple and immediate, their power is felt like a presence, and so, to quote Emerson once more, they make us happy. That is to say, they are successful words in successful poems, which compete with other successful poems in the world and hold their own.

Whitman's sense of such competition was more lively than he liked to admit. Sometimes he denied it altogether, as we know. He thought of himself as having been placed beyond comparison with the great poets of the past by being born just when and where he was. But he could also remember his peers, and as he did so could wonder whether he had been wise in cutting loose from their company. He had repudiated, for example, meter; he invented a long, loose line which would leave him free to fill it with whatever belonged there, whether this was little or much. He knew of course that Homer and Shakespeare had not been slaves to meter; in their hexameters and blank verse they were conspicuously free, for they were able to say anything at all in the precise way it should be said. A master of meter is not a slave for the simple reason that he *is* a master. The poets of Whitman's day whom he rightly despised were masters of nothing, and least of all their verse, which lacked energy as most verse does in most generations. Whitman, however, did not propose to restore the energy that had been lost—or never, it may be, even imagined; instead he abandoned the form, and loafed in the long line he preferred instead. The result is sometimes wonderful and sometimes woeful. But we are in no position to guess what he would have done within the form he turned his back on; he never mastered it, even in contempt. His stricter poems—"Edolóns," for example, and "Pioneers! O Pioneers!"—are monotonous and grinding; they do not truly move; or else, like "O Captain! My Captain!," they are singsong and sentimental. The author of "When Lilacs Last in the Dooryard Bloom'd," using the loose line for the same subject, did infinitely better. In such a masterpiece the poet is clearly in charge of his own form; and this was true of Whitman often enough so that we must say his own form is justified. There is only one dimension it lacks in his hands. He cannot be humorous with it. He can be witty, as Emerson pointed out, but he cannot be humorous in the way Carl Sandburg, his disciple, has been. There is Sandburg's fish-crier on Maxwell Street in Chicago:

> His face is that of a man terribly glad to be selling fish, terribly
>   glad that God made fish, and customers to whome he may call his
>   wares from a pushcart.

Or there is the famous question:

> Tell me why a hearse horse snickers hauling a lawyer's bones.

Or there is "Bas-Relief":

> Five geese deploy mysteriously.
> Onward proudly with flagstaffs,
> Hearses with silver bugles,

Bushels of plum-blossoms dropping
For ten mystic web-feet—
Each his own drum-major,
Each charged with the honor
Of the ancient goose nation,
Each with a nose-length surpassing
The nose-length of rival nations,
Somberly, slowly, unimpeachably,
Five geese deploy mysteriously.

Whitman could do nothing like that, having in fact no sense of humor. It is a genuine defect in a poet, though some great ones have survived it, and he did.

"Since me the universal," said Whitman to his muse, and there was something humorless in the injunction. Particular things are the stuff of poetry. The greater the poem the more universal we are willing to call it, but what interested us in it was the single thing with which it dealt, and which it managed to make real. Reality is of course a universal term, and the great poet knows where he stands with respect to it. The great poet was once, and still is in some deep part of himself, a philosopher. In his capacity as a poet, however, he has disciplined himself to deal, or seem to deal, with nothing whatever save things that can be seen, with individual things whose surface truth he is content to render, leaving us, the beholders of these individual things, as free as men ever are to judge and interpret their companions in creation. The true poem has a limited subject—or shall we say a limited object—to which the poet gives his unlimited powers, remaining with it, rendering it with strict fidelity, until there is no more of it that can be shown. Until, for example, Hector is buried; or until Hamlet, having said all he could say, observes that the rest is silence.

In his best poems Whitman remembers this. His worst ones are those he forced himself to write in the absence of such knowledge. Indeed, the trouble with *Leaves of Grass* as a whole book, a book that tries to be round and complete, is precisely that it has an unlimited subject, and has it all the time that it is conscious of itself. It strains to swallow the camel, not the gnat. Its author says:

I will not make poems with reference to parts,
But I will make poems, songs, thoughts, with reference
    to ensemble,
And I will not sing with reference to a day, but with
    reference to all days.

The program is not agreeable, and we yawn. We expect poets to take the parts, not the ensemble: as many parts as they have years to treat, and one at a time. Of Shakespeare we finally say, and so did Whitman say, that his knowledge of men was comprehensive, even universal; but play by play we have noted that he gave himself entirely to its characters and to no others under the sun. And if we say of Shakespeare too that he had a wonderful power to accept and love all kinds of persons, good and evil, brilliant and stupid, we say this only after the entire population of his poems has passed in review. While they were passing Shakespeare said nothing of this; he merely let them speak; it is we who think universal thoughts as a grand result of the specific lives we have seen lived, the specific deaths we have seen deserved or not deserved. Whitman, claiming as he does in many of his poems that his subject is all things and all men, and suggesting as he makes the claim that if anything else were true he would be a trivial fellow, takes a short cut to the universal which will not in fact bring him there. It will bring him rather to the deserts of listed things with which we grow impatient because there seems to be no reason why they should be of one size rather than another. The lists seem endless because Whitman cannot end them; there is no principle by which he could, just as there is no principle by which we could recognize that the end was reached. These are the pages we skip, willing to grant a few examples but staggered by the hundreds we are given. In the preface to the first edition, the preface Emerson read, tribute is paid to "the solid and beautiful forms of the future where there are now no solid forms." Solid form—Whitman on the whole does not have it because his theory, such as it was, made it impossible. If all things are equal in truth, beauty, and goodness, then no one thing is ever especially good, beautiful, or true. Without a hierarchy of goods, nothing in fact will be either good or bad, and no subject for a poem will exist.

Or at any rate no subject for a book of poems which is trying to be one poem in the large. Nothing will be possible except catalogues of this or that. And so we get the catalogues, as broad as they are long and as shallow as they are broad. Whitman, sticking stubbornly to his theory, has no way to focus his or our attention upon one object, one person, within whose outline all the meaning of the world may secretly and unobtrusively exist. The outline is the thing, and Whitman cannot draw it.

Most of the time, that is, he cannot. In his good poems he can and does, and that is why they are good poems. Indeed they are great poems because their outlines are so very sharp and because these outlines are filled in with everything they should contain— everything we had desired, and much, much more than that; for any great poet surprises us with what he knows, and takes us deeper into the territory of his theme than we could have imagined going. Also, Whitman's power of phrasing is constant here—not intermittent, not accidental, as it was in the ambitious but unsuccessful works with which *Leaves of Grass* is so unfortunately full, but ever-present and ever-pleasing, not to say ever deeply moving. The rhythm is now organic; the length of any line justifies itself; the beat of the music corresponds, we feel, to the beat of the writer's mind and pulse; and instead of poems which easily could be shorter or longer we have poems whose size is right for the subject, and whose energy drives them at the proper moment toward genuine conclusions. These great poems, though lyric in their genius, have beginnings, middles, and ends. Aristotle said that long poems should have those three parts, and it is one of the wisest things ever said; but it is true for short poems too, since short poems, if they aim to be powerful, must have their own dramatic tides, they must aim for some shore and reach it.

No reader of *Leaves of Grass* fails to find and to love for himself—almost as if a secret were being shared between him and the author—a number of very short poems which have the air of being notes, say, or sketches. For the most part they are descriptions of things Whitman has just seen, ideas that have just struck him, or memories miraculously just come back out of a past he had forgotten. Or so they seem, whatever may be the facts about their composition. We do not know such facts, nor does it matter; we have the individual object or idea—it may, actually, be only a state of mind or an excitement along some nerve—before us in its natural form, intensely rendered for us, but at no point swollen or deformed by the exaggeration to which Whitman at other moments was addicted. The stuff of these pieces is highly particular, though it is familiar to us too, or we can imagine that it is. Sometimes they are imbedded as it were in longer poems, they are single lines, with little or no context before or after, that leap out and ring in our ears. Such a line is this one from "Song of the Open Road":

> Why are there trees I never walk under but large and
>   melodious thoughts descend upon me?

For the most part, however, they stand alone, with titles, and beckon us to read them as we pass. "A Farm Picture" is three lines:

> Through the ample open door of the peaceful country barn,
> A sunlit pasture field with cattle and horses feeding,
> And haze and vista, and the far horizon fading away.

"The Runner" is four lines:

> On a flat road runs the well-train'd runner,
> He is lean and sinewy with muscular legs,
> He is thinly clothed, he leans forward as he runs,
> With lightly closed fists and arms partially rais'd.

And "Beautiful Women," which Rembrandt might have written, and somehow did with his etcher's tools, is only two lines:

> Women sit or move to and fro, some old, some young,
> The young are beautiful—but the old are more beautiful than the young.

Others of course are a little longer, though not very long, and never at all too long. "The World Below the Brine" penetrates the depths of the sea, peoples the darkness there with animals and plants, then emerges into our upper world again, remarking upon its difference from the one just left, and remarking too upon the host of further worlds concerning which we know as little as whales and sea-leopards, lichens and sea-lettuces, know concerning us; and it does this in 11 lines. "The Dalliance of the Eagles" reports a "sudden muffled sound," "the rushing amorous contact high in space together" of "four beating wings, two beaks," in 10 lines, no word of which is out of place or pace. "The Torch" is briefer, as it should be, because so little is seen; but it is well seen:

> On my Northwest coast in the midst of the night a
>   fisherman's group stands watching,
> Out on the lake that expands before them, others are
>   spearing salmon,
> The canoe, a dim shadowy thing, moves across the black
>   water,
> Bearing a torch ablaze at the prow.

"The Ox-Tamer" is of ampler scope because the man in it, "my farmer friend," "my silent, illiterate friend," has tamed a hundred oxen, and they are in the poem. Note that in each of these poems there is a single thing, or a single set of things, which focuses the poet's effort. "On the Beach at Midnight" has the entire sky in it, but only as seen by a man and a boy; and because we see through their eyes we see exactly what Whitman wants us to see:

> Amid a transparent clear belt of ether yet left in the east,
> Ascends large and calm the lord-star Jupiter,
> And nigh at hand, only a very little above,
> Swim the delicate sisters the Pleiades.

These are the great *little* poems of Whitman; and some of them are greater still because they are more than descriptions of external things, they are resolutions or interpretations of them, they make applications of them in the life of the speaker, as of course in the life of the listener too. There is, for example, the famous spider:

> A noiseless patient spider,
> I mark'd where on a little promontory it stood isolated,
> Mark'd how to explore the vacant vast surrounding,
> It launch'd forth filament, filament, filament, out of itself,
> Ever unreeling them, ever tirelessly speeding them.

And you, O my soul where you stand,
Surrounded, detached, in measureless oceans of space,
Ceaselessly musing, venturing, throwing, seeking the spheres
to connect them,
Till the bridge you will need be form'd, till the ductile anchor
hold,
Till the gossamer thread you fling catch somewhere, O my soul.

There is the equally famous Southern tree:

I saw in Louisiana a live-oak growing,
All alone stood it and the moss hung down from the branches,
Without any companion it grew there uttering joyous leaves of
dark green. . . .

And there is the picture of Whitman himself as he watches a world
he cannot change, and makes no move to change:

I sit and look out upon all the sorrows of the world, and upon
all oppression and shame,
I hear secret convulsive sobs from young men at anguish with
themselves, remorseful after deeds done,
I see in low life the mother misused by her children, dying,
neglected, gaunt, desperate,
I see the wife abused by her husband, I see the treacherous
seducer of young women,
I mark the ranklings of jealousy and unrequited love attempted
to be hid, I see these sights on the earth,
I see the workings of battle, pestilence, tyranny, I see martyrs
and prisoners,
I observe a famine at sea, I observe the sailors casting lots who
shall be kill'd to preserve the lives of the rest,
I observe the slights and degradations cast by arrogant
persons upon laborers, the poor, and upon negroes, and
the like;
All these—all the meanness and agony without end I sitting
look out upon,
See, hear, and am silent.

That is a catalogue, but for once Whitman knows why he makes it, just as he knows how to render, by it and other means, the sense he has of being suspended, powerless, staring at a world in which almost everything is bad but in which, so far as he himself is concerned, there is no possibility of improvement. This is how, with tensions such as we are moved by here, poetry accepts the universe. It does not talk of doing it; it does not promise to do it; it does it, now, in this present moment which has the feel of eternity and the face of authentic circumstance.

Two outstanding sections of *Leaves of Grass,* "Calamus" and "Drum-Taps," throng with such brief masterpieces. The "Calamus" poems are impressive by their very silence and shyness—Whitman whispers of the men he loves, and cannot be doubted as he assures us that in these whispers his most intimate, most honest voice is speaking. The vignettes of battlefields in "Drum-Taps" are silent too, somewhat as Brady's photographs are silent; they are time exposures, delicate and just in every detail, and unforgettable in the way that our own most fugitive, most vivid memories can be unforgettable, for reasons we shall never know. There is greater length and there is more action in "Come Up from the Fields Father," but it too is strangely stationary in its perfect, single stillness: a family gathers to read a letter about the wounding of its son, and about his death, if they but knew that it had happened. Only we and Whitman know that it has happened.

One of the "Calamus" poems puts a question—or makes a statement, for it is a rhetorical question—of the utmost importance to Whitman: "What indeed is finally beautiful except death and love?" His indubitable masterpieces, his extended and massive ones, build themselves on this foundation. The first of them, and there are three, does not rest squarely upon it, because it had not then been laid. "Song of Myself" is more interested in life than it is in either death or love; it celebrates the poet's discovery of his own life—of its outline, of its content, of its structure, of its color and inward form, of its eccentricity that yet is central to the life of man, of its strangeness which nevertheless must be lived with and adored because while it is strangeness it is also truth—and the celebration takes for the most part the form of argument; or if not argument precisely, then epigram and paradox. But implicit even here is the further discovery, to be announced at least as early as the second edition of 1856, in a poem then called "Poem of Wonder at the Resurrection of the Wheat" but now known as "This Compost," that life and death do not separate themselves in the imagination, that in some miraculous way they are one subject, one thing; and that if either one of them is pre-eminent for poetry it is death, since death is the limiting, the framing force, the beginning and ending act out of which the middle derives its meaning. Whitman, that is to say, had made the discovery that only great poets make: the supreme subject is death. Little poets may think they have made it, but all they become as a result is maudlin or morbid. Great poets rise through it to reality and power; life is still their theme, but death is their language, death is their symbol and motive force; only through death may life be understood. Death transforms itself for them into a living thing. It has positive dignity and beauty, to be accepted for the same reason that life is to be accepted, and on the whole to be accepted first.

The second of Whitman's masterpieces in the major mode came in 1859, three years after "This Compost." Published the next year in *Leaves of Grass* as "A Word Out of the Sea," it was subsequently reworked and much improved—this is one case where Whitman rewrote with excellent results—and given the title by which we now know it: "Out of the Cradle Endlessly Rocking." It is lyric, not argument; it is one protracted, impassioned song in celebration of death. It is narrative as well; it is a reminiscence, somewhat in the spirit of Wordsworth's *Prelude,* which reconstructs one moment in the poet's life when he was a boy by the seashore. *One* moment, we note; and we note too that in the very first line we are given the sea, which can be thought of as a grave, as also a cradle—death and life together. In some briers by the shore there had been two birds, "two feather'd guests from Alabama," alternately sitting on the eggs in their nest, one watching, "silent, with bright eyes," while the other flew out over the waves and then returned. But once the female did not return; hour after hour, day after day, she did not return. And so the boy listened as the solitary he-bird broke his heart in song.

O night! do I not see my love fluttering out among the breakers?
What is that little black thing I see there in the white?

High and clear I shoot my voice over the waves,
Surely you must know who is here, is here,
You must know who I am, my love.

O past! O happy life! O songs of joy!
In the air, in the woods, over fields,
Loved! loved! loved! loved! loved!
But my mate no more, no more with me!
We two together no more.

Then the boy's heart would have broken too, had he not implored the sea to send him the meaning of what he had seen and heard, and had not "the savage old mother incessantly crying" consented.

Whereto answering, the sea,
Delaying not, hurrying not,
Whisper'd me through the night, and very plainly before
    daybreak,
Lisp'd to me the low and delicious word death,
And again death, death, death, death,
Hissing melodious, neither like the bird nor like my arous'd
    child's heart,
But edging near as privately for me rustling at my feet,
Creeping thence steadily up to my ears and laving me softly
    all over,
Death, death, death, death, death.

Which I do not forget,
But fuse the song of my dusky demon and brother,
That he sang to me in the moonlight on Paumanok's gray beach,
With the thousand responsive songs at random,
My own songs awak'd from that hour,
And with them the key, the word up from the waves,
The word of the sweetest song and all songs,
That strong and delicious word which, creeping to my feet,
(Or like some old crone rocking the cradle, swathed in sweet
    garments, bending aside,)
The sea whisper'd me.

"My own songs awak'd from that hour." The discovery of death made Whitman a poet, and this is the way he tells us. Poetry could hardly be better, and very seldom is. "Out of the Cradle Endlessly Rocking" is not merely one of his masterpieces; it is one of *the* masterpieces, and alone would justify the reputation of its writer.

He was better only once: in the dirge for Lincoln, "When Lilacs Last in the Dooryard Bloom'd." The Civil War, just ended with Lincoln's life, had been not so much the making as the remaking of the great poet who slept in Whitman's bones. Death now had become tragic and particular: the deaths of soldiers, the death of America as Whitman had known it in the days of Eden, the days of the Children of Adam; and now the death of "the sweetest, wisest soul of all my days and lands." The greatest man in Whitman's world had died, a man not himself, a man quite outside himself; and that was an advantage too for the poet who was to begin his crowning piece, for the subject matter of poetry should be outside, must be outside, if one is to go and put oneself in it. Whitman went to the subject of Lincoln with good and evil defined in his imagination, with each of those great things limited and made lifelike by the other. And he bore with him a set of symbols which to the accompaniment of magnificent music he could weave and intertwine as plastic artists do their visible, their tangible materials. The lilac, the star, the bird are concrete, irreducible images; the poem organizes itself around them as if by a natural process, though it is of course the artistic process at its best. Whitman is there too; "Lilac and star and bird" are "twined with the chant of my soul." The importance of the subject is finally in the understanding Whitman has of it. But it is something to be understood; and once more the song of a bird assists the musician of the spirit to find his voice: once more there is a great hymn to death:

> Come lovely and soothing death,
> Undulate round the world, serenely arriving, arriving,
> In the day, in the night, to all, to each,
> Sooner or later delicate death.
>
> Prais'd be the fathomless universe,
> For life and joy and for objects and knowledge curious,
> And for love, sweet love—but praise! praise! praise!
> For the sure-enwinding arms of cool-enfolding death.

There is the summit of *Leaves of Grass*. It has other eminences, and on the lower ground there are foothills—the great little poems—which time will find it hard to wash away. Time and criticism. Already they have eroded the mountain, as is the way with all such things—a good way, since it leaves what ought to be left, and shows it in interesting shapes. Probably they will cut still deeper in. But certain rocks will endure as granite does. That, at this moment in time, is criticism's guess.

13
A CENTURY OF MARK TWAIN

The quarter of a century since Mark Twain's death has done as much as any equivalent period to give us the author we now possess. The first twenty-five years of his life gave him, of course, his best subject matter: the Mississippi River, the Valley frontier. The next twenty-five years brought him to the point of understanding this material and embodying it in his two masterpieces, "Life on the Mississippi" and "Huckleberry Finn." Another twenty-five years and he had become the white figure of the legend: eccentric, funny, and upon occasion fierce. But it is only since 1910 that criticism has been busy with him in a serious way, establishing him as an artist and considering him in perspective. Albert Bigelow Paine's massive and fascinating biography, following as soon as possible after its hero's death, prepared the ground for many particular studies; and the finest of these, Van Wyck Brooks's "The Ordeal of Mark Twain," is still a center about which opinion and interpretation can whirl. The contemporaries of Mark Twain were content for the most part merely to enjoy him. Already, however, he has grown into an object of thought, a stimulus to abstraction. For better or for worse he has become the author he never quite dared to hope he would have to be.

For better, because no writer perhaps can survive very long without the aid of an articulate criticism which isolates, describes, and keeps on talking about his special quality. For worse, because the special quality of Mark Twain is unusually difficult to describe without destroying, unusually delicate under the threat of analysis. It is delicate because it is not his alone. It is the quality of his people, the American people, and if it is notorious that we bungle when we dissect the heart of a nation it should be still more obvious that we have little reason to hope for success in the business of cutting the cord between a popular writer and his race. Mark Twain was almost indissoluably attached to America, and America to him; and this is still the case. He still can be read, and is read, for rapid enjoyment. So distinctly and happily so, in fact, that it is a question whether there is any better way to read him, and whether most of the criticism has not been worse than irrelevant. To say as much is not of necessity to take literally his words to Andrew Lang: "I have never tried in even one single instance to help cultivate the cultivated classes. . . . I always hunted for bigger game—the masses. I have seldom deliberately tried to instruct them, but have done my best to entertain them. To simply amuse them would have satisfied my dearest ambition at any time." Nor is it to suppose that he was thinking of himself when he dictated the following paragraph to Paine, pretending that it was what an Albany bookseller had said to Robert Louis Stevenson about the words of a hack named Davis:

Nobody has heard of Davis; you may ask all around and you will see. You never see his name mentioned in print, not even in advertisements; these things are of no use to Davis, not any more than they are to the wind and the sea. You never see one of Davis's books floating on top of the United States, but put on your diving armor and get yourself lowered away down and down and down till you strike the dense region, the sunless region of eternal drudgery and starvation wages—there you will find them by the million. The man that gets that market, his fortune is made, his bread and butter are safe, for those people will never go back on him. An author may have a reputation which is confined to the surface, and lose it and become pitied, then despised, then forgotten, entirely forgotten— the frequent steps in a surface reputation. A surface reputation, however great, is always mortal, and always killable if you go at it right—with pins and needles, and quiet slow poison, not with the club and the toma-hawk. But it is a different matter with the submerged reputation—down in the deep water; once a favorite there, always a favorite; once beloved, always beloved; once respected, always respected, honored, and believed in. For what the reviewer says never finds its way down into those placid deeps, nor the newspaper sneers, nor any breath of the winds of slander blowing above. Down there they never hear of these things. Their idol may be painted clay, up there at the surface, and fade and waste and crumple and blow away, there being much weather there; but down below he is gold and adamant and indestructible.

Yet both passages have their pertinence, and the second one has the additional value of perfectly illustrating what has just been said. An American is talking there, and no other kind of man. No American but would talk that way if he could: if he had, that is, the genius. Mark Twain had the genius. And the American people were first to recognize the fact. The critics were second, but it is essential to Mark Twain's reputation that millions of persons should continue capable of feeling the glory of such prose—feeling it immediately, without reflection and without recourse to the idiom of analysis.

Such prose has form, a thing Mark Twain is customarily accused of lacking. His books, as books, do lack it; they trail off, they ravel out, they are heaps of fragments. And in the long run this will doubtless work against him, since a book which does not hold together is doomed to a particularly hard battle with oblivion, there being much wind and weather there. Yet the very looseness of his structure has a certain advantage, for it means that if the good parts are indeed good they will be all the freer to separate themselves from the bad. The mortal parts will blow away in time, leaving the gold and the adamant all the more inviolable. And what are the immortal parts? They are the passages in which Mark Twain has done what he did in the dithyramb to Davis; in which he has exaggerated according to the laws of his own language and of his own people.

It is not enough to say of him that his humor consisted in exaggeration. His whole art consisted in that, and his only art. There was nothing else that he knew how to do with an absolute perfection. He did not think far, even if he thought clearly; he was often deficient in taste; he could be outrageously sentimental; he was in many respects an ignorant man, and could be in turn too proud and too apologetic about this ignorance. But whenever, as frequently happened, he got going about something, it was more than likely that he would develop the speed and the beauty and the form by which we have learned to recognize him at his height. At such moments and in such passages he was possessed by that ancient and noble thing, poetic rage. It possessed him at the same time that he controlled it for the purposes of his peculiar art. He mounted through his theme with an incredible celerity, riding the fieriest steeds known to rhetoric, and the broadest-winged: iteration, reiteration, and multiplied example. He mounted with gigantic ease and a vast naturalness, reaching the top of his subject at last and breathing the great air there with happy lungs; then suddenly descended to the ground and jogged along to the next inspiration. Or, to change the metaphor, he blew a bag up till it almost burst; at his best he did not let it burst, but tossed it lightly away and left it floating. Or, to change the metaphor once more, his prose was a river which regularly widened its banks, swelling and accelerating until there was danger that it should cease to look like a river; then it subsided and narrowed again, pulling us onward to new bays.

The story of the three matches in "Roughing It," or of Slade, or of the lost claim; the picture of Hannibal's indolence in "Life on the Mississippi," or of its animation when a steamboat lands at the wharf, or of the river itself as fearfully studied from a pilot house; the first description of Huck's father; the parody of Mrs. Eddy; the whole of "My Watch"; many an unmailed letter—any of these and a hundred other passages will serve as an illustration of what is meant. Such passages place Mark Twain against that portion of the American background where he belongs. It is not, incidentally, the portion which produces at least once each generation an Artemus Ward, a Mr. Dooley, a Will Rogers. Mark Twain could do what they do, but he never did it better than Artemus Ward, if indeed he did it as well. He was not a cracker-box philosopher, a homespun wit with the gift of sly, dry talk out of the corner of his mouth. Their forte is understatement. His was overstatement, and the tradition which supported him was the tradition of the tall tale, the mighty mendacity. Their pride is in the truths which they insinuate; his pride was in the boldness and grandeur with which he could lie. This is the finer tradition; or at any rate by doing what he did with it he has made it seem so. What he did with it was to realize all its possibilities and to prove that they were beautiful. They had seldom been actually beautiful; we can be sure that a majority of the Sellerses, both then and now, have been tiresome men who did not know when to stop or how as they went on to improve the quality of their utterance. Yet there is a deep instinct in any American which tells him that one liar may be better than another and which encourages him to listen for the perfect note. He heard it in Mark Twain and recognized a master: one who began where he did and who followed all the rules, but who somehow soared and sang; and who, furthermore, lied in a precise, a disciplined language which was so far from being ignorant of irony as almost to use that instrument as its grammar. One more example, a little-known one, must suffice. It is the letter, signed Samuel Langhorne, sent in 1871 to the New York *Tribune* proposing that a substitute be hanged in place of one Ruloff, a condemned murderer whose learning was being set forth in the press as remarkable. The contemporary fame of this letter is not wholly to be explained on the ground of its novelty; papers must have copied it across the country because it got going so well on the theme—not of Ruloff's learning merely, but of learning in general as the mass of men understand it:

I am not sorry that Ruloff is to be hanged, but I am sincerely sorry that he himself has made it necessary that his vast capabilities for usefulness should be lost to the world. In this, mine and the public's is a common regret. For it is plain that in the person of Ruloff one of the most marvelous of intellects that any age has produced is about to be sacrificed, and that, too, while half of the mystery of its strange powers is yet a secret. Here is a man who has never entered the doors of a college or a university, and yet by the sheer might of his innate gifts has made himself such a colossus in abstruse learning that the ablest of our scholars are but pigmies in his presence. By the evidence of Professor Mather, Mr. Surbridge, Mr. Richmond, and other men qualified to testify, this man is as familiar with the broad domain of philology as common men are with the passing events of the day. His memory has such a limitless grasp that he is able to quote sentence after sentence, paragraph after paragraph, chapter after chapter, from a gnarled and knotty ancient literature that ordinary scholars are capable of achieving little more than a bowing acquaintance with. But his memory is the least of his great endowments. By the testimony of the gentlemen above referred to he is able to *critically analyze* the works of the old masters of literature, and while pointing out the beauties of the originals with a pure and discriminating taste is as quick to detect the defects of the accepted translations; and in the latter case, if exceptions be taken to his judgment, he straightway opens up the quarries of his exhaustless knowledge, and builds a very Chinese wall of evidence around his position. Every learned man who enters Ruloff's presence leaves it amazed and confounded by his prodigious capabilities and attainments. One scholar said he did not believe that in matters of subtle analysis, vast knowledge in his peculiar field of research, comprehensive grasp of subjects, and serene kingship over its limitless and bewildering details, any land or any era of modern times had given birth to Ruloff's intellectual equal. What miracles this murderer might have wrought, and what luster he might have shed upon his country, if he had not put a forfeit upon his life so foolishly!

The words "serene kingship" mark the high point here, but there has been a steady climb to them, and as always the end comes shortly after, with an abruptness both expected and prescribed.

Of course there is more to Mark Twain than this. He had a heart and a brain, and he stood in a very interesting relation to the America of his time, a relation which has been stated quite differently by Van Wyck Brooks and by Bernard De Voto. But in the long run it may appear that his sheer literary energy, surpassed in amount by no American writer except perhaps Melville, may tell the tale most truly. Whatever the merits of our controversies about his "significance" and about what he reflected or represented, he still stands in a relation to us which will be valuable and delightful as long as we remain capable of responding to great language, the tall tale, the swelling theme. Much of him has ceased to mean what it meant fifty years ago, and his personality no longer dominates the land; nor is the same land here that he observed with such an all-seeing eye. Yet enough of it lingers, in ears born waiting for the magnificent word whenever and by whomever it may be spoken, to suggest that his reputation will be permanent. It is in this respect that he was a great writer, and it is in this sign that he will continue to conquer.

14

THE POEMS OF THOMAS HARDY

A text for any discussion of Thomas Hardy's poems might be the
373rd pensée of Pascal: "I shall here write my thoughts without
order, and not perhaps in unintentional confusion; that is true
order, which will always indicate my object by its very disorder. I
should do too much honor to my subject if I treated it with order,
since I want to show that it is incapable of it." Pascal's subject,
to be sure, was not anybody's poems; it was everybody's life, it
was the whole of experience as he tried to grasp it. Yet the text has
a peculiar fitness in Hardy's case, for it can be made to refer not
merely to the overwhelming volume and variety of his poetic output
but to the view he himself took of the world; or the views, for
there were many of these, and he never pretended that they were
consistent with one another.

In one of his prefaces he confessed how difficult it had been to
arrange the present poems in anything like a natural or rational
order. Indeed, it was impossible, and so he had given up. "I mean,"
he said, "the chance little shocks that may be caused . . . by the
juxtaposition of unrelated, even discordant, effusions; poems
perhaps years apart in the making, yet facing each other. . . . But
the difficulties of arranging the themes in a graduated kinship of
moods would have been so great that irrelation was almost un-

avoidable with efforts so diverse. I must trust for right note-catching to those finely-touched spirits who can divine without half a whisper, whose intuitiveness is proof against all the accidents of inconsequence.'' The problem, familiar of course to any poet, must have been particularly torturous for Hardy, who had been prolific for so long. The eight volumes of short poems he had published between 1898 and 1928—between, that is, his fifty-eighth and his eighty-eighth years—contained by no means all new matter. He was always bringing forward poems he had written in the 1860's, or in any of the three subsequent decades; for he started as a poet, and only because he could not get published in that capacity had he written novels. Now that he was determined to be known as a poet and nothing but a poet he ransacked his desk for "effusions" that might still do. No wonder he found it difficult to arrange the result.

The modern reader cannot do so either; nor can the modern critic decide with readiness which poems of Hardy's are the best, let alone the most characteristic. No poet more stubbornly resists selection. And this has not been to Hardy's advantage in the field where reputations are made. There is no core of pieces, no inner set of classic or perfect poems, which would prove his rank. Perhaps no poem of Hardy's is perfect; indeed, there is no great poet in whom imperfection is easier to find. Yet he is a great poet, and there are those who love him without limit even though they will admit his thousand failures and defects. With such persons it is the whole of him that registers and counts; one thing they would be reluctant to admit, namely, that out of his *Collected Poems* a *Selected Poems* might be put together which would contain everything pertaining to his essence. His essence, they would insist, is everywhere in the body of his work: in the capillaries, the tissues, no less than in the sinews and the heart. For them, in other words, the *Collected Poems* is neither too long nor too miscellaneous; its reputation with them depends upon the very richness that puts other readers off. They have made the effort the volume requires, and the reward of that effort is their knowledge of a poet who is great even when he is not writing well. He is great in himself, as one who thinks, feels, sees and speaks; and he cannot lose their allegiance.

This miracle is worked in the *Collected Poems* alone; not in the slight verse play, *The Famous Tragedy of the Queen of Cornwall,* or even in that more impressive drama in one hundred and thirty

scenes, *The Dynasts*. It is good to have read *The Dynasts* once, for
it contains curious and wonderful things; but few can have read it
twice, at least all the way through. It does not get close to its people,
whom Hardy too convincingly calls automata, cheese-mites, and
mackerel. The view he takes of them is from too far away. This of
course is the view he wants to take, since a theory rules him as he
writes: a theory not unlike that of Tolstoy as he wrote *War and
Peace* on the same subject, the wars of Napoleon. For neither man
did individuals count, at any rate so far as theory went: there was
no such thing as character or will, there was only mass movement,
and even in this movement there was no meaning. But Tolstoy so
far forgot his theory as to create Natasha, Andrey, and Pierre, to
name only three out of dozens of souls to whom his pen gave life;
whereas Hardy, with that stubbornness which his admirers will
always forgive him, refused to budge from the platform he had
erected whereon to stand and state his thesis—the calamity of
Napoleon was fortuitous, without design or moral, nor were the
sufferings of innumerable men so much as noted by the Immanent
Will whose unfeeling mind worked

> unconsciously, as heretofore,
> External artistries in Circumstance.

The Spirits with whom Hardy shares his platform, bodiless beings
who have no more control over the drama than he has, say magnificent things in a monotone their poet never violates; but they say
what he chooses to have them say, since they are nothing but spokes-
men for his metaphysics. When we descend into the action—battles,
conferences, love passages, riots, and duels—we do not find ourselves among people to whom warmth has even by inadvertence
been given. Nor do these people speak fine verse, as often the
Spirits do; they are not enough alive for that, nor does Hardy wish
them to be. He has been more eloquent in his stage-directions; it is
to those that the reader is most likely to return. For example, this
early one:

> The nether sky opens, and Europe is disclosed as a prone and emaciated
> figure, the Alps shaping like a backbone, and the branching mountain-
> chains like ribs, the peninsular plateau of Spain forming a head. Broad
> and lengthy lowlands stretch from the north of France across Russia like a

grey-green garment hemmed by the Ural mountains and the glistening Arctic Ocean.

The point of view then sinks downward through space, and draws near to the surface of the perturbed countries, where the people, distressed by events which they did not cause, are seen writhing, heaving, and vibrating in their various cities and nationalities.

That is eloquent, surely; indeed, it is brilliant; but it closes a door on drama which is something like the door of a tomb. Those of us who insist on entering must abandon all hope of making human sense out of what we see.

No, it is the *Collected Poems* upon which Hardy's reputation will be obliged to rest. And this is a volume, as has already been hinted, in which a traveler can lose his way. Its contents are a cavern the quality of whose darkness is always changing, and the number of whose recesses appears to increase as the explorer stumbles on. Lights gleam and then subside, only to be lit again in further corners. The reader, that is to say, is forever making new discoveries: either of Hardy or of himself. If of Hardy, they have to do with dimensions of his thought and feeling not previously observed. If of himself, they have to do with certain poems he seems to be reading for the first time; or reading with a sense of power in them that startles him, for there had been no sign of it before. No poet has so changeable a surface as Hardy, no poet maintains in his reader so changeable a mind. Which are his best poems, and which are his worst? The question never seems to get settled; no wonder that he becomes the anthologist's despair.

Hardy himself has been before us in the cavern, lighting candles that would seem to show the way. Only, they do not show it all. They show, in fact, only their own wicks and tallow. They are the "philosophical" poems in which Hardy states his theory of life. It is the same theory that he states in *The Dynasts,* and it is equally unilluminating of anything save his own conscious thought. They are good poems, but they are not the ones that move us to call him a great poet. We want more from a poet than a theory of life; we want, if such a thing is possible, the look, feel, sound, taste, and even smell of life itself. And that is what Hardy eventually provides, and provides so richly that his name is sure to last. Meanwhile there are these philosophical poems which tell us that he finds no intelligibility in events, no form or order in the world. They are such poems as only he could write; they say what they have to say in his own idiom, for he meant very personally what he said in them; and they make a solemn, piercing music which alone would certify their sincerity. But they are not the heart of the book as he must have supposed they would be. They take their place among the thinner tissues, the ones with the least blood in them. The heart of the book, assuming it can be located at all, is older and tougher than these poems are. The book was not a single effort like *The Dynasts,* conceived and carried through with little or no interruption; it was the work of almost seventy years, and Hardy himself changed much in all that time. Or if he did change, he submitted himself to many chances, and caught on the fly a bewildering number of perceptions which in the nature of things could not have been alike. An assiduous taker of notes upon himself, he rendered on a wide front his experience of the world, so that there is scarcely anything he has not understood and said before he is finished. This is not precisely to say that the rest of the book contradicts or denies the philosophical poems. Rather, it absorbs them; it finds a place for them and leaves them there.

In that place they say the same thing over and over: nature and man have come to a misunderstanding, and this misunderstanding will never be cured. Nature—sometimes the term is God—did not make man to think and feel; man was once unconscious, as other things still are, as mildews and mandrakes are, as stones and birds. That was the good time, when suffering of course existed yet could not tell itself it did; when no creature expected more than it could get; when the "disease of feeling" and the malady of thought had not yet been born in the brain of one creature, man, who now is doomed to pain by the very fact of this monstrous birth. The qualities we think distinguish us are the qualities that make us miserable. We long for what we can never have, just as we agonize over losses and failures of which nature takes only routine account. If we could be one with nature again, as Lucretius thought we could, and as naturalism says we must, we might recover that happiness of which we were unconscious when we had it; but this can never be. The gulf between us and our maker widens with every idea we have, and with every refinement of experience. Nature remains the same; we change, and in the process move away from her into a loneliness for which there is no remedy. The more we use our minds, the less we understand; yet we must keep on using our minds, as we must keep on hoping and despairing. Even nature is aware of all this, and laments her wayward child; though the only thing she can tell us is that if we came back to her we would be coming back to unconsciousness, we would be as toads and starts, as mushrooms and meteors.

> Maybe now
> Normal unawareness waits rebirth.

So in his last book, *Winter Words,* Hardy dares to hope; but it is the dimmest hope, and of the dimmest thing.

No wonder Hardy calls himself a tragic poet, and says on one occasion: "Comedy lies." No wonder he is at home with gloom, which he certainly is; or that he can note as a scientist would some signs that the world, like any other machine, is running down. In an uncanny poem, "Nature's Questioning," he even endows inanimate objects with the power to wonder what men wonder:

> When I look forth at dawning, pool,
>   Field, flock, and lonely tree,
>   All seem to gaze at me
> Like chastened children sitting silent in a school;
>
> Their faces dulled, constrained, and worn,
>   As though the master's ways
>   Through the long teaching days
> Had cowed them till their early zest was overborne.
>
> Upon them stirs in lippings mere
>   (As if once clear in call,
>   But now scarce breathed at all)—
> "We wonder, ever wonder, why we find us here!
>
> "Has some Vast Imbecility,
>   Mighty to build and blend,

> But impotent to tend,
> Framed us in jest, and left us now to hazardry?

> "Or come we of an Automaton
>   Unconscious of our pains? . . .
>   Or are we live remains
> Of Godhead dying downwards, brain and eye now gone?"

These are terrible questions, put with a terrible candor, which of course is Hardy's. There is one further question, more difficult for Hardy to phrase because it seems to him rhetorical:

> "Or is it that some high Plan betides,
>   As yet not understood,
>   Of Evil stormed by Good,
> We the Forlorn Hope over which Achievement strides?"

He phrases it rather stuffily; he is not convinced that it was worth asking; but then he closes with music—his music—on the note most native to him:

> Thus things around. No answerer I . . .
>   Meanwhile the winds, and rains,
>   And Earth's old glooms and pains
> Are still the same, and Life and Death are neighbors nigh.

"Are still the same." Perhaps the heart of Hardy is just there. Winds and rains, glooms and pains—those are the matter out of which he makes his art; they are the very folklore of his life, the familiar data, never to disappear, over which his imagination can pore without becoming tired. He would not know what to do without them; and once he said as much, in the poem he wrote refusing an invitation to the United States. Our claim to be young and happy was precisely what kept him away:

> I shrink to seek a modern coast
> Whose riper times have yet to be;
> Where the new regions claim them free

From that long drip of human tears
Which peoples old in tragedy
Have left upon the centuried years.

No, he must remain where men, bent under pressures unimaginable in a new world, were all but deformed by pain and failure. His allegiance was to irony; to the monstrous coincidence, the ghastly event, or else—reducing calamity's scale—to the queer outcome, the miniature misadventure, the misery no bigger than a mouse. It was characteristic of Hardy that his poem about the sinking of the *Titanic* dealt with only one fact: the building of the iceberg and the building of the ship at whatever moment in each case would bring it about that the two collided when and where they did. But it was just as characteristic of him that he should write, in "The Sun on the Letter," about the odd circumstance that sunlight played as brightly over bad news as it would have over good. The size of things did not matter to him so long as all of them, huge or minute, testified to the principle of chance—or, as he put it in an early poem, Hap. Crass Casualty was still another name for it. And in nature as men once knew her it would not have been noticed, since nothing would have been noticed. It is the disease of feeling that has made men hypersensitive to truth: they cannot take what must be and what is. They are skinless creatures, shivering in the winds of circumstance.

Now it might follow from the firmness with which Hardy held on to this view that he would have no sympathy with those who feel; that he would spend all of his strength, as Lucretius did, in lecturing them upon the absurdity of their error; that he would, in other words, be cold and heartless. The contrary, as any reader of him knows, is true. In all the world there is no more feeling poet. He proves it in a hundred ways, no one of which is logically defensible; has he not demonstrated, even to monotony, the foolishness of tears? It is now that the great poet emerges, the poet whose humanity is profounder than his thought. He is that most moving kind of man, the kind that tries not to feel yet does; he is that most convincing of lovers, the one who begins by thinking he does not believe in love. Hardy should scorn the emotions of himself and others; instead of which, he lets them break his heart.

The intensity of his concern may show itself in bizarre, unlikely ways, but there is no mistaking the intensity, as for example in "The Head Above the Fog," which gives life to a mistress in the very act of decapitating her:

> Something do I see
> Above the fog that sheets the mead,
> A figure like to life indeed,
> Moving along with spectre-speed,
>   Seen by none but me.
>
> O the vision keen!—
> Tripping along to me for love
> As in the flesh it used to move,
> Only its hat and plume above
>   The evening fog-fleece seen.
>
> In the day-fall wan,
> When nighted birds break off their song,
> Mere ghostly head it skims along,
> Just as it did when warm and strong,
>   Body seeming gone.
>
> Such it is I see
> Above the fog that sheets the mead
> Yea, that which once could breathe and plead!—
> Skimming along with spectre-speed
>   To a last tryst with me.

The intensity in this case is not Hardy's, it is the ghost's, and the skimming speed of the ghost is what conveys it to us. Hardy is never without the power, indispensable in any ambitious poet, to endow his creations with an energy that seems to be their own. It is he who speaks, but it is they who have the final word. "The Head Above the Fog" treats of a tryst: a favorite subject with Hardy, for nothing interests him more than meetings between lovers; the most moving number for him is two. The meetings are more often sad than successful, but no matter; his deepest sympathies are engaged, and there is always something beautiful in that depth. He may or may not be recording a personal experience; most of the time, he tells us in his prefaces, he is not. It is clear enough that twenty-one poems in *Satires of Circumstance* have to do with the death of his first wife, with whom he had lived thirty-eight years; and these poems are seldom matched in all the literature of grief. Usually, however, we are willing to assume that he is dramatic, or as he himself liked to say, "personative." Whether or not the rule applies to the poem *Near Lanivet, 1872,* we could no more take it for unreal than we could so take *Othello* or *King Lear.*

There was a stunted handpost just on the crest,
    Only a few feet high:
She was tired, and we stopped in the twilight-time for her rest,
    At the crossroads close thereby.

She leant back, being so weary, against its stem,
    And laid her arms on its own,
Each open palm stretched out to each end of them,
    Her sad face sideways thrown.

Her white-clothed form at this dim-lit cease of day
    Made her look as one crucified
In my gaze at her from the midst of the dusty way,
    And hurriedly "Don't," I cried.

I do not think she heard. Looking thence she said,
    As she stepped forth ready to go,
"I am rested now.—Something strange came into my head;
    I wish I had not leant so!"

And wordless we moved onward down from the hill
    In the west cloud's murked obscure,
And looking back we could see the handpost still
    In the solitude of the moor.

"It struck her too," I thought, for as if afraid
    She heavily breathed as we trailed;
Till she said, "I did not think how 'twould look in the shade,
    When I leant there like one nailed."

I, lightly: "There's nothing in it. For *you,* anyhow!"
  —"O I know there is not," said she . . .
"Yet I wonder. . . . If no one is bodily crucified now,
  In spirit one may be!"

And we dragged on and on, while we seemed to see
  In the running of Time's far glass
Her crucified, as she had wondered if she might be
  Some day.—Alas, alas!

His lovers are sometimes faithful, sometimes faithless; though as often as not the faithless ones are merely feeble of purpose, perhaps for a reason they cannot understand—they change, and are bewildered by the change. If they are cruel, it may be unintentionally so, or else they remain unaware that they were cruel. "A Maiden's Pledge" is the song of an absolutely faithful girl who will continue so even if her lover never hints of marriage:

Your comet-comings I will wait
With patience time shall not wear through.

Hardy takes pleasure in that, as in one of his best-known songs, "Let Me Enjoy," he says he takes pleasure in countless sweet things that are not for him.

Let me enjoy the earth no less
Because the all-enacting Might
That fashioned forth its loveliness
Had other aims than my delight. . . .

From manuscripts of moving song
Inspired by scenes and dreams unknown,
I'll pour out raptures that belong
To others, as they were my own.

His singular devotion to birds—one could almost say, his obsession with them—has something like this for its source. The intensity of birds, equal to his own, caught him up in their ecstasies as they sang or sported; or suffered, for he had no defenses against the spectacle of one in pain, particularly such a one as he addresses in "The Blinded Bird." His rage against men who run red-hot needles through the eyes of songbirds to increase the sweetness of their voices is stated only by indirection, yet the rage is strong enough:

> Who hath charity? This bird
> Who suffereth long and is kind,
> Is not provoked, though blind
> And alive ensepulchred?
> Who hopeth, endureth all things?
> Who thinketh no evil, but sings?
> Who is divine? This bird.

For Hardy, it would seem, birds were omens: they had been sent to tell him something. In "The Darkling Thrush" the message is that hope may have some meaning after all, for this bird if not for him. But another thrush, seen out of his window on Christmas day, told him something else again:

> There, to reach a rotting berry,
> Toils a thrush,—constrained to very
> Dregs of food by sharp distress,
> Taking such with thankfulness.
>
> Why, O starving bird, when I
> One day's joy would justify,
> And put misery out of view,
> Did you make me notice you?

Hardy never ceases to take testimony, to read the world as if it were a book, now closed, now open, with too many pages in it ever to let him finish. A tree in London can strike pity out of him because it is not in the country where it belongs. But sometimes it is he who is being read, as in the case of the fallow deer that looked in upon him one night:

We do not discern those eyes
  Watching in the snow;
Lit by lamps of rosy dyes
We do not discern those eyes
  Wondering, aglow,
  Foorfooted, tiptoe.

A poet's power to feel is best proved in the stories he tells, provided he can tell stories. Hardy could; that was where his genius lay; and so it may be that the heart of the *Collected Poems* beats in the narratives that throng it like so many persons, each one of them powerful in his or her own right. The final richness, perhaps, is here. Hardy is the envy of those who would be infinitely fertile in narrative ideas if only they could; it would seem to have been easy for him to be just that. Doubtless he worked harder than appears; there is evidence that he scoured newspapers for material, and took copious notes on stories he overheard in his native Wessex. The appearance, nevertheless, is of a fountain that cannot stop flowing; and its waters are strong waters that thrust forth from deep places. Hardy's stories are little melodramas, sensational, unrelenting, and if need be mournful beyond bearing, as the great ballads are.

In "The Burghers" a man who has planned to ambush his wife and her lover—to kill them with two strokes of his sword as they flee from his house—brings them home with him instead and heaps gifts upon them, of clothes and jewels; then he lets them go, knowing that his kindness to them is a wound which will never heal.

In "Her Death and After" a dying wife tells her former lover that she wishes the child she has just borne were his; her husband is not kind to her, and she fears for the child's future, since it is lame. The lover haunts her tomb until it becomes noticeable that he does; the husband himself notices it, and comes to ask him why; then without premeditation he tells the husband that the lame child is his. The child is sent to him and he brings it up, happily because this is what the dead woman would have wished, unhappily because he has hurt her name.

In "The Dance at the Phoenix" a woman of sixty who in her youth had been free with her favors, especially to "sundry troopers of the King's Own Cavalry,'' is now the virtuous wife of a gentle fellow who knows nothing of this past; and she would have died peacefully in good time had not on a certain evening the King's Cavalry come to the Phoenix Inn for a dance like those of the old days. Jenny, sleeping by her husband, hears the music and cannot refrain from slipping away to join the merriment, old as she is. She dances all night; is escorted home; slips back into bed; and dies of exhaustion which her husband attributes to some natural cause—"The King's said not a word.''

In "A Sunday Morning Tragedy" a mother tells how, having failed to persuade her daughter's lover that he should marry her because she is with child by him, she procures from an herb woman a drug that will dispose of the child; only after she has administered the drug does she hear that the lover, repenting, has published the banns in church; but it is too late, for the drug proves fatal to the daughter.

In "The Noble Lady's Tale" the lady's husband, an actor who has given up the stage to please her father, begs her for permission to go back and play for just one night; she consents; he goes; but when he is home again he accuses her of having followed him to the theater, nor does he believe her oaths to the contrary; he finally decides that her wraith had followed him rather than herself in flesh and blood; but this distresses him quite as much, since it suggests that she had not trusted him; he wastes away, and so does she, unable to be sure whether a projection of her had pursued him; yet those who listen to her tales are left with further questions:

> Did she, we wonder, follow
> Jealously?
> And were those protests hollow?—
> Or saw he
> Some semblant dame? Or can wraiths really be?

In "The Moth-Signal" a woman, sitting with her husband one night, tells him she pities a moth that is burning in the candle flame; she goes outdoors to see how the weather is, and her lover comes to her from a tumulus nearby; he remarks that the moth she put out of the window as a lure to him is "burnt and broken," as he is, for he has shattered his own marriage vows; and an ancient Briton speaks from the tumulus, saying people are what they used to be.

In "The Sacrilege" a woman of the roads promises her lover that she will go no more to meet his rival, Wrestler Joe, provided he will steal treasure from the cathedral shrine with which she can buy ear-drops and rings; the lover sets off to do this, but only after engaging his brother to murder her in the event that the theft is traced to him (whereupon he will be hanged) and she then takes up with Wrestler Joe; things do go that way, and the brother drowns the woman, whose screams as she dies he will never cease to hear.

In a companion story, "A Trampwoman's Tragedy," the heroine pretends, for no reason she can understand in the sequel, that the child she carries is the child not of her "fancy-man" but of "Jeering John," his rival. Her fancy-man stabs Jeering John to death; is hanged; and leaves the woman wondering why she had done such a mad thing; her only comfort being that she can reassure the ghost of her lover whenever it appears and pleads to be told the truth.

In "The Statue of Liberty" a man is asked why he scrubs with mop and water the statue that stands in a city square; his answer is not that he is paid by the city guardians to do it, or that he loves liberty, which the statue symbolizes; it is simply that his daughter was the sculptor's model, and that she had died in this city, distant from his, before he could visit her; what he does now is the only favor he can do his darling, whose good name he thus preserves; but he does not know that he is speaking to the sculptor himself, and that the sculptor knows what happened to the daughter—she died "in the dens of vice."

And so on. The list seems to be endless, for Hardy's narrative vein does not run out. Now and then there is a hearty, humorous tale, since Hardy had that in him too: "The Bride-Night Fire," or "The Homecoming," the latter with a fine refrain:

> Gruffly growled the wind on Toller downland broad and bare,
> And lonesome was the house, and dark; and few came there.

But the prevailing tone is somber, and the accidents of love or hate, of innocence or guilt, are lighted by an artist in the wings who knows everything about shades and shadows.

He knows everything about time as well. Not only do his stories happen, as all stories do, in time; time is also his very subject. No poet has known better how to move forward and backward in this strangest of dimensions. The poem "One We Knew" concerns an old woman whose memories were pictures for others to study as well as herself:

> She said she had often heard the gibbet creaking
>   As it swayed in the lightning flash,
> Had caught from the neighboring town a small child's shrieking
>   At the cart-tail under the lash. . . .
>
> With cap-framed face and long gaze into the embers—
>   We seated around her knees—
> She would dwell on such dead themes, not as one who remembers,
>   But as one who sees.

She resembled Hardy in that, for his own memories were like things printed on a wall; anything that had happened to him, or had happened to his imagination, was real as present things were unable to be.

He lived in his own gallery of paintings; nor could he be sure how many of the figures there were ghosts. This philosopher who prided himself upon his hardness of mind saw ghosts; he had no business to, but he did. They were the spirits of murdered persons, or of persons otherwise wronged; but then too they could be of the mildest sort, like those in "The Garden Seat":

> At night when reddest flowers are black
> Those who once sat thereon come back;
> Quite a row of them sitting there,
> Quite a row of them sitting there.
>
> With them the seat does not break down,
> Nor winter freeze them, nor floods drown,
> For they are light as upper air,
> They are light as upper air!

Perhaps the most touching of them all is to be found in the tale of the dead sailor's mother who comes nightly to the house where she used to live and waits for her son to appear; it is the only house he remembers, and so is the only one he can haunt.

Old houses interest anybody, but for Hardy they were tombs in which time was buried. But buried as it were alive, so that it moved there, and even spoke or sang there, like one of his authentic ghosts. An old mirror, he assumed, must be haunted by the images that had been made upon it; one of his poems, "The Cheval-Glass," tells of a man who bought at an auction the mirror before which a woman he once had loved stood nightly and brushed her hair; he said he saw her in it still, and would keep it with him till he died. Old furniture must remember, Hardy thought, the people who had used it; indeed it must reflect them:

> Hands upon hands, growing paler and paler,
>   As in a mirror a candle-flame
> Shows images of itself, each frailer
>   As it recedes, though the eye may frame
>   Its shape the same.

There was not too much difference for Hardy between an Old English house and a prehistoric tumulus or barrow, or a Roman ruin: those had been houses too, if only for bones. The bones still slept there; they even dreamed, and he could hear them talking in their sleep. But the official antiquities of his island were really no older for him than things he himself had seen or done long years ago. Time, that relative thing, was so relative in his case that a certain Roman road on which as a child he had walked with his mother was ancient to him rather for this reason than for the reason that helmed legionaries once marched along it. His imagination had always a temporal cast. His genius could endow things with age that had none otherwise, just as it could read into a single moment, recollected and reconsidered, eternities of meaning which as it passed had not been recognized; the present moment, he is forever saying, contains all time and more, but nobody knows this then. Railway trains and stations, despite their bleakness, which he never minimizes, take on in his poems the dignity of timeless crossroads where anything on earth can happen, or anything in hell or heaven.

His love of music is chiefly the love of country singing—old singing, of songs and hymns not much remembered now. His poems ring with the quaint names of former tunes, just as they shake with the feet of dancers: not merely her of the Phoenix Inn, but countless young and old performers of forgotten steps. Church choirs, and groups of warblers by night, serenading bridegrooms or celebrating births and deaths—these have a peculiar, almost a sacred importance for Hardy, who knows the names of ancient instruments, too, and is learned in the folklore of bells. One of his best stories, "The Chapel-Organist," deals with a woman who would rather die than cease to play

> Old Hundredth, Saint Stephen's
> Mount Zion, New Sabbath, Miles-Lane, Holy Rest, and Arabia,
> and Eaton.

And the whole subject comes perfectly into focus as he watches some young girls in a winter street singing songs whose origins are venerable beyond their comprehension:

> Yea, old notes like those
> Here are living on yet!—
> But of their fame and fashion
> How little these know
> Who strum without passion
> For pence in the snow!

Hardy hugged time to himself as he hugged pain and gloom; they were the three dimensions of his universe, in which he felt so much at home that he could be surprised when readers complained of its barrenness. It was thick and warm for him, like an old coat that exactly fitted him, even if it looked a little long, and indeed dropped to the ground. It was what he recognized as reality, the one thing to which he was entirely committed. The bitterness of the world did not forbid him to embrace it: a poor thing, but his own. At times, to be sure, he wondered whether he missed something that others saw; he peered hard, and had the reward of any pessimist—something was better than he expected. For that matter, many things were; even all things, if one did not mind their being just what they were. Now and then he would offer an apology for the low tones in which he spoke: he but sang his part, as others must sing theirs. There is in fact much kindness in him, a sort of subdued good nature which shines through his frown as well as his smile; for he smiled and was humorous, too, he had a nice sense of the absurd. He was susceptible to superstitions for which his philosophy would have had no use. Oxen *might* kneel on Christmas Eve; and of course there were all those ghosts; there was true love, too, a thing that mechanism would not explain.

His mind was complicated, and so was his art. The effect of plainness in his poems can make us overlook their skill: a conscious thing with him, and the product of study. He seems to be interested in nothing but accuracy of statement, even if this means that he must sometimes sound clumsy and crude; exactness is what he wants, and he will sacrifice everything to it. This is true; and it is true of any great poet; there is nothing else that causes us in the end to love poetry at all. But accuracy is itself an art, a fine and high one which all the muses conspire to praise. Hardy's muses, he said in 1887, were five in number: Form, Tune, Story, Dance, and Hymn. The last of these may surprise us a little until we read him through again and realize how often he was lyric in the rich, free, leaping way of the Elizabethans:

> This is the weather the cuckoo likes,
>   And so do I;
> When showers betumble the chestnut spikes,
>   And nestlings fly:
> And the little brown nightingale bills his best,
> And they sit outside at "The Travellers Rest,"
> And maids come forth sprig-muslin drest,
> And citizens dream of the south and west,
>   And so do I.

Or until we remember how various his stanzas are; he studied the stanza like a musician, and made it his idiom, whether intricate as in "The Discovery":

> I wandered to a crude coast
>   Like a ghost;
> Upon the hills I saw fires—
> Funeral pyres
> Seemingly—and heard breaking
> Waves like distant cannonades that set the land shaking;

or simple as in "The Pine Planters (Marty South's Reverie)":

> We work here together
>   In blast and breeze;
> He fills the earth in,
>   I hold the trees.
>
> He does not notice
>   That what I do
> Keeps me from moving
>   And chills me through . . .
>
> I have helped him so many,
>   So many days,
> But never win any
>   Small word of praise.

Hardy was a musician; he was also an etcher. It was not for nothing that he had practiced architecture; the draftsman in him is always coming out. He has the keen eye that feeling cannot confuse— an old man's eye, we are tempted to say, which misses nothing. Some of his poems are pure studies in black and white of things he saw in passing: "An East-End Curate," for example, or "No Buyers: A Street Scene" or "Nobody Comes." Others are master-pieces with weather for their theme: any kind of weather, for Hardy liked it all, but his specialty was rain, as in "A Sheep Fair":

The day arrives of the autumn fair,
　　And torrents fall,
Though sheep in throngs are gathered there,
　　Ten thousand all,
Sodden, with hurdles round them reared:
And, lot by lot, the pens are cleared,
And the auctioneer wrings out his beard,
And wipes his book, bedrenched and smeared,
And rakes the rain from his face with the edge of his hand,
　　As torrents fall.

The wool of the ewes is like a sponge
　　With the daylong rain:
Jammed tight, to turn, or lie, or lunge,
　　They strive in vain.
Their horns are soft as finger-nails,
Their shepherds reek against the rails,
The tied dogs soak with tucked-in tails,
The buyers' hat-brims fill like pails,
Which spill small cascades when they shift their stand
　　In the daylong rain.

Not that these particular sheep were before him as he wrote; a third
stanza of the poem says it was long ago that he went to Pummery
Fair, "and the hoarse auctioneer is dead." But time had not faded
the impression—time, the sixth muse of Thomas Hardy.

The world of the *Collected Poems* is a great world. It is *the* great
world, seen always as Hardy saw it, with quizzical, deep eyes that
both formed and deformed it. But the deformation was no crime; it
was rather a style, a way of twisting things into the shape his genius
saw. This is often a queer shape. What other poet, wishing to tell
his beloved that he would be hers even in the grave, ever expressed
the hope

　　　　That thy worm should be my worm, Love?

Worms were as much his specialty as weather.

> The leaf drops: earthworms draw it in
> At night-time noiselessly.

That is a small event among the many that take place in the great world. But Hardy noticed it, and having noticed it he must put it down. Of the several epitaphs he composed for himself, none is more simple and true than "Afterwards," with this refrain to be spoken by his neighbors:

> "He was a man who used to notice such things."

15
NOTHING TO SAY:
ON VIRGINIA WOOLF

With Virginia Woolf, rather more than with any other contemporary novelist except James Joyce, life breaks up into "writing." Her novels have been triumphs of expression. And so here, where the English families whose fortunes she follows from 1880 to the present day are of less importance than the style she has chosen to stipple them with. Her brief and brilliant sentences are dabs at a surface which she would never dream of covering to the corners, or for that matter at the center. There is no center, as there are no corners; there is only an extension, as far as Mrs. Woolf cares to push it, of glistening dots and patches with speckled shade between. The result is something more admirable than interesting, provided life is still interesting.

For Mrs. Woolf one can guess that it is not. The weariness of twentieth-century England had received no more perfect expression than is to be found in "The Years," whose author, one would think, could never lift her pen again; except that it is a light pen, capable of dancing by itself and sufficiently enamored of its own nimbleness to want to go on forever. It goes on here with a kind of fine strength, shedding delicate traces of itself over a large scene and a long one; unifying a world under images of rain, snow, wind, down-drifting leaves, and small quick birds that fly in and out of the chapters. Mrs. Woolf has lavished the art of a lace-maker upon these images; which interested her more, I think, than the Pargiters of the narrative, unless the Pargiters are to be understood as having been for her also a collection of threads and holes, a generation of creatures born to the needle.

Their lives establish a record for inconclusiveness. No beginning leads to an end, unless the skepticism written into the final section is an end for everybody. Colonel Pargiter and his many children promise rather well in the first section, if only because Mrs. Woolf must in the nature of things endow them with attributes and desires in order that we may distinguish between them. But the progress of the work is the dimming out, not the development, of these desires and attributes. Mrs. Woolf's central people are quite literally snowed under by her style; and the infection spreads to other branches of the family. There is cousin Sara, for instance, not to mention her sister Maggie, and not to mention many another relation with whom something valuable could have been done. They all tend to merge into a population of intelligently bewildered spirits: frightfully knowing souls for whom it is inconceivable that one gesture should be more meaningful than another, and for whom most gestures come in the end to be impossible. They talk well, but in broken sentences which do not refer to anything. Sara talks best, and is indeed the clearest person in the book; but that is only because in her witlessness she can dare to be fantastic, to interrupt conversations with scraps of romantic books she has read and with phrases repeated irrelevantly from the lips of others. Mrs. Woolf's only interesting character is therefore fey; and the fact has its significance; though it is also significant that even Sara pales into parrotry by the time the last party is over and the last sigh drawn.

There is a moment when Eleanor Pargiter, who comes as near as anyone to being the heroine of the volume, wonders whether life says something:

Does everything then come over again a little differently? she thought. If so, is there a pattern; a theme, a recurring, like music; half remembered, half foreseen? . . . a gigantic pattern, momentarily perceptible? The thought gave her extreme pleasure: that there was a pattern. But who makes it? Who thinks it? Her mind slipped. She could not finish her thought.

The experience is typical. Nobody in the book can finish his thought; or can follow another's, the conversation being no less directionless than beautiful. A few pages later Eleanor is overcome by the conviction that she is or might be "happy in this world—happy with living people." But this conviction is canceled in the reader's mind by the loathing which most of Eleanor's relations have for one another: a loathing that expresses itself in the language of bored tolerance. And Eleanor herself must resort still later to dreaming about a better existence.

There must be another life, she thought, sinking back into her chair, exasperated. Not in dreams; but here and now, in this room, with living people. . . . There must be another life, here and now, she repeated. This is too short, too broken. We know nothing, even ourselves. We're only just beginning, she thought, to understand, here and there.

Yet this is not Eleanor's conclusion, as it certainly is not Mrs. Woolf's. The conclusion of the novel, stated or unstated, is that life has grown intolerably old; that everything possible to do has been done; that there are no new people; that the graces by which we suffer one another are worn to the thinnesses of an illegible sixpence; that the world, and particularly England, is a garden of last year's thistles whose stings have been softened by time. And that there is no other life.

No one has ever said this, even in our age when most writers are saying it, better than Mrs. Woolf. And no one has indicated more clearly that a new start should be made. Perhaps it has been made in those novels which indict the middle class of decay and welcome into the world of fiction, in accents less silken than Mrs. Woolf's, the classless class of the future. But perhaps it has not, at any rate on the level of Mrs. Woolf's power and truth. One thing however is plain. Neither Mrs. Woolf nor anyone else can proceed much farther in the direction of "The Years." There is such a thing as growing weary of weariness, of being tired of having nothing to say.

16

JOSEPH AND HIS BROTHERS: A COMEDY IN FOUR PARTS

To say that Mann's *Joseph and His Brothers* is primarily a comic work is to say no more than the author himself said in his foreword to the new edition of 1948. He called it then "a humorous song of mankind," an "epic undertaking" in the spirit of Goethe rather than of Wagner, a narrative written "playfully," with many "pleasantries" in it which he hoped would "cheer those who come after us," though with "pathos" in it, too, which at some later time might still be touching. He spoke of it, that is to say, as a comic poem of vast proportions. And so it is. Its "seventy thousand calmly flowing lines"—someone else might say its twelve hundred continuously intelligent pages—make up a modern masterpiece with which there are few things to be compared, though Marcel Proust's *Remembrance of Things Past* is surely one of those. That equally vast work depends equally with *Joseph and His Brothers* upon our sense of time; or, if you prefer, upon our sense of eternity; or, if you insist, upon our sense of the present moment. For when we have succeeded in giving ourselves to the present moment we are as near to eternity as we shall ever get. Eternity is not a lot of time; it is no time at all, and so is this moment that passes before we know it has come—except that we do know some moments when they come, and it is these and only these from which we learn.

The comic genius loves to speculate about such matters. It has not always done so as explicitly as in the two outstanding cases of Proust and Mann; but then ours is an explicit age which struggles to be conscious of everything, so that we are not surprised when Mann discusses at length a number of things that Chaucer, say, could take for granted. The comic genius has never been more alive than it was in Chaucer, but it does not appear that he thought he needed a theory of time, or at any rate a statable one which in effect would constitute his subject matter. Neither of course does Mann think simply that; his subject matter after all is never anything but Joseph and his father and his brothers, and the wonderful world of Egypt where he spent his most brilliant years, just as in *The Magic Mountain,* Mann's other masterpiece which deals with time, the subject matter is whatever the persons of the story talk about when their excellent brains catch fire in the cold solitude of an Alpine sanatarium. Yet it is true that Mann must think out loud as he writes, and what he thinks about is the bottomless well of time which threatens, if looked into deeply enough, to obscure every individual character and countenance—even those of Joseph himself—and to silence every event so that we who come long after may have doubts that it occurred, or in any case that it made much noise in the universe it could not manage at the end to alter. The prelude to the work, called Descent into Hell, might have been called instead Descent into Time. The genius of story can never dispense with time, but the genius of comic story stands in a peculiar relation to that commodity. It both believes in it and does not. Tragedy believes furiously, even obsessively, in time; time always presses there, leaving the hero unfree to act in the wise way he might if he had the leisure. Comedy, on the other hand, relaxes and disperses time; spreads it out or draws it thin so that it looks a little like eternity. It is not eternity, and cannot ever be; but enough of it will establish the perspective that comedy likes and indeed must have. Only, given the maximum perspective, movement comes to a stop and men are reduced to resembling one another so closely, even so absurdly, that merely man is left; or, to put it abstractly, human nature.

Perhaps it was human nature that Mann lived with during the sixteen dreadful years between 1926 and 1942, when he was composing *Joseph and His Brothers.* One could also say that he lived with Joseph, the individual upon whose image he had settled. But the image enlarged while he studied it, as did the image of every other person in the tale, so that at last he had before him something like the whole spectacle which human life provides when nothing operates to distort it. In the Germany of these years it was outrageously distorted, and there were those who said it would never regain its ancient shape. Here, though, was that very shape; and Mann has testified to the satisfaction he derived from contemplating its breadth and depth. "It was my refuge, my comfort, my home," he says, "my symbol of steadfastness, the guarantee of my perserverance in the tempestuous change of things."

Yet he would have done substantially as he did in any case. Mann's genius was entirely comic; which is to say that it was contemplative, discursive, skeptical, tender, mocking, and loving all at once. It was contemplative because it desired the oldest and the widest view of things, somewhat as they are, supposing man can know this, in their eternal aspect. It was discursive because man's mind is most at home in conversation, in endless talk that considers, measures, analogizes, and compares. No reader of Mann needs to be told how irresistibly he was drawn to language, and how much pleasure he took in imitating the various dialects of thought. The comic genius is among other things a mimic; so in America, where Mann wrote the fourth section of his epic, it was natural for him not merely to see a parallel between Joseph the Provider and Roosevelt the prophet of abundance, but also to adopt so many idioms of the time and place as to incur the charge that he no longer wrote in German, though of course, he did, to the enrichment of that none too lively language. *The Magic Mountain,* like any pure comedy, tends to be all conversation; and if this is not quite true of the Joseph books, it is nevertheless true that what its people say to one another, and what Mann says about them as he converses with his reader, can be understood as carrying most of the burden. Nor can one miss the fact that Joseph's own gift, his distinguishing art, is the wonderful way he has with words, so that he entrances all who come within the sound of his voice or—the same thing—the reach of his mind. When he read aloud to Potiphar it was as if he were creating a new beauty in the text. The intellect of any person is perhaps most swiftly revealed by the way he reads a page he has never seen before. Potiphar knew the pages by heart, but never had they sounded like this. "Joseph read . . . capitally," we hear; "was fluent, exact, unaffected, moderately dramatic, with such natural command of words that the most involved literary style had a happy conversational ease. Literally he read himself into the heart of the listener; and when we seek to understand his swift rise in the Egyptian's favor we must by no means leave out of account these reading hours." He knew his way among intricate phrases as Hamlet, speaking to the players, knew his; no mind, no tongue, has ever been more nimble than that. But this was Hamlet in his comic aspect: his original aspect, which tragedy, as Ophelia divines, has already overwhelmed and lamentably deformed.

The genius of Mann is skeptical in the finest sense of an often misapprehended term. It was not that he believed nothing; he believed everything; he liked ideas, and could live with all of them at once. No sooner did one start up in his brain than another came to reinforce, illuminate, or check it. This was why he could turn so soon from tenderness to pathos, and why he could mock the very man he loved the most. These transformations of his mood will bewilder anyone who does not comprehend how serious at last the comic spirit is. Nothing in man is more serious than his sense of humor; it is the sign that he wants all the truth, and sees more sides of it than can be soberly and systematically stated; it is the sign, furthermore, that he can remember one idea even while he entertains another, and that he can live with contradiction. It is the reason at any rate that we cannot take seriously one whose mind and heart have never been known to smile. The gods do not weep; they smile. Eternity is something like the sun.

The comic spirit has a perfect sense of time, as of a good comedian we say that he has perfect timing. The comic spirit knows that time both does and does not exist; it can look like sheer illusion, though the illusion is one in which comedy will luxuriously live. Comedy takes its time, as truth and history do. The good story-teller is never in a hurry, nor do we want him to be; his digressions, his elaborations, his hesitations, his gestures are in the end more interesting than the action he unfolds; we do not, in fact, want him to reach the end, for then we shall no longer hear his voice or relish with him the way he looks at life, of which the story at hand is but one illustration. While it was being told it amply sufficed our hunger for understanding; it replaced all other stories; was, in effect, story itself, was poetry in the flesh. It treated of only a few people and things, and it treated them in some present moment which absorbed us so that we forgot the rest of time. Yet it had also something to do with the rest of time, which hung about it like a haze, beautifying and validating its apparently random, its artfully accidental details. "The form of timelessness," says Mann, "is here and now." He can say this because he knows how to see Joseph and Jacob as men who lived both long ago and now. They lived so long ago that if time were altogether and simply real they would have no identity today; their figures, their faces, would be woefully indistinct, and the thoughts they had would be mere puffs of desert dust. But time is not that real; Joseph and Jacob can exist not only again but yet; because they existed so intensely in their moment they live always, in all moments. These things are forever happening. History, with a monotony which comedy loves rather than deplores, repeats itself ad infinitum. All thoughts, all things, all men are simultaneously true, as somehow in God's mind they are. The mind of comedy is not that great, but it is the greatest possession of the one creature made in God's image—unless, as Mann playfully suggests, man was the maker of God: in the person of Abram was none other than His father. But in that case it would still be true that the greatest thing in man is his power to know and remember many things at once; to master time; to be in a word the receptacle of the comic spirit.

Any story that is worth telling can be told either briefly or at length. Ideally these alternatives are absolute: the teller takes no time at all, or else he takes an infinite amount of it. Since neither of those miracles is possible, the narrative artist must be content with a choice between abridgement and amplitude. Mann certainly did not abridge the story of Joseph. His work is forty-five times as long as the section of *Genesis* which deals with the hero alone, and fifteen times as long as the section which covers in addition, as Mann himself does, the careers of Abraham, Isaac, and Jacob. This is amplitude indeed, and there have been those who wondered whether Mann did not achieve too much of it for any earthly purpose. The answer ought to be clear. His purpose was comic, and comedy takes its time. It insists upon leisure, of which it is confident that there cannot be too much. Also it is addicted to talk, its own and others', and entertains itself with as much of that as the subject suggests, or as we shall listen to. The subject of Joseph suggested everything to Mann; nothing he knew or thought was alien to it, and no idea was irrelevant. So for sixteen years, with major and minor interruptions, he happily spun his web until it draped like a silken veil the whole figure of the world.

Even *Genesis* had lingered over the story as it did not in the cases of Abraham, Isaac, and Jacob. There was something special about Joseph even then and there; he had nothing of the patriarch about him, and in after times his name dropped out of the *Bible*. God appeared to Moses as the God of three great men, not four. Joseph had saved the race in Egypt, but he was never to be honored as one of its founders. He was not simple enough for that. Neither in a sense was Jacob, yet Jacob's name lived on as one of the never to be forgotten three. Jacob for one thing did not become an Egyptian; he never became anything but what he was, so that when Joseph met him in the Land of Goshen there was a fantastic difference between the two figures: the younger one brilliant with linen and gold, the older one as plain as the wagon seat on which he had ridden all the way from Israel, through dust and among the remnant of his herds. It was not easy for the father to recognize his son in the splendid prince he saw step out of a chariot; nor, when the time came to talk, did he hesitate to say some things that may have sounded bitter to the young man whose mind was full of the glittering deeds he knew he had done. "God has . . . given you back, but yet not quite, for He has kept you too. . . . He has elevated and rejected you both in one, I say it in your ear, beloved child, and you are wise enough to be able to hear it. He has raised you above your brothers just as in your dream—but He has raised you in a worldly way, not in the sense of salvation and the inheritance of the blessing. . . . You are blessed, my dear one, . . . blessed with blitheness and with destiny, with wit and with dreams. Still, it is a worldly blessing, not a spiritual one. . . . Through you salvation is not to reach the peoples and the leadership is denied you. . . . You are not like the fathers, my child, for you are no spiritual

prince, but a worldly one.'' This is Mann writing, not the author of
Genesis, but it is what the whole *Bible* means in spite of its silence
on the subject. The *Bible* is silent like the patriarchs; Mann, like
Joseph, is eloquent as civilization and comedy are eloquent. He is
even loquacious, for there is nothing he would rather do than put
into words what simple men suppose cannot be said, or for that
matter has no need to be said.

There can be no comedy about patriarchs. They come before
civilization is in flower, and comedy is the finest of the flowers.
They are the foundation, for the most part hidden from sight; it is
the cornice, the gables, and the roof. Or, to change the figure once
again, they are the blood and it is the complexion. Mann's Joseph
is all grace, all light, all intellect at its highest. He can do anything
except be the silent, tremendous man each one of his ancestors was.
In Egypt he remembers the faith of his fathers, and characteristically
gives a lucid account of it whenever asked. But it is not a part of
him; it is not in his bones as it is in the bones of Jacob. If anything
he understands it too perfectly; it is one of the works of art he
knows like a connoisseur; it is outside of him, and he can leave it
there when he likes. He leaves it there during his sundry flirtations
with other faiths and other deities: Tammuz, Ashtaroth, and Osiris.
What Mann calls ''the soul's love-affair with matter'' fascinates
him if anything too much. There was a youthful moment when he
almost worshipped the Moon and subscribed to its cult. ''As a
cult,'' says Mann, ''it was vague, confused, and prone to degenerate—
calculated to alarm the careful father—but just on that ground
intoxicating, because mental and physical emotions were therein so
enchantingly mixed.'' Egypt, the Kingdom of the Dead and therefore the embodiment of all that Jacob had taught him to abhor,
was not visited by Joseph voluntarily; Jacob's other sons, the
red-eyed sons of Leah, sent him there; but once there he again
became the connoisseur of customs, in this case exquisite ones
which the artist in him could not but admire. He did no more than
admire and master this new way of life; he remained faithful to his
fathers, and said so often enough; yet none of his fathers could
have done what he did—could have become more Egyptian than
any son of Egypt, and worn its manners like so many jewels. It is
impossible to imagine Isaac, for example, flattering as Joseph did

the guide who was about to take him in to his first audience with Pharaoh. Isaac would never have been there in the first place; but supposing that he was, and supposing that the guide asked him whether he knew how to salute the god, it could never have occurred to him to smile and say: "I wish I did not, for it would be pleasant to learn it of you." This was flattery, and it was mockery too; it came from the top of Joseph's mind, that touched the stars.

Joseph is material for comedy precisely because he is civilized. Both comedy and tragedy depend on civilization for their power. The stories of the patriarchs belong perhaps in neither category; they are too primitive, possibly they are too important, to be classified at all. They simply exist and tell themselves, as seeds germinate in the ground. The first fathers were to be sure the heroes of great stories; they were this side of God in whose life there are no events; but they were nowhere near as far away from absolute simplicity as Joseph was. Joseph was secular; he could believe anything and everything; he was advanced; he was free; and his only illusion was that he had none. He had several concerning himself, the chief of these being that there was no real difference between him and Jacob. Even at the end he was not too certain as to what the difference was that Jacob had tried his best to put into words. This supremely intelligent man did not, that is to say, know everything. And just there is the point at which he becomes available for comic treatment. The stupid person who knows nothing is of no interest to the comic spirit. The brilliant person who nevertheless is blind to something as visible as the ground before his feet—he is the one upon whom wit delights to sharpen its knives. And so with Joseph in Mann's case. Loving his hero as he loved himself, Mann still could mock him because he was not God. And in the same breath he could adore him. He lavished upon him all the understanding that he had, all the elaboration of which his wit was so abundantly capable. His marvellous reconstructions of the Egyptian court, intricate perhaps beyond any imagination but his, and ornate as only he could delicately achieve ornateness—witness for example the entrance of Nefertiti, "with swaying tread, faintly smiling, her eyes cast down, the long, lovely neck thrust anxiously out: the bearer of the seed of the sun"—still do not match the work he did inside of Joseph's mind, where recess upon recess opens as it were into the very caverns of genius. And this work is endless; it fills a fearsome multitude of pages; nor was any of it done in *Genesis*. It is all Mann, all modern, and all comedy.

Sometimes, to be sure, Mann wonders to himself about his method, and lets us know that he does so. "There is too much abridgement and condensation about this," he suddenly remarks of the Biblical narrative where it puts in two sentences the decision of Pharaoh to set Joseph over all Egypt; "it is too dry, it is a drawn and salted and embalmed remnant of the truth, not truth's living lineaments." Within a few lines, however, he has remembered the contrary principle. "Of course," he continues, "there is really nothing against condensation in itself. In the long run it is quite impossible to narrate life just as it flows. What would it lead to? Into the infinite. It would be beyond human powers. Whoever got such an idea fixed in his head would not only never finish, he would be suffocated at the outset. Entangled in a web of desultory exactitude, a madness of detail. No, excision must play its part at the beautiful feast of narration and recreation; it has an important and indispensable role. Here, then, the art will be judiciously practised, to the end of getting finally quit of a preoccupation which, though after all it has a distant kinship with the attempt to drink the sea dry, must not be driven to the extreme and utter folly of actually and literally doing so." Yet three hundred pages before this he had burst out in the same way, and in the same way had taken his words back. The question then was how Potiphar's wife had offered herself to Joseph. "To tell the truth," exclaimed Mann on that occasion, "I am horrified at the briefness and curtness of the original account, which does so little justice to life's bitter circumstantiality. Seldom have I felt more acutely the harm done to truth by abbreviation and compression. Yet let no one think that I am deaf to the reproach—whether expressed or, out of politeness, not expressed—which hangs over my account, my entire exposition: to the effect that the laconic terseness of the original text cannot be surpassed, and that my whole enterprise, which is already of such long continuance, is so much labor lost. But since when, may I ask, does a commentator set himself up in competition with his text? And besides, is there not as much dignity and importance attached to the discussion of the 'how' as to the transmission of the 'what'?

Let us remind ourselves once again that before the story was first told, it had to tell itself—with an exactitude of which life alone is master, and to attain which a narrator has no hope or prospect at all. He can only approach it by serving the 'how' of life more faithfully than the lapidary spirit of the 'what' condescended to do. But if ever the fidelity of a commentator can justify itself, then surely it does in the story of Potiphar's wife and of just what, according to the tradition, she is supposed to have said." Doubtless in such passages Mann protests too much, and in doing so loses his good humor. The comic spirit cannot afford to worry about its right to exist. And most of the time in Mann it does not commit that fault. Most of the time it is vigorous and blithe, and goes about its business with its head high in the air. Nor does it call that business commentary. It calls it story, and lets us add that it is comedy, too.

Mann's method of amplification is simple in one sense; it is the method of filling in, of stuffing interstices with matter he thinks belongs there. The Biblical narrative is famously bald; it leaves almost everything to the imagination, after of course giving the imagination great work to do. Mann cannot be said to desire that nothing be left for his own reader to imagine; he, too, gives him work, and it can be a life's work if one chooses to do it; but the reader in this case has ideas to contemplate rather than actions to complete. And the ideas are Mann's. Claiming to know in full detail what the people of the ancient tale said to one another in this crisis or that, he supplies conversations which themselves are food for the soul, so delicate and deep they are. The colloquies between Jacob and his favorite son explore the entire field of filial and paternal feeling. What Pharaoh said to Joseph tells us more about Egypt than the archaeologists can. And what Potiphar's wife confessed to him in her third-year agony of love is the climax of a whole fine novel of which she has been the distinguished heroine— though in Mann's opinion, Joseph has not been its distinguished hero. He gives us that opinion—just as he always lays bare for us the process of his own thought. We are continuously in his confidence; the book could in fact be described as a conversation between the author and the reader, or rather as a monologue which the reader is expected to overhear. To that extent it *is* a commentary.

But the method is not as simple as all that. Sometimes it involves the addition of circumstances and deeds, the outright invention of narrative details, none of which we could have worked out for ourselves unless our talent and our scholarship had been identical with Mann's. And the richest number of these is to be found in the Potiphar section, which Mann himself called "the artistic zenith of the work." Potiphar's household becomes a fascinating world all by itself. The dwarves, the parents of the master, the eunuch master and his tragic wife—these are the central figures, and each one of them is a triumph of creation, yet they are surrounded by others still, in a busy and beautiful house which for the time being absorbs our entire attention. And none of this is in the *Bible*. Perhaps it did not need to be, but we do not think of that; and even if we did we would find nothing that contradicted or violated the primitive fable. It is simply that Mann has moved us up close enough for us to be able to see what happened in this household day by day—it may be minute by minute—during the three years it was a part of human history. There is the day, for instance, of the ladies' party, when Potiphar's wife, incapable any longer of bearing alone the crushing burden of her love for Joseph, invites her friends to come and eat oranges with her. Each of them is given a little, sharp knife with which to open the precious fruit; each starts to do so at the moment when Joseph appears to pour the wine; and down each snow-white wrist runs a stream of crimson blood. For so much beauty, so suddenly entering the hall, has captured each lady's eyes, so that her knife knows not where it should cut. And this was exactly as Mut had planned it when she told Joseph he must come in among them at such and such a moment. It is an unforgettable moment; nor did Mann need to invent it. His scholarship, which surely was enormous, found it for him in the *Koran,* in seventeen Persian poems, and in "countless renderings by pencil and brush." Those are the sources he reveals to us; but if we have access to none of them we can go to Louis Ginzberg's *Legends of the Jews* for a version graphic enough.

Not that Mann inserts the episode of the ladies' party with a flourish of narrative trumpets or with any brave show of art. Here also he is true to the comic tradition of story-telling, which plays down the narrative art. It says that history is more interesting than fiction; so history is what it pretends to write. Chaucer has his "author" whom he merely follows; Cervantes has his Arabian biographer whom he merely translates. The comic artist will not admit that he has invented anything; the truth is enough for him— Mann says "the facts"—and all truth is as old as the hills anyway; there can be no new stories, just as there can be nothing new under the sun; see the *Bible* as to that. Every man knows everything; except of course that some men forget what they know, or do not wholly realize it, and so commit the only sin that comedy is designed to deal with, namely, folly. Folly is not a fatal sin, though there are those who unaccountably grow fond of it in themselves; therefore it either can be cured or can be rendered harmless as a spectacle at which we wiser ones may smile. It is rendered harmless by understanding: the fool's understanding at last, or if this is not to be expected, then ours; and probably, too, that of several other persons in the story. The essence of comedy is its love of understanding. That is why it goes in so heavily for talk—or rather, we hope, lightly: deliciously and lightly. The dialectic of comedy may seem queer, but it is dialectic nevertheless; and they are right who credit Plato with having perfected both philosophy and comedy in his matchless dialogues. Now it would be saying too much, if not too little, to say that the essence of tragedy is misunderstanding. The errors of tragic heroes are too vast to be so trivially dismissed. Yet they do misunderstand their situations and themselves; and in the rush of events which their own blindness accelerates they do dreadful things which with more time and light they would never have done. Tragedies are dark and short; more light, more time, more talk would make literally all the difference in the world; but those blessings are not available. Whereas they are the very stuff of comedy, which like John Tanner keeps on talking though the heavens fall. But in fact they do not fall. In comedy there is neither the midnight of utter confusion nor the sudden blaze of a belated dawn. In comedy the hour is always noon.

And nothing much happens then. The action of any comedy is less interesting—certainly less memorable—than the discussions it contains. A tragedy whose plot cannot be remembered in the strict order of its events is no tragedy at all; the events create their own order, from which there is no escape, or else they have no meaning for the mind. This must have been what Aristotle meant when he said the soul of a tragedy was its plot; the action was everything. In comedy there is action too, or we should have no story; but it is most interesting for what can be said about it before and after it is done. Which throws still further light upon the fact that comic poets underplay their plots and take no responsibility for them in the first place. By the same token they are indifferent to dramatic or narrative effects; they ignore the conventional devices for securing such effects; they lean over backwards to avoid melodrama, which to be sure they may approach as a possibility, but which they would rather parody than embrace.

So Mann in his great comedy refuses to make what tragedy would make, and what the *Bible* did make, out of certain recognition scenes. The recognition scene is essential to tragedy, which lives on such bursts of feeling as it perfectly provides. There was an opportunity for Mann to contrive a meeting between Joseph and Mut-em-enet after Joseph came home from prison. But he discusses the possibility only to reject it. Romancers, he says, have tried their hands at such a scene, and the result is "Persian musk," is "attar of roses," which is to say, sweet nonsense. For one thing "it has nothing to do with the facts." For another, their story was done. And even the recognition scenes which he is bound to accept because they come down to him and are a part of his duty—those between Joseph and his brothers at the climax and between Jacob and Joseph at the very end—he deliberately muffs, and here and there even mocks. Of course they are moving; but Mann does not want them to break our hearts, and he knows how to keep them from doing so. He wraps them in talk the principals murmur to each other even while they weep; dialectic still holds the center of the stage. And as for the weeping, what would a tragic poet have to say of one who in the immortal scene between Joseph and his brothers transmogrifies the Biblical "he wept aloud" into: "His nose began to prickle inside, he sniffed a little, and his eyes all at once ran over?" Granted, on a later page—much later, for the scene is long—we are told that "glittering tears ran down his cheeks." This to be sure is more like drama; yet even there we are forced to suspect that the tears of Joseph *would* glitter, since everything about him shines. Nor at the moment when the great scene was preparing had the author kept us in suspense as to whether it would happen. The comic artist cares nothing for suspense, which indeed is never as indispensable to narrative as commonly it is thought to be. It is at best a second-rate device for generating interest where no interest naturally exists. At least this is true if it consists of no more than the artificial withholding from us of some information we need for understanding and would normally have. When it consists of telling us that a given thing will happen but letting us wait to see how it happens, and precisely when, it is a powerful because a natural narrative tool. And it is thus that Mann uses it, and confides to us that he does. "Joseph's suspense was great," he writes on one occasion; "on this point depended his future relations with the brothers. We, of course, are in no suspense: we know all the phases of the story by heart. . . . So in our wisdom we may smile at him."

Such, remarks Mann on an earlier occasion, is the advantage of having an old story to retell. "If I were here a mere inventor of tales, what I have to tell would certainly expose me to the reproach of drawing too long a bow, and presuming far too much upon a credulity which after all has its limits. Luckily, such is not my role. I rest upon the traditional facts, which are not less sound because some of them ring as though they were newly minted. Thus I am in a position to state what I have to tell in an assured and tranquil tone that in the face of all doubts and reproaches carries conviction." A tragic poet who stopped his story to address his audience thus would instantly break his spell and lose all power to convince. For the comic poet there is no spell; or if there is one and its name is truth, it is just in this offhand way that he invokes it.

The truth about Joseph is of course a complicated thing which it is the main business of the book to convey. Mann's hero is perhaps not different from the one we meet in *Genesis,* nor is his father altered from the ancient Jacob; nor for that matter is their relation to each other built here upon ground which the original text did not at least lay out. But Mann's refinements are as many as they are marvellous. The brilliance and beauty of Joseph have few parallels in the fiction of the world. And the vanity. The problem was to make the vanity palatable, and it was solved by suggesting, not indeed in so many words, that it was like the vanity of a golden mirror which can no more help being what it is than a bright person

can help being bright. Joseph might have bitten off his tongue, as
Potiphar's poor wife all but did; yet he did not; he kept on saying
with it the most fascinating and impudent things; and we are as
glad of this as Jacob was, or Benjamin, or even the ten sullen half-
brothers who in spite of themselves adored the speaker of them,
too, at the same time that they wanted to kill him, or at least to
remove him from their sight forever. It was Jacob, however, who
resisted Joseph least; which is a mild way of saying that he committed the sin of idolatry by elevating him to the rank of favorite
son, somewhat as he had committed that same sin by loving Rachel
for herself and not in God. Mann is willing to say that the doting
father was the chief source of his son's misery, if misery it was.
Perhaps it was never that; for the pits into which this youth was
cast, first in the desert and then in Egypt, yielded in every case an
experience he could dramatize; and there was no exercise he loved
more. In no crisis of his life did he die so that he might be reborn.
He does not look to us at the end like one of those truly great men
of whom it can be said, not that they have lived a lot but that they
have died a lot—have been, we sometimes say, in hell. No, in some
amazing way he has not been touched by the bonfires he walked
through. For one thing, though he would deny this, he has never
ceased to assume that others must love him more than they love
themselves. The assumption had been wrong both in the case of his
brothers and in that of Mut-em-enet, and now he knows that it was
wrong. Yet he has not changed in the secret depths of his heart
where he still knows that he is like nobody else. "Have you ever
heard the voice of self-denying love?" Jacob asks him this in the
Land of Goshen, and the question answers itself. When on the last
page of the book Joseph insists to his brothers that they are to
forgive him, not he to forgive them, he speaks in the character he
has enjoyed from the beginning. "If it is a question of pardon
between us human beings, then it is I myself must beg for it, for
you had perforce to be cast in the villain's part so that things might
turn out as they did." The hero's part had been so naturally his
that he still needs no rehearsing in it.

Not that we love him less because all this is true. The triumph of
Mann is that we love on every page the hero he himself loves this
side of idolatry. Idolatry in Mann would have destroyed his comedy

since comedy admits no gods that are made of earth. That he resisted the sin, tempted though he surely was, is a triumph more stupendous still. The sign of his resistance is the impression of Joseph he leaves with us at last: the impression of one whose understanding is so fine that the light in his mind almost puts out the stars—yet not those stars at which his great-grandfather Abraham, that wonderful old man, stared without speaking a single word. "One can easily be in a story," Mann has Joseph say, "and not understand it." Joseph understood everything in his story except himself. His light never shone altogether inward, producing perfect silence.

17

THE LETTERS OF
JOHN JAY CHAPMAN

Mr. Howe recommends John Jay Chapman to us as "a rich and significant product of American civilization." It is a pity that Mr. Howe thought he had to talk this way about a man whom he calls in another portion of the same sentence "unique" and to whom in a further sentence he pays the compliment of saying that in any civilization he would have been just what he was in ours. Nobody who reads these letters can doubt that Chapman was a very rich sort of person, but I for one cannot discover what it is of which he was or is significant. His life is typical of no life that I know; his ideas have astonishingly little relation to one another; many of the things he did and said were mad or half-mad; and the final feeling I have as to his personality is that it charged into the world like a wild bull out of chaos, pawing and snorting for decades in a manner peculiar to itself. Quite a splendid spectacle, but representative of nothing else, either on or off the earth.

He was something of a mystic and he loved Christ, but his behavior during the World War was that of any over-heated, upper-class savage. He thought highly of William Lloyd Garrison and the Abolition movement, he participated in the political reforms of the 1890's and he was so shocked by the news of a lynching at Coatesville, West Virginia, in 1911 that he went down there a year later, hired a hall, and prayed publicly (to an audience of two) for the town's soul; yet he raved against the Jewish and Catholic "menaces," campaigned against Al Smith because of his religion, and publisted a sonnet called "Cape Cod, Rome, and Jerusalem" in the *Ku Klux Kourier.* In January, 1887, being in love with Minna Timmins without knowing it, and being unable to account for a reciprocal disturbance in her except on the theory that some other man had caused it, he looked for the man, thought he found him, beat him with a stick, rushed home to his lodgings in Cambridge, and thrust his left hand into a coal flame until the bones were exposed and amputation was necessary. When one of his sons by his first wife was drowned in Austria he said to his second wife as she hurried to him: "I would rather it had been you." When he opened the telegram informing him that his son Victor had been shot down as an aviator at Verdun his only words were: "That's good." The list is almost repulsive. And so would the man be if one felt the obligation to make sense out of him or to establish him as the product of something. The man in fact is most attractive. But that is because he had a genius for writing letters, a very small portion of the high heap he wrote being the excuse for Mr. Howe's present volume.

Chapman once wrote of William James: "It was easy to differ from him; it was easy to go home thinking that James had talked the most arrant rubbish, and that no educated man had a right to be so ignorant of the first principles of thought and of the foundations of human society. Yet it was impossible not to be morally elevated by the smallest contact with William James." He might, except for the word "morally," have been talking about himself; and perhaps even that exception should not be made. He will make most of his readers pity their own paleness, their mildness, their shortness of breath; they will seem to themselves undersized as they read, and will wonder whether they have ever had a good time in the world. He is more than a breeze, he is hurricanes and waterspouts. He can and does say anything, and says it with the effortless rush which there is in all good letter-writing. Usually it takes anger to get him going, but when he is not angry he can do with poetic fury, the manifold licenses of which seem to have been understood by his friends, and forgiven, even when there had been an insult in every line; for the last line of all might have honey in it, though of course it might on the other hand strike like the scorpion's tail.

The letters are first of all a key to Chapman's character as a literary critic. Most books to him were merely writing, and he hated writing; it was so largely "gamboge and style," with "its 'howevers' and 'moreovers' and semicolons" and the tendency of its words to be all of one size and weight, as in the case for instance of a new book by President Eliot, all phrases in which, said Chapman, "excite the same emotion—i.e., that of a woodchuck eating a carrot." "A man," he insisted, "who spends his whole time in writing—as I do—knows it futility. Writing is for people who believe that what they say is true and that their analysis is the thing. For people who know that all statements are gross illusions it's almost *fraudulent* to write." Yet he wrote, impatiently and with many dashes, separating often with the finest insight the bogus in any author from his best gold. At bottom extremely serious, he expected much from any book, and he wanted it direct. Seldom, he said, did he find poetry as good as Michael Angelo's—"as good," that is, "as prose." Lowell was "all barnacled with quotations and leisure, too much culture—too many truffled essays and champagne odes and lobster sonnets." Stevenson was "sham." The Carlyle correspondence was "all clotheslines and bedbugs and not enough to eat—hairpins-in-the-soup sort of people." Shelley could induce a mood all right, but "it's a weak, vegetarian, sinking-of-the-stomach mood." His praise of Shakespeare, Rabelais, Balzac, and other writers who somehow had not "written" was correspondingly high. Most of Rabelais bored him, but the best was so good that he could only conclude he had written it himself. As for the New Testament, "You cannot criticize it. It criticizes you."

But the letters are not all literary criticism. There are incomparable portraits of persons: Charles Pierce, George Herbert Palmer, Robert Bridges, and John Cowper Powys. There are epigrams which will have to be remembered, such as this one at the end of a letter to James: "A thing is not truth till it is so strongly believed in that the believer is convinced that its existence does not depend on him. This cuts off the pragmatist from knowing what truth is." And there are half-humorous, half-momentous, outbursts like this one (aetat fifty-four):

My dear Dr. Drury: Do you really think that if I *had* any ideas on the parent-and-child question I'd waste them on you? But just now I am taking a loaf and trying to forget the whole subject. Is the education of the young the whole of life? I hate the young—I'm worn out with them. They absorb you and suck you dry and are vampires and selfish brutes at best. Give me some good old rain-soaked clubmen—who *can't* be improved and make no moral claims—and let me play checkers with them and look out the club window and think about what I'll have for dinner.

There are, in short, a dozen God's plenties.

18

MUSIC OF A MIND:
ON DELMORE SCHWARTZ

Delmore Schwartz's book is less miscellaneous than it looks, and
in fact it is not miscellaneous at all unless the play at the end, "Dr.
Bergen's Belief," is felt as falling a little outside of the magic circle
within which Mr. Schwartz finds poetry. I do not say, "Finds *his*
poetry," for what is in this book is more important than anything
personal could be. It is the thing, rare enough at any time but certainly rare now, toward which a reader's mind can move as if
toward rest, for it is poetry which seems to depend for its existence
less upon the writer and the reader than upon itself. It originates,
educates, nourishes, and warms itself. There is perhaps no magic
circle here, or at any rate no secret which Mr. Schwartz would
claim that he alone knew. Mr. Schwartz makes few claims for
himself, even though the word "I" is frequent in his prose and
verse. And the last claim one can imagine him making for himself
is that he inhabits a private world. The distinction of his poetry,
considering it first as literary news, is that it restores a rich, wide
world of reference which latterly has been lacking to the art: it has
memories, it has feeling, it even has morality. Considered in itself,
it is what very little poetry has been for a long time: it is interesting.
There is of course a connection between the two statements, though
I do not wish to suggest that this poetry may be less interesting in

some other time which does not need it. I do not assume that it will lose its interest any more than that it will lose its goodness. For by calling it interesting I have meant to call it good: as good as any poetry has been for a long while, say at least a literary generation.

By Mr. Schwartz's poetry I strictly mean the thirty-five poems which make up the third section of his book. I also mean, however, the short story which gives the book its title, and certain portions of a long philosophical poem in prose and verse which rewrites "Coriolanus" for a dream performance. The short story is itself a dream, and a highly elaborate one because what the narrator is dreaming on his twenty-first birthday is that he sits as a boy in a moving-picture theater several years before he is to be born and watches on the screen a young man and woman who will be his father and mother. That sounds ingenious, as indeed it is, and it is a reminder that Mr. Schwartz is often busy with psychological materials. Yet the ingenuity is there for the sake of feelings in which Mr. Schwartz wants us to be interested, and psychology neither here nor elsewhere is one of Mr. Schwartz's ends. It has helped him to revive two individuals out of a dead past and to isolate them for an instant somewhat as a movie screen isolates itself in oceans of surrounding darkness; it could not have taught him the accents of pity and terror with which he renders their loneliness. So in "Coriolanus and His Mother" the ghost of Freud sits in a box and offers his analysis of the hero's problem as an individual. But Mr. Schwartz does not accept this analysis as any more final than that of Marx, another ghost, or than that of Aristotle, a third phantom and in fact the wisest; as Mr. Schwartz, who is very well educated, knows without exactly saying so. If any analysis is accepted it would appear to be that of Shakespeare himself, whose play gains singularly little after all from the elaborate apparatus of a commentary and re-phrasing here provided; though readers of the book as such are gainers from several brilliant lines and from the prose interludes which the ghost of the author speaks from the stage. These are witty, valuable and various.

To come now to the thirty-five shorter poems is to arrive at the heart of the book, and at a body of writing which will be gone over by many future readers and critics. They will not fail to see with how much concentration Mr. Schwartz has put the whole of "Dr.

Bergen's Belief" into the four pages of "Father and Son," and how in the process he has thickened and enriched the theme. But what is of more importance, if they have ears they will listen everywhere to the music of a mind which knows the art of enjoying its own existence, as well as the existence of a vast world full of meat and flowers upon which it can feed forever. When I say "enjoy" I do not mean childish pleasure, nor do I wish to suggest the ecstasies of a romantic who lacks a proper object for his contemplation. All I mean, and in the present literary scene it is much, is that Mr. Schwartz has kept the avenues open between his poetry and himself, and that he has seen himself not as the "surd irreducible" which Coriolanus was but as an individual for whom self-knowledge signifies knowledge of existence. When Socrates said "Know thyself" he seems to mean: "Know all human things including thyself, with the emphasis upon the all." Socrates and Aristotle are Mr. Schwartz's teachers, along with Freud and Marx, and—standing to one side—Shakespeare. That is why, since his personal endowment is so great and happy, he can write poetry in which we seem to miss nothing important. By constitution able to feel tragedy, by thought he is able to understand it and by art he is able to create it; his book is drenched with its tears and its wisdom.

> For we are incomplete and know no future,
> And we are howling or dancing out our souls
> In beating syllables before the curtain:
> We are Shakespearean, we are strangers.

19
THE POEMS OF THOMAS MERTON

In the summer of 1953 Thomas Merton wrote to me from Gethsemani: "Our cow barn burned down in little over twenty minutes or
half an hour—like a pile of brush. We could do nothing to put it
out. Everybody thought it was a really beautiful fire, and it was. I
am sending you a poem about it." The poem was "Elegy for the
Monastery Barn," and I liked it so much that six years later, when I
knew I was going to write this preface, I wrote Merton saying I
hoped it would be among the poems he had selected. He replied:
"I forget whether or not I included the Barn on the original list,
perhaps I was shy about it. As a matter of fact it is for me sub-
jectively an important poem, because when I was a kid on a farm
in Maryland (yes, even that, for a while) a barn burned down in the
middle of the night and it is one of the earliest things I can remember. So burning barns are for me great mysteries that are important.
They turn out to be the whole world, and it is the Last Judgement."
Well, the poem is here, and it is as good a place as any to start
looking at and listening to the poet in Thomas Merton. But one
further document has a bearing on the subject. The preface to
The Strange Lands, 1957, ends with these sentences: "'Elegy for
the Monastery Barn' was written after the cow barn at Gethsemani
burned down, one August evening in 1953, during the evening

meditation. The monks left the meditation to fight a very hot fire and the poem arrived about the same time as the fire truck from the nearest town.'' The bearing is in the humor, which Merton never is without, and in the knowledge he keeps of the way things go in this world. The slowness of the truck, the swiftness of the poem, the childhood memory: all of these are somehow there, illuminating if not explaining the happy power awakened in Merton's mind as it races through the realities of his theme. For the burning barn is really an old lady dressed for her last hour in unaccountable finery, nor is any distinction to be made between her proud cries and the crackling of the flames. And she leaves us when she is gone with delicate memories of what she had been during the years when we ignored her: of her solitude, her peace, her patience as she waited for this end. The fifty invisible cattle, the fifty past years, are just as real; and so at the close is Merton's flight into another dimension where the Holy One sits in the presence of disaster. All is real; nothing is made up; this, we instantly believe, is the true content of the subject, which like any other subject starts on earth and gets in its own natural way to heaven.

Such, I take it, is what Merton means in the note on "Poetry and Contemplation" which he appends to the present volume. He says there, better he thinks than he did ten years ago, and in this I believe him to be right, that poetry at its best *is* contemplation—of things, and of what they signify. Not what they can be made to signify, but what they actually do signify, even when nobody knows it. The better the poet, the more we are convinced that he has knowledge of this kind, and has it humbly. "The earliest fathers," Merton wrote me in 1954, "knew that all things, as such, are symbolic by their very being and nature, and all talk of something beyond themselves. Their meaning is not something we impose upon them, but a mystery which we can discover in them, if we have the eyes to look with." The right eyes for the purpose are keen and honest, and there had better be some humor in them too. At least that is where poetry begins, whether its aim is religious or not. And certainly, if its aim is religious, it must begin there if it is ever to move us deeply. Religious poetry is rooted in things as much as any other kind of poetry is. Without that root it is merely pious, as its secular counterpart is merely poetical.

The sight and sound and feel of things is everywhere in Merton's poetry. Consider the first line of "Trappists, Working":

> Now all our saws sing holy sonnets in this world of timber.

The sound, so sudden and robust, brings with it a sense of the joy with which it is made, and the context of that joy. Perhaps there is no sound at all in the beginning lines of "The Trappist Cemetery—Gethsemani":

> Brothers, the curving grasses and their daughters
> Will never print your praises.

But no sound was intended; the prim alliteration in the second line is like a finger laid upon the lips, forbidding speech where no speech would be proper. The silence asked for here is nothing like the heavier sort that states itself in the first of "Three Postcards from the Monastery":

> The pilgrim passes swiftly.
> All the strange towns,
> Wrapped in their double cloaks
> (Of rain and of non-entity)
> Veil their elusive faces.

The wit of the parenthesis is no less deadly for being all but voiceless, as befits the faceless towns behind their veils of rain. What a plenitude of sound, however, comes to us out of eleven words in "The Trappist Abbey: Matins,"

> where some train runs, lost,
> Baying in eastward mysteries of distance.

And again it is true that the thing we hear speaks of more than itself; its skillful music is in the service of a thought so wide that all the world at dawn, near by and far away, is sleepily included. Elsewhere we read:

> But sound is never half so fair
> As when that music turns to air
> And the universe dies of excellence.

Those lines from "A Psalm" bring sound to a dead stop, drowned as it were in itself, and signifying by its very extinction the universe beyond sense.

Sight and sound and feeling. I have spoken so far only of sound, and indeed that may be enough, for in the poetry of Thomas Merton all the senses work together to one end, the letting of things declare themselves. Which of the senses is dominant, for instance, in this passage from "The Sowing of Meanings"?

> For, like a grain of fire
> Smouldering in the heart of every living essence
> God plants His undivided power—
> Buries His thought too vast for worlds
> In seed and root and blade and flower,
> Until, in the amazing light of April,
> Surcharging the religious silence of the spring,
> Creation finds the pressure of his everlasting secret
> Too terrible to bear.
> Then everywhere we look, lo! rocks and trees
> Pastures and hills and streams and birds and firmament
> And our own souls within us flash.

It is something to be seen and heard and felt in one miraculous moment; also, to be wondered at and contemplated, thought about and blissfully forgotten. Yet sound is somehow for Merton the carrying sense, the medium through which experience of any magnitude makes itself seen and felt. Of any magnitude—a reminder that Merton is a noticer of little things as well as huge ones. Of children, for instance, and their

> little voices, light as stems of lilies.

Are these voices heard or seen? Or felt? It does not matter, in view of the unearthly sweetness they signify, any more than it matters how we decide to explain the magic by which St. Agnes, with no thought of us in her small head, steals all our love as we behold her.

> Hear with what joy this child of God
> Plays in the perfect garden of her martyrdom, . . .

> Spending the silver of her little life
> To bring her Bridegroom these bright flowers
> Of which her arms are full. . . .
> Her virtues, with their simple strings,
> Play to the Lover hidden in the universe.

The foregoing would suggest that the special reputation of Merton's poem "For My Brother: Reported Missing in Action, 1943" is not an accident. No poem in the book is better known, and the reason may lie in the music it makes. It is the kind of music that only poetry can make: not pure sound, of course, but something buried in the words and (in this case) mourning there. *The Seven-Storey Mountain* tells the story of the brother's death in prose that moves the reader too; without, however, assembling the sounds that are climaxed here in two paradoxical verses:

> The silence of Whose tears shall fall
> Like bells upon your alien tomb.

The poem, having created its own silence in preparation for these lines, drops them into our imagination where it is possible for tears that make no noise to sound nevertheless like delicate, distinct bronze, hopelessly far away. The figures of the poem are justly celebrated: the sleepless eyes as flowers, the fasts as willows, the thirst as springs, and the money of breath and death and weeping. Yet figures alone do not make a great poem. There must be a music that absorbs them and relates them, and gives them in the end a power for which we cannot assign the cause. We can say that the very intensity of the poet's fear that he will fail is somehow the reason for his success; we can guess that inarticulate grief manages here, simply because it must, to become articulate after all; but it is truer to say that in such a poem sadness sings—a low note, in perfect pitch, that carries around the world.

For Merton there is another world beyond this one where his brother died, and where he himself writes poetry. But the poetry is a way to that world. Indeed, given his endowment, it may well be *the* way, so that mystic and poet, seer and singer, in his case are one.

20

JOHN BERRYMAN: 1914-1972

The death of John Berryman by suicide on January 7, 1972, was a shocking event for many reasons other than the one that must be obvious. The chief of these is the loss to American letters, and indeed to the world of letters, of a brilliant poet who in his fifty-eighth year was well on his way to a position among his peers that would have given both him and them an enormous pleasure. For he was ambitious as well as brilliant, and latterly his books, coming close upon one another, and meeting in almost every case with sensational success, had brought him a joy that he made no effort to conceal. He was not vainglorious; he was simply and naturally proud of the eminence he had attained after a good many years of something less than that. I knew him well through all of those years, from the time he was a freshman in Columbia College to the time, not long before his death, when he wrote me from Minneapolis a characteristically sanguine letter about the work he said he had just realized now lay ahead of him: thirteen books to match the thirteen he had already published.

The thirteen new books would be both verse and prose, both poetry and scholarship. John had never ceased to think of himself as a scholar in the great field of Shakespeare—a "Dr. Dryasdust," as he put it in this letter—and there were other fields he was frantically impatient to explore. He admitted that he was frantic, just as he insisted at other times that he was no such thing. "There are three reasons, I believe," he said in this same letter, "for my never having finished anything important except the Sonnets, the Crane, the Bradstreet poem, and the Dream Songs. First is: *some* bone-laziness but mostly DOLDRUMS, proto-despair, great-poets-die-young-or at least unfulfilled like Coleridge & Co., all that crap. Two: the opposite, fantastic hysterical labour, accumulation, proliferation. . . . The man I identify with is Housman, pedantic and remorseless (though with a lyric style far superior to mine), a really bifurcated personality—and I mean to deal with him some time. . . . Third is over-ambitiousness. Part of this is temperamental grandiosity but more of it—unless of course I am wrong—is legitimate self-demand on the largest conceivable scale."

So on and on, this all but infinitely energetic and excitable spirit whom those who knew him loved for a generosity to others that equalled the delight he took in his own career, actual or imagined. I have known few poets more lavish than he with praise for work altogether different from his own. He rejoiced in the successes of his friends, and he had many friends whom it pleased him to praise publicly. In a word, he was an overflowing man, a man who was never self-contained, a man who would have been multitudes had there been time and world enough for such a miracle.

His poetry, after a relatively mild beginning, first announced its full force in *Homage to Mistress Bradstreet,* a poem in fifty-seven stanzas which he published in 1956, though it had appeared four years before that in *Partisan Review.* The strength in this poem was a weird thing, difficult to define: a muffled thing, as if it were struggling up through dense layers of resistance, but in the end a darkly musical thing which those who had ears to hear were captivated by; and the wrenching of idiom and syntax, the forcing of attention upon every word of the text, the putting of pressure upon the reader such as translations from great dead languages bring sometimes to bear, created a still deeper regard for the talent now so splendidly on display. Berryman's poetry, coming to maturity in *Homage to Mistress Bradstreet,* was to go through further developments before his death, but no matter what the direction in which he moved, he continued as in the Bradstreet poem to search for styles that fitted his vision, and the fact is that he found them.

This was conspicuously true in the case of his famous *Dream Songs,* of which he finally published as many as three hundred and eighty-five: a large number, but it was justified because in the idiom he here discovered and used he was able to say all that he saw, thought, felt, imagined, and understood. In other words, he had broken through into his own deepest recesses, a region where few poets or writers of any kind ever come, and where he was free to be as witty, as serious, as ribald, as tender, as tough, as terrible, as downright funny as he pleased. To reread the *Dream Songs* is to recognize with rushes of pity how much went out of the world with their author. And this is not to speak of the other works, all of them comparable, each of them unique. The extent of our loss is still of course to be measured. It has only been hinted at here.

21

AUGUST 1914

The world we all live in, West and East, was born during the war whose first two weeks are the subject of this vast novel—vast quite truly, for the volume at hand is only one of several that the author will require to render his vision complete. The vision, which Solzhenitsyn says came to him in 1936, when he was leaving secondary school, has yet of course to be defined, but who can doubt that it will embrace the military defeat and breakdown of Russia in World War I, the chaos that resulted, and the steps taken by Russia to collect its strength again? I shall not presume to anticipate more than that much of the vision; I prefer to wait and see.

Meanwhile, Solzhenitsyn is downgraded and despised by the very government whose existence his vision includes; for I cannot suppose that he will treat the revolution of 1917, when he comes to it, as anything but necessary for a society as rotten at the core as the one whose military failure was but a symptom of its general weakness. To be sure, in a great novel, *The First Circle,* he interrupted his vision to write of another corruption, the thing called Stalinism, that later struck like a disease and spread until it too was threatening—as it still is—the life of Russia even as Czarism had threatened it. By a series of acts, the Soviet government has demonstrated a stupidity so dense, so terrifying, that chaos would seem to have come again. Solzhenitsyn is nothing less than persecuted by the authorities who might be grateful to him for being the first Russian novelist of modern times to write masterpieces comparable with those of Tolstoy, Dostoevsky, Gogol, and the rest of the giant tribe we all recognize as supreme in fiction. And more than that, the first to tell the truths that most need telling, whether or not they flatter the rulers of the people—the truth, for instance, about the tyranny that governs by fear, the censorship that claims to regulate what cannot be regulated: the imagination of artists, the speculations of philosophers. Solzhenitsyn's books, incomparably the finest of their time, cannot be published in Russia; they must be smuggled out and printed in Paris, London, and New York; and when their author is given the Nobel Prize for literature he is not permitted by his government to go to Stockholm to receive it. He would have been welcome, doubtless, to go and not return; but he loves his country, he says, and cannot live in any other. It is his life, it is the source of all his images and ideas. So he did not go to Stockholm; he merely wrote a message of acceptance that is already one of the heroic, heartbreaking documents of the contemporary world.

All of which is possibly irrelevant to the question of whether or not *August 1914* matches in beauty and power the novels of Solzhenitsyn we have hitherto known: *The First Circle, Cancer Ward,* and *One Day in the Life of Ivan Denisovich,* the last one of which he will certainly never be forgiven for in Moscow, because it reveals the horror of the work camps where countless Russians, including Solzhenitsyn himself in one period of his life, would have been destroyed as individuals if those who had absolute power over them had been able to do what they intended: abuse their bodies and obliterate their souls. Many individuals, of course, were indeed destroyed, and the process undoubtedly continues; but a remarkable number were unkillable. And that is what Solzhenitsyn's books— all of them—are about. That is to say, they are about a people so tough, so wonderful, that nothing whatever can subdue them: not even a tyrannical government, for the Russians have never known any other kind. They emerge from any acquaintance with them as a people whose perennial failure to achieve freedom for themselves remains one of the human world's deepest mysteries. They are brilliant, they are fascinating, they are possessed of a tremendous intellectual and spiritual strength yet they continue to be slaves. How can this be explained?

I am one of the many who do not know, and so, I take it, is Solzhenitsyn, who in any case has no time to explain it in this narrative of the first fantastic defeat the Russian army was destined to endure before it crumbled in 1917 to nothing but a mob of soldiers wandering without aim in the streets of helpless cities. To the question whether *August 1914* matches its predecessors in beauty and power, my own answer is emphatically Yes. I have seldom encountered so much power in any modern novel, or so much beauty. Those who compare it with the greatest of all novels, Tolstoy's *War and Peace,* are amply justified in doing so. For one thing, it has something like the same structure: at its center the movements of armies, for the most part desperately confused, and at its edges the fortunes of families whose fathers and mothers and sons and daughters we become identified with as we did with the Bolkonskys and Rostovs of *War and Peace.* The rich Ukrainian farmer Tomchak and his daughter Xenya, to name no others, promise to hold our attention throughout whatever future awaits them. They are the stuff of which classic fiction is always made: passionate, independent, unpredictable spirits whose every action, whether or not it be a surprise, is something we watch without precisely knowing why we do—except, to put it simply, that the author does not permit us to look elsewhere.

The truly central person, however, is General Samsonov, commanding the Second Army as it advances into East Prussia with instructions to destroy the German army it will find there. But that army remains mysteriously invisible, as Samsonov's forces, sent on their mission before they were ready to start and commanded in many units by generals who are criminally incompetent, not to say incredibly obtuse and hopelessly vain of their nonexistent virtues, are encircled and either massacred by the thousands or captured by the tens of thousands. Samsonov, whose suicide at the end is one of the most touching spectacles I have ever encountered in fiction or drama, is himself the victim of an inefficiency in the high command that is so massive as almost to defy belief. Yet we do believe it, and like Colonel Vorotyntsev, invented by Solzhenitsyn to be the one honest witness in a universe of knaves and fools, we shudder as we learn in the final chapter that the faithful account he gives of what really happened—of how Samsonov was betrayed, both before and after his death, by false witnesses who had nothing but their own skins to save—was not accepted by the Grand Duke whose duty it was to review the events leading up to the disaster.

For all was disaster, as anyone might have predicted who knew how unworthy of salvation Russia itself had become. Nothing was left but the future, which all of us must wait to see.

22
SELECTIONS FROM "GREAT BOOKS OF THE TWENTIETH CENTURY IN LITERATURE"

The latest work of literature in *Great Books of the Western World* was Dostoevsky's *The Brothers Karamazov* (1880). On the assumption that a modern *Great Books* may some day exist, and if so that it will embrace the period, roughly a hundred years, between 1880 and whatever date at which the twentieth century shall by that time have arrived, what works of literature should be included in it? I have been asked to speculate concerning this, and in the following pages I shall do so in the spirit of one who guesses rather than knows. For there is no science of the future, and it is with the future reputations of modern authors that I shall be concerned. Nothing whatever can be known about such things. The mortality of reputations, literary or otherwise, is notoriously high; many a book considered by its contemporaries to be a classic has been ruthlessly beached upon the shores of time. And so it could be with some, or even many, of the books that I shall name. All I can do is use the judgment available to me.

The word *literature,* I must furthermore confess, embarrasses me at the very beginning. How does it happen that the word has come to mean only one kind of book out of the many kinds there are? And worse yet, how does it happen that this kind has been distinguished by the qualifying term *imaginative?* History, philosophy, and science are imaginative too; or if not, they are nothing. The best word would be *poetry;* but that too has lost most of its traditional content. In essence it meant *story:* The lives of invented individuals; or if not wholly invented, then individuals reshaped to suit the poet's purpose. Story is not history, though the two are related; it is not philosophy, though if philosophy is totally absent from it we cannot believe it; it is not science or mathematics, though if the elegances of those are missing in it we shall yawn. Story, then, is story; or as Aristotle put it, poetry is poetry. And Aristotle's three kinds of poetry are still the only kinds there are: epic, dramatic, and lyric. Modern epic poetry is represented by the novel; dramatic poetry by the drama; and lyric poetry by the song and the short story. Even lyric poetry, when it is powerful, has epic and drama at its roots: as song, it implies story; as short story, it implies still more story than it states. I trust it is clear that I have accepted Aristotle's refusal to identify poetry with verse. When either verse or prose is powerful, poetry is present. It is the power that matters.

For practical purposes I shall assume that the modern *Great Books* which may some day exist will have room for as many as ten volumes of literature—I return to the term, again with the desire to be practical, and with the certainty that I shall be understood. And I shall assume that the ten volumes will be generous in size, for I intend to pack a great deal into each one. If in some cases this is too much, the editor can decide what must be trimmed; I shall not be the editor, God forbid. I am not deciding, I am suggesting. I am guessing what books of recent or present time will live. Or perhaps I am only saying what books I hope will live for the simple reason that I especially like and respect them. Here then are the ten volumes.

Ibsen, Shaw, and Chekov

It would be unthinkable, for me at any rate, to begin this volume of plays with any others than Ibsen's. The only question is, which ones? For this dour, embattled Norwegian (1828-1906) tried his hand at many types of drama: tried, and nearly always succeeded. In verse, in prose, in tragedy, in comedy, he had done massive work; and by the time of his death he was acknowledged master of the European theater. Playfulness, perhaps, was the only thing his genius lacked. In retrospect he seems a grim figure, even a scowling one, with eyes set firmly in search of significant themes. And that is the only figure which many see when they hear his name. But this, I am confident, is only because they have not been reading him: have not been in contact with his unparalleled intensity. For he is unfailingly intense; and since he is a highly skilled playwright, he therefore is unfailingly effective. There is a darkness in his plays, indicative of the cold country where he was born and died—though he lived in voluntary exile from it for twenty-seven years. But the intensity is never absent, nor the attention to dramatic detail which distinguishes him among the playwrights of the world.

I have selected *A Doll's House* (1879), *Hedda Gabler* (1890), and *John Gabriel Borkman* (1896). It has been painful to leave certain of the others out, but of these I am sure. *A Doll's House* is well-nigh perfect in its rendering of the young wife Nora who leaves her husband and shuts the door behind her—a famous door that nobody forgets. Nora's husband, Torvalt Herlmer, is perfect too in his less than admirable way; he has thought to make a child of Nora, and he thinks he has succeeded until the dramatic moment when she tells him she must go forth into the real world and find out for herself what it is like. *Hedda Gabler* is not less successful in the handling of its heroine, but she is far from being another Nora, with sweetness in her as well as strength. In Hedda there is nothing but a cold, contemptuous strength, an unexplainable unrest, a cruelty of heart, which makes us fear her at the same time that it fascinates us. She is a Medea of the North, with no children to kill but with two men to hurt—her husband and the author whose manuscript she burns—before she ends the play by shooting herself: good riddance to all-but-divine rubbish. *John Gabriel Borkman,* whose hero, a disgraced banker, at first is only heard, not seen, as he walks overhead and broods upon the good he had intended to do with the money he embezzled, is powerful not only because of him but also because of his wife Gunhild and her twin sister, whose mutual loathing at the start is like something out of Greek tragedy. A Greek tragedy the whole play is: dark and bitter, yet beautiful too in the way it works itself out.

It has been equally difficult to choose among the fifty-odd plays

of Bernard Shaw (1856-1950), that inexhaustible fountain of comedy
who when he stopped bubbling at the age of ninety-four had established a reputation quite as firm as Ibsen's. If he had any hero
among his contemporaries it was Ibsen; not that he was anything
like Ibsen save in his insistence upon candor as he anatomized the
society of his time. He always met resistance and always overcame
it—in his case, as he once modestly remarked, by being "unbearably
brilliant." His high spirits, an impudence on occasion, his absolute
fearlessness, and his genius for dialectic—his complete understanding of whatever it is that makes good talk—these were his comic
weapons, and they never failed him. He is the master of comedy in
modern times, and that alone would explain his presence here. As
for his dialectic, the distinction of it lies in his power to comprehend
those persons in his plays who think differently from him; he gives
them ample chance to refute him and even to ridicule him, though
he never abandons the position he assigns to some character who
more or less represents his own thinking. He had stout convictions,
but so do all of his people, every one of whom he seems to like at
the same time that he finds him—or her—absurd. His plays have
sometimes been dismissed as nothing but talk—the essence, as it
happens, of the comic spirit. Tragedy is action, comedy is talk.
And there is always something more to say.

It has been difficult to choose, but here are my choices:

> *Caesar and Cleopatra*
> *Man and Superman*
> *Major Barbara*
> *Heartbreak House*
> *Saint Joan*

Caesar and Cleopatra (1898) conveys among other things the
conviction of Shaw that Julius Caesar was one of the great men of
all time, and therefore superior, Shaw thought, to the figure Shakespeare gave him to cut in the great play that bears his name. Shaw's
Caesar is witty—of course—and strong-willed: two qualities with
which he endows all of his heroes. The story is of how Caesar came
to Egypt before Antony did and found another Cleopatra than
Shakespeare's. *Man and Superman* (1903) has in John Tanner a
man who preaches, somewhat in Ibsen's vein, a doctrine of the
"life force"—Ibsen, in his gloomy vein, was forever praising life

and light—but John Tanner is Shaw's own man: opinionated, headstrong, eloquent, yet wittily aware of his own absurdity if someone like Ann, whom he loves in spite of his resolution never to yield his freedom to any woman, has the audacity to point it out. This may still be Shaw's masterpiece, despite all the fine work that followed it. It is endlessly engaging. *Major Barbara* (1905) contains in Andrew Undershaft a further vehicle for Shaw's conviction that strength of intellect and will is everything. Undershaft, a munitions-maker, justifies his trade on the ground that it may help men to shoot and kill such abominations as poverty, which he thinks the Salvation Army, in the person of Barbara, sentimentally encourages rather than cures. The dialectic is between these two, and again the adversaries are generously matched. *Heartbreak House* (1919), written in the shadow cast by World War I, is subtitled by Shaw "A Fantasia in the Russian Manner on English Themes." The reference is surely to Chekov (1860-1904), of whom more later; but Chekov nowhere has a character as positive in force as Captain Shotover, another of Shaw's frank heros whose conversation is perpetually salted with surprises. But the fabric of the play sym-bolically expresses a society which has seen its own fabric shattered by falling bombs. *Saint Joan* (1923) is Shaw's only tragedy, if indeed it is a tragedy; and doubtless it is, since the death of Joan at the end is truly painful. But even here the razors of Shaw's dialectic go on flashing, for the heart of the play is the series of conversations between Joan of Arc and the authorities—religious, secular—who either try to tell her how she can be saved or else explain to her why she has to die. Once more we have a conflict of wills, and once more the balance is even; for the death of Joan does not absolve those who burned her, even though they had the best reasons. They represented authority, and authority makes sense, as over and over Joan is told. So, however, does a conscience like this girl's: there is the irreducible difference.

Of Chekov's plays it would be a temptation to say, as many have done, that their chief value is as a record, or perhaps a revelation, of the decay into which Russian society had fallen by the close of the nineteenth century. And it is true that the prevailing mood in these plays is despair, or if not precisely that, then a sort of witless wonderment as to what life has come to mean. The people are restless; they feel that they are caged; no prospect is satisfactory; they want to be somewhere else; they remember better times than these, and they dream of better times to come; they are absent-minded; they are bored. So the temptation is to say: Ah, that is how it was then and there; now we know what Russia was like before the Revolution. Once more we are faced by the question of poetry and history, of the root and the flower. And we cannot dismiss the reality that surrounds Chekov's scenes. But we must remember that if the only merit of these scenes is their truth to a perishable moment in time, then the chances of their surviving into future ages are bound to be slight, since that moment will surely be forgotten. Was Falstaff, a decayed knight, true to his type in fourteenth-century England? The absurdity of the question is its own answer.

If I did not believe that Chekov's plays would survive, these three would not be included here:

Uncle Vanya
The Three Sisters
The Cherry Orchard

Sonia and her Uncle Vanya (1897), left at the end in the same predicament that they were in before the pompous Professor Sere-bryakoff came to muddle their existence, see only monotony ahead of them, only a dreary round of days. "What can we do?" asks Sonia. "We must live out our lives. . . . You have never known what it is to be happy, but wait, Uncle Vanya, wait! We shall rest. We shall rest." This is not the speech of a woman who typifies something; it is the speech of a woman indeed, and she could have existed in any play at any time. The delicate compassion of Chekov transcends time and place. So does it in *The Three Sisters* (1901), whose heroines are stifled in the atmosphere they must breathe; they dream of Moscow, where they fancy life would be perfect, but they will never get there. Which does not mean at all that the only aim of Chekov is to expose the limitations of provincial towns. It is, I think, to give us Olga, Masha, and Irina, along with their brother Andrei, exactly as they are: alike, yet different, and all of them unhappy as people anywhere, given the present situation, might reasonably be. *The Cherry Orchard* (1903) could seem to be the best case of proving, if proof was desired, the documentary nature of Chekov's dramas. The irresponsible Liuboff Andreievna and her still more irresponsible brother Gaieff, who imagines he is playing billiards when he is supposed to be thinking seriously about the future of the estate—his mind is never where *he* is—are so vivid before us that we can have the illusion of being onlookers at a certain moment when the history of Russia opens itself for our inspection. Yet the vividness is the answer. These people are not copied from anything. They hold their places in the long line—but not too long—of persons that drama has managed to make live and keep on living.

Lyric Poetry

Great Books of the Western World made no attempt to represent the lyric poetry of Europe. The reason is that lyric poetry suffers more than any other kind from translation. The language of lyric is a highly specialized thing, so fine in its effects that only a comparable genius in another tongue can be trusted to carry it over without fatal loss. Rilke's German, Mallarmé's French, Lorca's and Neruda's Spanish, to cite no further instances, have so far failed to find the comparable English, so that readers of existing translations, some of which are of course better than others, still have to believe rather than know how good the originals are. We are left, then, with six poets of England, Ireland, and the United States who in my opinion cannot be ignored. The lyric poetry of the period under review has substance and beauty, and I cannot imagine a corpus of modern literature that would leave it out.

William Butler Yeats.—I can imagine no person who would challenge the right of Yeats (1865-1939) to a high place in this volume. Perhaps the highest; yet, who knows? It is sufficient to say that from his early years in Ireland to his death at 74 he was a poet of commanding importance in the mind of the world. He began with song, he went on in middle life to matters more metaphysical, and then in his old age he returned to song—not with a lilt as in the old days but with a dagger: the dagger of wit. He was a superbly accomplished craftsman at the same time that he reached deeply into the mysteries of existence. He is the most quoted of modern poets in English, and with good reason: he thought priceless

thoughts, and for each one of them he found the proper dress.
Here are the poems of his that belong, I think, without question:

> To an Isle in the Water
> Down by the Salley Gardens
> The Lake Isle of Innisfree
> When You are Old
> The Lamentation of the Old Pensioner
> The Ballad of Father Gilligan
> The Everlasting Voices
> The Lover tells of the Rose in his Heart
> The Song of Wandering Aengus
> To his Heart, bidding it have no Fear
> He wishes for the Cloths of Heaven
> The Fiddler of Dooney
> The Folly of Being Comforted
> Never Give all the Heart
> O Do Not Love Too Long
> His Dream
> A Woman Homer Sung
> Brown Penny
> To a Friend whose Work has come to Nothing
> The Cold Heaven
> That the Night Come
> A Coat
> The Wild Swans at Coole
> The Cat and the Moon
> Easter 1916
> The Second Coming
> A Prayer for my Daughter
> Sailing to Byzantium
> Leda and the Swan
> Among School Children
> For Anne Gregory
> Byzantium
> Crazy Jane talks with the Bishop
> Under Ben Bulben

Edwin Arlington Robinson. — Time has not tarnished the reputation of E. A. Robinson (1869-1935). It was a reputation for wisdom, wit, and singularly delicate feeling which nevertheless delivered its discoveries coolly, with impeccable phrasing. My list of his poems is not long, partly because two of them are longer themselves than might seem to justify my calling them lyrics. Yet "Ben Jonson Entertains a Man from Stratford," possibly Robinson's most famous poem, is one protracted note of extraordinary music; and "Isaac and Archibald" sings likewise to itself. I am certain that this poet will live.

> Miniver Cheevy
> Old King Cole
> Luke Havergal
> John Evereldown
> The House on the Hill
> Mr. Flood's Party
> Isaac and Archibald
> The Sheaves
> New England
> The Dark Hills
> Variations of Greek Themes
> Ben Jonson Entertains a Man from Stratford

T. S. Eliot. — Here is a modern poet in the special and restricted sense which we have in mind when we say "modern art," and mean by that a kind of art that self-consciously breaks with the past. Eliot (1888-1965) was so respectful of the past, so drenched in tradition, that he felt free to continue it in his own brilliant fashion; he never thought of himself, nor should we think of him, as one who ran wild without knowledge of where he was running. His attempt in fact was to restore the greatest tradition of all, the tradition that forces poetry in any age to face the spirit of that age and reflect it without loss or blur. That he succeeded with our age is attested by his great fame; for his vogue, if vogue it was, has never diminished. If at first he sounded strange, and seemed to be in love with disorder, the reason was the view he took of a fragmented culture, a wasteland of poorly remembered things. As soon as this was understood, he ceased to be altogether strange; though the uncanny perfection of his verse will remain strange in the way that perfection always does. His subject matter, satirical in the beginning, slowly moved toward a high seriousness; he became a powerful religious poet. Yet his mind never ceased to play, nor do his final poems truly contradict the poems by which he originally got to be known. He is a haunting figure, destined to last.

> The Love Song of J. Alfred Prufrock
> Rhapsody on a Windy Night
> Morning at the Window
> Mr. Appollinax
> The Hippopotamus
> Sweeney Among the Nightingales
> The Waste Land
> The Hollow Men
> Ash-Wednesday
> Journey of the Magi
> A Song for Simeon
> Marina
> Eyes that last I saw in tears
> The wind sprang up at four o'clock
> Choruses from "The Rock"
> Four Quartets

James Joyce (1882-1941) is a literature in himself, and all of his books would belong here were there space enough in a single volume. His genius is such, and his reputation is such, that students of him spend their lives inside his work alone, as if there were no other work in the modern world, no other author worthy of attention. Their devotion is excessive, and yet it is comprehensible. Once he fixes your attention, it is hard to look away. I must be content, however, with the following selection, and even that is long:

> "The Dead," from *Dubliners*
> *A Portrait of the Artist as a Young Man*
> *Ulysses*

One of the fascinating things about Joyce is his own fascination with language. I do not mean by this merely that he studied many languages other than English and used them more and more steadily from book to book. In college in Dublin he is known to have studied Latin, French, and Italian, and even Norwegian so that he might read Ibsen in the original, for Ibsen was one of his literary heroes. I mean rather, and especially, that language as such—English as such—was the very medium of his imagination, which loved words inordinately, obsessively, and played with them as if they alone were the substance of literature. They are not the substance of literature, nor is it true that Joyce thought so, since his own books have much to say—or, since they are narratives, tell. But his final work, *Finnegan's Wake* (1939) is so tortuous with its puns and double meanings, so imbedded in what seems a quagmire, a quicksand, of reference and cross-reference, that only scholars in Joyce have a right to say that they can read it at all. It was the end product of an evolution that conceivably could be called tragic, since it culminated in a book from which most readers are shut out. *Ulysses* (1922) before it had seemed difficult, and it still is difficult for all the familiarity we now have with its contents; but the difficulty of *Ulysses* is less in language, though that is there too, than in its arrangement, than in the order of its parts. *Dubliners* (1914), at the commencement of this fabulous career, was lucid as any finely written book can be lucid. Yet even *Dubliners* took ten years to get published, and then not in Dublin; for it was considered an insult to Joyce's native city, concerning whose people its stories maintain a detachment so icy as to seem cruel, though the cruelty is now no longer apparent—certainly not in the great short story "The Dead," the last in the book. Indeed there is warmth and depth in "The Dead," though there is no sentiment, a thing foreign to Joyce. The discovery that Gabriel Conroy accidentally makes of a young man in his wife's past, a young man who had died for her in a distant part of Ireland, is deeply touching as Joyce discloses it and immediately after muffles the pain of it in a superb passage describing the snow that begins "falling faintly through the universe and faintly falling, like the descent of their last end, upon all the living and the dead."

The absence of sentiment in Joyce has much to do with another fascinating fact about him, namely, that although Dublin is the scene of all his fiction, and the center of all his thought, he was unable to live there after 1904; the rest of his life was spent in Switzerland, Italy, and France; he was self-exiled as Ibsen was, and possibly for the same reason—a sense of confinement, a fear of being smothered by what each of them felt to be a national sentiment, an organized conspiracy against candor and right judgment. However that was, Joyce at any rate devoted the whole of his art in absentia to the streets and pubs of Dublin, no inch or corner of which he seems to have been able to forget. It was not nostalgia; it was simply that his imagination had all it needed in the region he knew best. And if the tissue of langauge in which he wrapped this region became ever thicker and richer—well, distance may have had something to do with that, and a consequent sense of Dublin as existing both in and out of place and time: eternally there, a city abstract as well as concrete.

A *Portrait of the Artist as a Young Man* (1916) is generally understood to have Joyce's own youth in Dublin as its moving subject. Its hero, Stephen Dedalus, in other words, is Joyce himself, with whatever differences art may account for, and doubtless there are many of those. One important difference is that Dedalus was not about to leave Ireland; he is still there in *Ulysses,* where he is one of the two leading characters, the other being Leopold Bloom, who was to have appeared in *Dubliners* except that the story Joyce planned for him was not written then; it was saved for his masterpiece. The story of Dedalus in the *Portrait* is the story of a gifted young man who learns what it is that he no longer believes, and what it is therefore that he must cast out of his mind if he should ever be the artist he hopes to be. The story, then, is the story of how the author became an author: a familiar theme in modern fiction, and one that we shall find again in Proust. What Dedalus rejects is the religion that has been taught him, and the national sentiment. "Look here," he says at the end, "I will not serve that in which I no longer believe, whether it call itself my home, my fatherland, or my church: and I will try to express myself in some mode of life or art as freely as I can, using for my defense the only arms I allow myself to use, silence, exile, and cunning." This was Joyce's own program, as the sequel showed; nor was the final entry in Stephen's diary irrelevant to that program: "So be it. Welcome, O life! I go to encounter for the millionth time the reality of experience and to forge in the smithy of my soul the uncreated conscience of my race."

"The uncreated conscience of my race"—a deeply interesting phrase in view of the Dublin, and the Ireland, we find laid open to our gaze in *Ulysses,* whose world is as far removed from the glory of Homer as the world of T. S. Eliot's *Waste Land* was removed from the time when Shakespeare wrote the beautiful unearthly lines that now and then drift into the text as if to underscore the fall from grace that twentieth-century man has committed. The point in either case, if the word "conscience" be remembered, was that the modern world was degenerate without knowing it was; was even, in fact, proud of its ignorance of all that it once had been. The title *Ulysses* is of crucial importance; the parallel with Homer is always present. Stephen Dedalus, still an unformed youth, stumbling through Dublin with no sense of direction, is searching for his spiritual father, and finds him, more or less, in Leopold Bloom, the central character of the novel. Bloom, a Dublin Jew, has come to little or nothing in his own life, and Molly his wife is about as far from Penelope as a woman could be—her reverie at the close, a single sentence forty-six pages long, is quite as obscene as the censors thought, who for decades prevented the book from being sold above the counter—but Bloom has a rich inner life which he keeps wholly to himself, so that only the reader knows it. He has a scientific imagination; he remembers all the things he has ever read, and he is well-read; he is decent and sensitive; he would be a hero if he could. The scene in which he takes Stephen home with him at the end of the twenty-four hours which the entire action of the book covers is in some sense an unsatisfactory scene, and intentionally so; there is nothing like the recognition of Odysseus by Telemachus; the climax is anticlimax at the best. Yet it is a kind of climax; the one, Joyce seems to be suggesting, that Dublin now deserves, just as Molly's reverie is all that Bloom, poor good fellow, has the potency to inspire.

Of course I have mentioned only three persons in a book that seems to contain thousands, so rich it is in character and event, so noisy with novels, it rages with energy throughout, and is brilliant everywhere. To read it is a discipline, but the discipline is something that any successful reader must consider to have been worth acquiring. Most of the world's fiction since its day has been formed or influenced by it. It is a monument that time will not overturn; or so I guess.

Marcel Proust—Remembrance of Things Past, that endless novel—but endlessly absorbing too—in which Proust (1871-1922) recaptured his life, appeared between 1913 and 1927 in seven parts:

> *Swann's Way*
> *Within a Budding Grove*
> *The Guermantes Way*
> *Cities of the Plain*
> *The Captive*
> *The Sweet Cheat Gone*
> *The Past Recaptured*

Doubtless not all of its thousands of pages can be crammed into the present volume, but it would be wonderful if they could, for the work, however long drawn out, is still one piece, and I can merely recommend that as much of it as possible, beginning with the beginning, be included. If it has to be cut off after *The Guermantes Way,* so be it. But what a pity to lose *Cities of the Plain,* and the next two parts dealing with Albertine, and the final part that draws so many threads together.

I shall discuss it all, for I do not know how to separate its themes that are one theme, any more than Proust knew how to hurry his novel toward its end. Asthmatic since childhood, he sealed himself at last into a cork-lined room and did nothing but write in a race with death; the last three parts appeared posthumously in France, when the fame of the work was already firmly established; yet he never skimped his task, he continued at the leisurely, looping pace he had started with. The pace is leisurely without ever seeming slow, or, at any rate, dull. The analysis of action and motive, the description of landscapes and rooms, the carrying out of every impression and thought to the finest end—these ought to make for tedium, but strangely they do not, in spite too of sentences so long that sometimes they run for pages. The reason is the author's saturation with his subject, which infects us so that we are with him wherever he is, wanting to know what he wants to know; for the story is of how he gradually learns the truth about a number of things—the truth from other points of view in the beginning, then finally, or more or less finally, from his own. More or less, because the relativity of truth is constantly announcing itself in this novel that seems to occupy all space, all time.

I remarked of Joyce's *Ulysses* and indeed of all the works of Joyce that their central subject was the preparation of the author for becoming the author he was; and I said that this would also be true of *Remembrance of Things Past.* It is still more true. The narrator of *Remembrance of Things Past,* a boy named Marcel who grows older with every volume, and who writes the entire work in the first person, has ambitions to be a writer; it is assumed by his family and friends that that is what he will become; and he does, he tells us, from the moment when as a man he tastes a little cake, a madeleine soaked in tea, such as he had loved when he was a child—tastes the cake, and there by some miracle his own past lies around him like a living thing. So he starts to put it down in words; goes on; branches out into further landscapes that are folded within these like Chinese boxes; remembers persons, places, things; peers at them passionately in order to make sure that he understands their relations to one another; thence on and on to what of course could never be an end, except that one is satisfactorily present in a final sentence which shows him still wanting to live long enough—naturally he did not—to understand absolutely everything.

The narrator is named Marcel, and much of what he remembers is what Marcel Proust remembered. Yet the novel is so much more than this that it lives in its own right as a work of the imagination. It finally makes no difference which Marcel is telling us these things, the author himself or a person he has invented. I for one, notwithstanding the parallels that scholars in the subject keep finding between persons inside and outside *Remembrance of Things Past*—so-and-so is identified as so-and-so—prefer to take the whole thing as a glorious fiction, illuminated by laws of its own making and true as poetry is true. In other words, I insist on believing that it is the Marcel of the book, not the Marcel whose last name was

Proust, who tells what he remembers. And what he remembers! The list of persons whom *we* shall remember is long and long, beginning with Marcel's mother and grandmother in the country house at Combray, and Francoise, the old servant whom Marcel will never be able to do without, either at Combray or later on in Paris, when he will live in a house connected with the great house of the Duc de Guermantes and the Duchess—live there with Albertine as his prisoner. But this is to anticipate, as it also is to make any mention of the fabulous Guermantes, although they are neighbors of Marcel's family in the country too, and never indeed are out of Marcel's mind; as M. Charles Swann is not, a friend of his parents who made a disastrous marriage with the courtesan Odette— disastrous, yet he survived it, and in fact their daughter, Gilberte, was the first girl whom Marcel loved, long before he met Albertine at Balbec, the seaside resort on the coast of Normandy where she and the girls who were her friends came and went from sight like little waves from the deep, and she herself was to obsess Marcel through most of the years of his life, though he was finally to banish her from his bed and she was to die of an accident in Balbec.

I realize suddenly how hopeless it is to attempt a synopsis of this book whose component parts weave in and out of our attention, entangled from beginning to end in a tissue which holds them all and never lets any one of them fly off by itself. I know I am suggesting confusion; but there is no confusion. Every detail, of person or place, is clear as dreams are clear, even though, as is true in dreams, emphasis and meaning are constantly in process of change: of change into still greater clarity, for many things that Marcel begins by thinking of as fixed are by no means fixed, and characters will shift and recombine as the bits of colored glass do in a kaleidoscope, or as details in a magic-lantern picture are clarified when the focus is perfected. The focus here is always being altered as Marcel learned more and more; as for instance in the case of the Baron de Charlus, another friend of Marcel's family who never disappears out of the work, though he grows more and more monstrous as the work proceeds. He is the arch-homosexual of a book that contains many of his tribe, not only in the section called *Cities of the Plain* (the French title is *Sodome et Gomorrhe*) but everywhere else as well. The jealousy that devours Swann is not only of the men who may be Odette's lovers but of the women who perhaps have been, or for that matter still are. And the jealousy that consumes Marcel—for the novel is among other things a study of this universal passion in all of its phases—has the same base: a suspicion, which time makes a certainty, that Albertine's girl friends are Lesbian friends.

But I still have only begun to name the persons who throng this book. Bloch, Marcel's friend, Bergotte, the novelist. The Marquis de Norpois. The Marquise de Villeparisis. The composer Vinteuil and his daughter (also a Lesbian). The Verdurins, who maintain a salon which they think is the last word in elegance, but they are absurdly ignorant of who anyone is. Robert de Saint-Loup, who deserves a paragraph to himself. Elstir, the painter. The Prince and Princesse des Laumes. The Princesse de Parme. The actress Berma. And there are hundreds more, for all of France seems to be here; not only the Faubourg Saint-Germain where the nobility have fabulous parties in fabulous houses, but seaside inns as well, and apartments of the middle class, and at the bottom of the scale the terrible room where Charlus, far gone in his vice, hires young men to flog him with a cat-o'-nine-tails studded with nails. These young men have no idea who the Baron is; and neither in the last analysis does Marcel think *he* does; for he refrains from judging his old friend, as indeed he exercises a similar restraint throughout his unending memoir. It is as if he thought of himself as a historian merely; such and such things happened, and he slowly became aware of what they meant.

Remembrance of Things Past is not the history of France between 1880 and 1920, though the Dreyfus case is at one point much in evidence, and World War I is important in the closing part. Nor is it sociology, though the wealthy and functionless nobility of the Faubourg might seem at moments to be the object of a student's scrutiny. No, it is fiction; which is to say that it is poetry. Seldom has any poem contained so much, or been so memorable. If portions of it seem evanescent and trivial, if the dukes and duchesses have their preposterous side as well as their overwhelming reality in Marcel's dream, then we can say, as I have said in another place, that *Remembrance of Things Past* lacks the solidity of Homer's and Tolstoy's poetry, where the whole world is somehow present and looks exactly like what it is. This world is a special one, even a decayed one, and doubtless that is a limitation. Nothing like it, nevertheless, has come to view in modern literature, and it would be as wrong to leave it out of the present set as it would be to leave out Ulysses, or certain other large works still to come; or as it would have been to leave out *Huckleberry Finn,* the stories of Sholom Aleichem, and the plays of Ibsen and Shaw.

William Faulkner—Once again the question of poetry and history raises its head. Does Faulkner's distinction lie in the report his novels made of life in northern Mississippi, or does it lie in the use he made—as a poet—of that life as he knew it, remembered it, and understood it? Certainly he knew it; he lived there; and he did unquestionably make use of it, for it supplies his landscape and his atmosphere—not to speak of his people, who may or may not be portraits of particular persons but who have the air of belonging in a world outside his fiction to which he can go whenever he pleases for individuals as well as types. Once again, however, it is the inside world that finally matters: the created world which has a consistency, a hue, that only imagination can explain. The world of William Faulkner (1897-1962), one of the richest worlds in modern fiction, is a world transformed; it is not copied, it is not drawn from what we are in the habit of calling life. It has its own life, and the source of it is Faulkner's genius. Otherwise he would not be here.

Of his many books I have chosen these:

> *Sartoris*
> *The Sound and the Fury*
> *As I Lay Dying*
> "Barn Burning"
> "A Rose for Emily"

Sartoris (1929), the opening novel in the long series dealing with life in and around the fictitious town of Jefferson, Mississippi—Faulkner lived in Oxford—introduces the two families that always will figure in the series: the Sartorises and the Snopeses, who represent respectively the top and the bottom of Jefferson society. The Sartorises are the aristocracy, the Snopeses the scum. Colonel

Sartoris, who had a career in the Confederate Army and who subsequently built a fine house for himself outside of town, is the progenitor of the clan as we encounter it, though in *Sartoris* it is only the ghost of his importance that makes itself felt; he had been murdered, as Faulkner's own great-grandfather, Colonel William C. Faulkner, had been. Now Bayard Sartoris, an old banker who will die in this book, represents the family, along with young Bayard who has just returned from being an aviator in World War I, and along with Miss Jenny, the ancient sister of Colonel Sartoris, whose tart tongue has much to tell us about the wildness of the tribe— the wildness yet the beauty too, for this is the only family, except for the de Spains, the Sutpens, the Compsons, the Benbows, and the Griersons, that holds on to the decent, gracious traditions of a past now threatened by the Snopeses. A Snopes, who has worked his way out of Frenchman's Bend, a filthy, degenerate village not far from Jefferson, is working in the bank, of all places; and he is writing anonymous letters to Narcissa Benbow which disgust and terrify her. Narcissa is to fall in love with young Bayard Sartoris and marry him; but wildness in him, after his return to find his first wife dead, has taken the form of racing a car madly about the neighborhood in the hope that he may kill himself: a consummation he achieves at the end, not in his car but in a plane, and this is a fitting death because another thing that haunts him is the death of his twin brother John in France, an aerial death he fancies he might have prevented. There is much more than this in the book. There is the love, for instance, of Horace Benbow for his sister Narcissa, a love that hovers on the edge of incest, like the love of Quentin Compson for his sister Candace in *The Sound and the Fury.*

The Sound and the Fury, also published in 1929—Faulkner, once he conceived the series, rushed to realize it—is perhaps more powerful than *Sartoris* because it is more concentrated; but the concentration is so intense, and the torment of its people so terrible, that Faulkner scrambled his time-scheme in an effort to make all the events seem simultaneous. The result has puzzled and confused many readers, though the passion in these people is authentic passion, and the book has found an audience that justly admires it. The invention of Faulkner is most impressive, as is the capacity to identify himself, then us, with the suffering of the Compsons. His plot is rich with

complications that remind us of Dostoevsky; his eloquence is likewise comparable with that of the Russian master. If it is true, as has
been said, that he caught fire midway of *Sartoris* and burned steadily
thereafter with a purpose that did not rest until the entire series was
finished—if indeed it was finished by anything other than his death—
then we have the spectacle of an artist profoundly involved with his
material, and an artist, furthermore, who gave it the kind of devotion for which there is no other word than love. By which I do not
mean sentiment, for a certain humor in him kept sentiment down.
In *The Sound and the Fury,* for instance, Jason Compson reveals
himself as more a Snopes than a Compson, let alone a Sartoris. He
is one of the meanest characters in fiction and as such stands in
cold contrast to the Compsons around him: people with hearts and
minds, people with voices that have music in them, as of course
Jason's voice has not.

Within a year (1930) Faulkner had published *As I Lay Dying,*
which some students of him consider his masterpiece, though if it is
a masterpiece it is a minor one, since the subject matter is slight.
Perhaps that very slightness is what recommends it to readers who
feel that other novels by Faulkner are thickets of conversation and
events through which they must fight in order to reach open air
once more. Read with the care he deserves, Faulkner does not
justify such a feeling any more than Dostoevsky does, though it is
true that his fare can be at moments all but unbearably rich. In *As I
Lay Dying,* however, we have nothing but a backcountry family on
its way to bury Addie Bundren, wife and mother, in Jefferson
where she had always wanted to lie. The father and the children—
grown sons and daughters—are of an irreducible simplicity. One
of them is making a coffin even before the poor woman who is to
occupy it has drawn her last breath. The others, including Dewey
Dell, who is pregnant out of wedlock and looks forward to finding
some medicine in Jefferson that will make all well again, manifest
their simplicity in monologues which give Faulkner full rein with
the humor he has in ripe abundance. The story is of the trip to
Jefferson in a mule wagon with Addie and her coffin properly
displayed. The only trouble is that there has been a heavy rain, so
that as they ford a swollen river the mules are drowned and the
wagon turns over; but it is righted, coffin and all, and at last the

burial takes place—in good time, too, for days have passed since the little procession started, and people along the way are offended by what they smell. It is an idyll for all of this, a perfect rendering— wry, ridiculous, charming, moving—of one far-off moment in Faulkner time.

Faulkner's short stories fill in the crevices between the novels; it is as if he could not bear the thought of incompletion. "Barn Burning," one of the best, brings a Snopes and a de Spain together. This Snopes, certainly one of the worst, a savage, cold terrible man, is given to burning the barns, or threatening to burn them, of land-owners to whom he is bound as a sharecropper; any insult from the landowner, real or imagined, brings swift retribution by night. In the present case Snopes is angered by the de Spains: by the lady because she is outraged over his defilement of her house—he has walked through cow dung and he grinds the residue into her finest rug; and by de Spain himself who gets a judgment against him in court. The story is told from the point of view of Snopes's young son, a boy who cannot bear to accompany his father any longer with kerosene and kindling. He is forced to do so this night, but afterward, when his father has been shot, he walks away as if he were going on forever out of a world whose ugliness he has ceased to be able to tolerate. "A Rose for Emily" deals with a Grierson, Miss Emily, who poisons the man she loves and shuts herself up in her house for forty years with his skeleton on her bed. A grim tale, yet even then a grace note to Faulkner's incomparable saga.

Kafka, Camus, and Orwell

I put these three together because of one thing they did in common: they wrote parables. Not Utopias, not satires, though sometimes they are credited with that intention, but parables—stories with something abstract in them, something of the universal under the guise of here and now. Our age has produced many such works, for it is an age even more nervous about the future than appalled by the present; it is an unhappy age, as perhaps all ages have been, but with the difference that commentary grows ever sharper and sharper, and the reference to conceivable perfection—only, alas, conceivable—grows more and more pointed. These three men are not alike, either in subject matter or in power; yet neither are they absolutely unlike, for each of them in his way is writing fairy tales of the mind: a valuable thing to do, now or at any time. And all of them have done it with a distinction that will not be forgotten.

The chief of them for me is Franz Kafka (1883-1924), whose two posthumous novels, *The Trial* and *The Castle,* were to have been burned by his friend Max Brod, as Emily Dickinson's poems were to have been burned by her sister Lavinia; but Brod, to our good fortune, saved them and published them. They are among the most brilliant and fascinating works of the present century, and commentary upon them has been various as well as endless. They are often taken to be satires on contemporary society, but I take them to be something deeper and higher than that. For me they are theological in their bearing: *The Trial,* I think, deals with damnation and *The Castle* with election; or, if you prefer, one is a parable of guilt and the other is a parable of grace. This may sound strange in view of the fact that Kafka was a Jew of Prague (he wrote in German), but it is relevant to know that he had read the Danish philosopher Kierkegaard, and almost knew by heart his *Fear and Trembling.* In any case he penetrated to the center of Calvinist dogma, where he discovered things that most people today are ignorant of—and that, incidentally, is one of the things his books mean.

The hero of *The Trial,* called Joseph K., is arrested one morning for reasons he does not know and never will find out. He is not only arrested; he is interrogated; he himself interrogates the court that has condemned him; and finally he is executed, still ignorant of the cause. There is no cause except that he has been picked out of thousands to be damned—something that is plain to us but is not so plain to him. The women of the novel find him attractive, as they find any condemned man attractive, and in our minds too he takes on a certain distinction because of the mystery that attends his fate. Mystery is the word. Why does God hate this man and love that other? Naturally there is no answer, any more than there is an answer to the famous question, as old as the world, What does he see in her, or she in him? Love, like the absence of love, is not to be explained, though the heroes of these two novels break their very brains in search of reasons why they should be treated as they are. For the hero of *The Castle* has been offered grace, again without discernible cause, but he does not know how to accept the gift, and eventually it seems to be withdrawn, though of this we cannot be sure because the novel does not end.

The courts that condemn Joseph K. are unimaginably complex and impenetrable, so that some commentators have assumed that Kafka intended satire upon the law's delays. Not so, I believe. The parallel is inevitable; and hence the parable. But the gist of the matter is unearthly, not earthly. Joseph K. is damned for all eternity, not because he has broken any law, but simply because it suits the universe to damn him. So with K. in *The Castle,* who comes to a snowbound village at the foot of a hill on which a mysterious building stands, expecting to be admitted because he bears a letter inviting him to be a land surveyor. But he never finds anybody who knows about the letter, and every attempt he makes to communicate with the Castle ends in frustration—the telephone does nothing but buzz, and the offices up there are too busy with documents to consider his case. The only official whose name he ever hears, Klamm, is so far from being available that K. can imagine he doesn't even exist, in spite of evidence—Frieda, Klamm's former mistress—that he does. The people down in the village cannot understand the aggressive eagerness of K. to gain admittance and be recognized. They belong to the Castle even though they live downhill from it, as Piccarda in the *Divine Comedy* says she belongs in Paradise even though she does not inhabit its inmost circle. The villagers suggest that if K. could relax he might eventually understand that he is already in and of the Castle, but this is something he cannot do. He remains bewildered by the barriers between him and Klamm, somewhat as visitors to modern business offices are thwarted by telephone operators who say their bosses are in conference, or by receptionists whose desks cannot be passed. So *The Castle* has often been taken to be a satire on bureaucracy and paper work, but again it is vastly more than that. Our paper work provides its symbol, but its essence is something more ethereal altogether, just as its moral, supposing it has one, is simpler than a child could say: When grace is given us we should know how to accept it and should not ask for proof that as a gift it is genuine.

In one sense I am misleading about Kafka: my exegesis of him sounds too solemn. His nimble style—short, plain words that run on and on till the reader, enchanted, is out of breath—and his charming invention—delicious details, always so logical and at the same time so surprising—these are primary virtues in one who would write, as I am certain he did, of supernatural things. Then add to all this that he is often amusing; he is said to have laughed uncontrollably when he read the manuscripts aloud. Amusing, yet under the aspect of eternity, terrible. Eternity is real in these parables, even though we are not permitted to inhabit it. We merely note that those who stray from it into time—into the ordinary world where we ourselves live—soon become weary, and find it hard to breathe. They are God's fish out of water. And who could suggest this but Kafka? It is my way at last of saying that in his two priceless narratives he came as near as mortal man can come to stating the truth about the moral universe. At any rate, we have from him a pair of classics of the highest and purest order.

The Plague, to which some readers may prefer *The Stranger* or *The Fall,* also by Albert Camus (1913-1960), is a parable in a special and perhaps a limited sense. Published in France in 1947, it is ostensibly an account of something that happened in the African city of Oran, namely, the coming of the plague and the long quarantine of the city in consequence, but who has ever doubted that it is really about the German occupation of France, and particularly of Paris, during the painful years between 1940 and 1945? The model for it is surely Defoe's masterpiece of reporting, *A Journal of the Plague Year,* which seems for all the world to be the account of an eyewitness, though Defoe was only five years old when the plague devastated London. This was a good model for Camus to take, because he must have wished to be as plain, and to sound as unimpassioned, as it was possible for him to be, considering how hard he had taken the occupation of his own beloved city. The parallel is all the deadlier for this calm in the narrator's voice. The details of the plague at Oran are wonderfully conceived and placed. It is a permanent work, and its final paragraph, speculating about the possible return of the plague at some future time, cannot be lost on any reader.

Animal Farm, by George Orwell (1903-1950), which preceded *The Plague* by two years (1945), is of a different order altogether. It reads like a children's story, which certainly it is not; or if it is, it is for children much older than their years. I might have chosen his *Nineteen Eighty-Four,* a savage Utopia in reverse, a Swiftian prophecy so bitter that it is all but unbearable, but the year 1984 will soon be here, and what of the prophecy then? Here even now, one might declare, but I prefer to represent this mordant critic of the modern world by a book that so far as I can see need never seem out of date. It is a tale of some pigs who suddenly were seized with the desire to form a perfect society. They did so, and then the society, perhaps like all such things, let corruption in. The corruption in this case consisted of letting human beings in, with the result that before too long the men could not be told from the pigs, nor the pigs from the men. A summary all too brief, but it may suffice to show Orwell's intention. His fable, or if you please his parable, continues to the end to read like a children's story: a bedtime one, perhaps, to be read in the last evening of the world.

Alexander Solzhenitsyn

Russian fiction since 1917 has not been notable for any qualities that would remind us of the great novelists—Gogol, Turgenev, Goncharov, Dostoevsky, Tolstoy—of the nineteenth century. Not, that is, until now, when Solzhenitsyn's *The First Circle* has stolen its way out of Russia and been recognized as the masterpiece of horror—and of beauty, too—which I agree with others that it is. I know I am taking a risk when I select for this hypothetical set of great modern works so recent a one as *The First Circle,* but it is a risk I do not hesitate to take, for two readings of it have convinced me that Solzhenitsyn belongs with the masters who preceded him so long ago, when literature in Russia, whatever difficulties beset it, still was not forced to consider itself an arm of government, a celebration of things as they are. No reader of him will doubt that he deals with things as they are, but neither will any reader be surprised to learn that what he has written could not be published in his own country. The wonder is that he could write it at all, and then get it somehow into the hands of the rest of the world.

Once again, and for the last time, I have to remind myself of the difference between poetry and history. *The First Circle* is history to the extent that it satisfies our curiosity concerning one phase of life in Russia under Stalin. The time it covers is four days in 1949, and the scene is a prison on the edge of Moscow where several hundred scientists are confined while they work on projects assigned to them by the authorities above. They are all political prisoners, and most of them—like Solzhenitsyn himself as it happens—had served terms in Siberian labor camps before they were sent here to work in relative comfort; but only relative, since they still were prisoners of an absolutist government and scarcely needed reminding that they had not escaped from hell; they had merely been moved up to its first circle, as the pagan philosophers in Dante had been sent to spend eternity in Limbo; and they could always be sent down again, as in fact the hero of the novel, Nerzhin, finally is, for no other reason than that he refuses a new assignment. He will never see the bright world again, nor be again with his wife, Nadya, its chief ornament for him as he is for her.

To speak thus of Nerzhin and Nadya, whom we see only once together during a thirty-minute visit she is permitted to pay him—they may not touch each other, nor say what they really mean except with their eyes—is all at once to make it clear that *The First Circle* is poetry: is a story with a hero and a heroine. Before Nerzhin was told that the visit would be paid, he had been tempted to make an assignation with a girl, Simochka, in the Acoustics Laboratory where he works, but now the sight of Nadya sweeps all such desire away, and when the time comes he tells Simochka so. Were there nothing else in the book, this love story would distinguish *The First Circle* among the novels of the world.

But there is much else—so much more that the range of it can merely be suggested here. There is the prison itself, with dozens of men in it whom we come to know intimately as we hear them talk and watch them work. And the central man among them is Nerzhin, whose integrity—of which he never boasts, for it is something he scarcely knows—provides one of the most moving spectacles I have ever encountered. It is this that I had in mind when I spoke of beauty: the human spirit of Nerzhin, doomed though he may be, is a star in the gloom of a prison so dreadful that the mind reels considering it, a star whose light no cruelty or stupidity can extinguish. The specific nature of this cruelty we discover from what happens to a man on the outside, Volodin, whose story begins and ends the book; and his story has a crucial relation to the story of the prisoners, notably Rubin, who will identify in the Acoustics Laboratory the voice of Volodin as that of the man who had tried to telephone a warning to Professor Dobroumov not to put himself in danger from the secret police. The telephone call had been taped, and it is Rubin—Nerzhin's friend—who makes the identification. The consequences for Volodin are too terrible to print, but that is not my present point, which is rather that Solzhenitsyn's art has thus placed the prison itself in a perspective where we shall always see it. Volodin, a hitherto happy denizen of the bright world, is the focus through which we suddenly peer into the grim interior of a circle, a cavern, a pit, where excellent men who cannot be aware of what they are doing do inhuman things.

Even then I have not exhausted the contents of this long and powerful work. To do so might require as much space as the work itself occupies. But that is true of any masterpiece. I am content to call it that, and to put it last, if only in point of time, among its peers.

PART 3

HOW PRAISE A WORLD?
A MARK VAN DOREN
MISCELLANY

INTRODUCTION TO PART 3

The essays here, while certainly general and miscellaneous, are nonetheless designed not only to demonstrate different facets of Van Doren's career but also to give further indication of his prose style.

The lead essay was written as a speech for a chapter of Americans for Democratic Action in New Jersey. Van Doren's books had been removed from a junior college library for "alleging opinions and associations of mine as evidence that in any case I was an undesirable person who should be listened to on no subject whatsoever." The statement was made in the midst of the Joseph McCarthy era and represents Van Doren's faith in the principles of justice and the American way of life. The published text originally appeared in The American Scholar.

"Know What You Want" originally appeared in Harper's Magazine *in 1957. Among other things, it shows the affection Mark Van Doren had for his older brother Carl, and Carl's lasting influence on him.*

For many years Mark Van Doren wrote film criticism for The Nation *and the essay "Let the Movies Be Natural" is a summary of his views about the film industry. It also appeared first in* The American Scholar, *in 1937.*

"The Kinds of Knowledge" presents Van Doren's view of the academic life and "The Joy of Being Serious," also delivered with an undergraduate university audience in mind, gives a further dimension to his views.

The short essays on Robert Frost and John Kennedy appeared after the death of both personages. The first, on Kennedy, was delivered at a local Connecticut church on the national day of mourning after the assassination of Kennedy. Characteristically, Van Doren did not mention the ties he had with the young President, for whom he had served as chairman of the artists and writers committee in support of the Nuclear Test Ban Treaty. His ties with Frost, of course, were long-standing and have been amply documented elsewhere. Valuable here is Van Doren's personal selection of some forty poems of Frost's, a poet whom he had reviewed at various stages of his career.

The next two essays show Van Doren's particular interest in place: the first a simple river near his beloved Connecticut homestead, and the other, on Greece, is based on a personal visit and his lifelong love of Greek literature. Both essays are hymns of praise, as is the final one, on praise itself. It was first delivered at St. John's College in Santa Fe, New Mexico, not long after Van Doren recuperated from a heart attack. It concludes with a poem that may serve as a king of epitaph to a man and writer whom Archibald MacLeish referred to as "one of the ripest, wholest talents of our time in any art."

23

IF ANYBODY WANTS TO KNOW

I understand that I am here tonight, not to be investigated or tried, or to speak in defense of anything I have ever done or said, but to assist in the discussion of an important principle. I hope that none of you came with the expectation that anything would be proved, either about me or about the Board of Education of this city, one or more of whose members have seen fit to order the removal of four of my books from the library of Jersey City Junior College. It appears that they did so without knowledge of what was in those books. All my books are about literature, or else they try to be literature themselves, and so it is safe to assume that the four in question may be so described. It further appears that the Board of Education was soon made aware of this; but that it decided not to alter its original position, alleging opinions and associations of mine as evidence that in any case I was an undesirable person who should be listened to on no subject whatsoever.

A few anonymous letters that I have received express agreement with the Board. But the great majority of those who have written or spoken to me have expressed emphatic disagreement, and have gone on to say that the action of the Board was either ridiculous or outrageous. I myself make neither charge. I am more interested in the principles and procedures that seem to be involved, and in the question whether Americanism and democracy have been well served in Jersey City. I come entirely alone to discuss this question. I represent nobody but myself; though I recognize how many friends of mine, some of whom I never knew before, hope that some degree of clarification will result. I gather that the issue is as important to them as it is to me; and, frankly, it is in their interest as well as mine that I am here, against my own natural inclination to live without trouble in the country I love.

Some of these friends have pointed out to me that the incident which inspired this meeting is already in some measure out of date. A rapidly growing number of citizens, from President Truman on down, have in recent weeks and days indicated their doubt that our program of security—in itself an absolutely necessary thing—is being handled to the best advantage: to the advantage, that is, of our own health and strength at a time when we need health and strength as never perhaps before. A religious leader in New York, for example, was all but stating a commonplace when in the newspapers for February 11 he said: "That American security is endangered is undeniable; but the greatest threat to our security is the fear that drives us to limit the very freedoms that have made us strong. Investigations and oaths and complex security laws—which in effect censor opinion rather than control conduct—are not providing the strength we need to meet the challenge of the international situation. . . . Scholars are becoming suspect, distinguished thinkers are discouraged from government service, and the spirit of free inquiry at great universities is in danger of being curtailed. . . . By making one's associations the test of loyalty, by identifying any unorthodox viewpoints with communism, we put a premium on conformity and stifle the spirit of freedom, the right to criticize, by which democracy lives and grows." The statement, however, is still not commonplace enough; that is why we are here tonight.

By a coincidence more pertinent yet to the reason for our meeting, I received only week before last, from the American Library Association, a copy of its Library Bill of Rights. This document is a welcome sign that groups of Americans are taking their own steps these days to safeguard their existence. I quote its third paragraph: "Censorship of books, urged or practiced by volunteer arbiters of morals or political opinion or by organizations that would establish a coercive concept of Americanism, must be challenged by libraries in maintenance of their responsibility to provide public information and enlightenment through the printed word.'' The application of these excellent words to the Board of Education's act in removing my books from one of the libraries for which it is responsible may not appear on one count to be perfect, and indeed by my own judgment is not. I happen to believe, and I have often said, that the right of school authorities to select the books their students shall read is not to be infringed. But on another count the application is clear. The Jersey City Board of Education, after conceding that my books are unobjectionable, still call their author objectionable—do so publicly—and still presume to protect the students of at least one college from contact with his mind.

They do this to me, it might appear, because they disagree with some of my opinions and disapprove of some of my associations. I say "it might appear," for I am not at all certain that they know any more about my opinions than they do about my books; though it is clear that they jump to conclusions, and want others to do so, from the associations they list and allege. I do not propose to challenge their list, though to the best of my knowledge it is sometimes erroneous, and at other times, if not erroneous, misleading. I am not here to repudiate anything I ever said, or to deny that I joined others in saying it—often through organizations which at the time were objectionable to nobody. An example would be the Independent Citizens' Committee of the Arts, Sciences and Professions, which I joined with many others in 1944 to assist in the election of Franklin D. Roosevelt as President of the United States, and from which I subsequently resigned. Nor is there time to argue the merits of my beliefs—either their present merits or their merits in the context (sometimes five, sometimes ten, sometimes twenty years old) which produced them. I am here to consider with you the inference which the Board of Education has publicly drawn from them—whether or not to my personal damage may not for the moment matter; or whether to the damage of the Board of Education's prestige, which might be supposed to depend upon its conduct of any affair involving logic and justice.

The one thing the Board did not do—indeed, by saying that the case was "closed" it showed it did not want to do it—was to discover what my opinions actually were and are, to consider their truth or untruth, and if they seemed untrue, to refute them by fair means. The Board seems not to be interested in the good old institution of argument. If I have ever been wrong in anything I publicly said or joined others in saying, I deserve to be proved wrong and in fact should welcome it. I could have been wrong; I can be wrong now; and certain of my friends who disagreed with me about particular matters have told me so, and given their reasons why, and sometimes I have found these to be good reasons. This, I take it, is the process of civilization. By the same token it is not, I take it, the process of civilization to say of someone with whom you disagree either that he is your personal enemy—which does not follow at all—or that he is the enemy of his country and of civilization itself. To be called irrelevant and erroneous names in argument is not agreeable, and it does not settle the argument. It is a dangerous method even for those who use it, since it can be turned against them. If I am your enemy then you are mine, and I may be forced to question your motives for thinking and saying what you do. I do not call in question the motives of the Board of Education in doing what it has done; I do not insist on knowing why they exaggerate and insinuate as in my case they do; I do not accuse them of joining with others in some sinister cause. I merely point out that they have not proceeded in what I am old-fashioned enough to believe is the American fashion—has been, still is, and always must be the American fashion if our oldest tradition is to keep its meaning.

My faith in the American people and their government—even though some members of that government have shown signs of panic—is still so great that I say this here and now: Whenever I shall be asked my opinion on any crucial matter, and when I have an opinion that I feel deeply, I will express it and join others in expressing it, and I will never bring pressure to bear, by prejudicial publicity, on anybody who disagrees with me, though I will argue with him as capably as I can, and if he is more capable, or proves that he is better informed, I will change my mind and admit that I have done so.

This for me is the essence of Americanism. But there seem to be Americans (I do not know how many) who are so bent upon having everybody agree with them (I don't know exactly about what) that they take another line. If they cannot have agreement in fact, they want it in the form of silence. Nobody must say anything or belong to anything. For the penalty, if he does, is that they will accuse him of supporting a foreign force. That force, it goes without saying, is communism; or it is Russia, which gives communism today whatever force it has. But there is an astonishing similarity between the two dogmatisms. In Russia also there is no third alternative to agreement or silence. I still believe with all my heart that for us this third alternative exists—and not only exists, but is necessary to our survival. I still maintain that it is obligatory for all Americans to speak their minds on matters of common importance, with the understanding that the proper penalty for their being wrong, if they are wrong, is that someone prove them so.

Whether they are right or wrong is infinitely more important, I think, than whom they happen to agree with. The current assumption sometimes seems to be that no man ever thinks for himself; he thinks only with a group, or as a group dictates. But it is American, as it is democratic, for men to make up their own minds. I for one can say that it is nobody's business why I ever said what I said, but that I am willing to say why. I meant what I said, and believed it to be true. If I sound naïve, it is perhaps because many have grown cynical. And I am sorry to say that I must include among the cynical not only those members of the Board of Education who assume an alien source for my ideas, but certain very well-meaning friends of mine who talk as if there were nothing to be done in this situation, which they themselves deplore. I thought there was something to be done. I came here tonight, and I did not think it was useless to do so. Nor was I in the least afraid to come. The Board says it is afraid of me, and the friends in question act as if they were afraid of the Board. So far as I know, I have no fear, and I see no reason why I should have any. Some of the letters I got were letters of condolence, as if I had died. I feel very much alive, and furthermore I am confident. I know I am not alone in my confidence; though even if I were, I should have to act as I am acting now. In the America of Lincoln and Thoreau there is no good reason for fear.

Yet many Americans are afraid today. And if enough more become so, we shall have lost our freedom. Freedom and courage come and go together, like liberty and argument. It has been insinuated that I "support the proponents of a change of government by force.'' Nothing could be more absurd. If I believe anything, I believe that the only force that can change or destroy our common life is the force of fear, which by its very ability to operate among us would seem to indicate a doubt that we really do have (as I am sure we have) the best way of life in the world—if we only stick to it with free minds and pure hearts. The last thing we should fear is communism itself, which some Americans denounce in one breath as contemptible and then in the next breath honor by trembling before its supposed power. It would have no power if they believed in themselves. It could not dominate them if they knew it couldn't. An American poet—poets sometimes do speak of serious matters— recently published his opinion that we as a people are already dominated by communism. He meant, by fear of communism, and by an obsession with it that prevents us from thinking of any other subject. I do not like to think that this is true. There is still time, I trust, for us to come back to the business of being ourselves, and of making our own life as free and strong as men can make it. This means, of course, preparing ourselves against our enemies. It also means remembering who and what we are. We have been the admiration of the world; but the world shows signs of distrusting us because we do not trust our own tradition.

Courage, said Socrates, is the knowledge of what is to be feared and what is not to be feared. Some things, therefore, are to be feared. One thing we can fear is that we should go the way of Germany, our former enemy, or of Russia, our potential present and future enemy, or of both combined, in the suppression of thought and discussion, and of political action harmonious with these. We are not so hard up that we need to do that. We are not hard up at all. There may be those who think we are, but they have already despaired. They think there is nothing left except for us to become indistinguishable from our foes. They are already beaten. For if they mean this, and if the rest of us come to agree with them, there will indeed be nothing left. The shortest way to weaken ourselves for any struggle we may have with Russia is to throw away the one imperishable strength we have, our faith in individual liberty and dignity, and our faith that the life of any democratic society is measured by the number of its members who believe it to be necessary, for the common good and for their own, that they think as well as they are able, and speak as sensibly as they can.

A letter to me last week assured me that I would have perpetual immunity from such challenges as the present one if I became forever silent. In such a case the silence would not be greatly noticeable. I do not flatter myself that I have been a person of public importance. I have actually said very little; and if the list of organizations with which I have been associated seems long to others, it does not seem long to me, particularly since the association has been for the most part slight and in almost no case active—I signed something I wanted to sign, or I sympathized with certain objectives when I thought all Americans should. But I have no intention, even within these modest limits, of becoming silent. Silence in democracy is death, and I do not want democracy to die. Whenever I believe something I will say it, without any other illusion, if illusion it be, than that in difficult times it is good for thinking to go on.

I have never forgotten the face of a Connecticut farmer I know, a Republican of course, as he turned to me from the radio where he had been listening to a transcription of the latest proceedings of the Un-American Activities Committee. It was a face filled with fear. And fear of what? Of the Committee.

"I've never heard anything like that in this country," he said. "I wouldn't want them to be asking me questions."

"Why not?" I asked.

"Because they were bullying that fellow. He may have done something bad, but I think they were worse. Can't anything be done?"

Perhaps there was nothing for him to do, but with him in mind I protested—like thousands of others—against the method and spirit of the investigation then going on. Communists protested too, doubtless for a different reason. I had my own reasons, which were as American as those of the Connecticut Yankee who was scared. If I also was scared, it was only lest nobody think it safe to object. When thousands did I was reassured—not for myself, but for a country that had still not lost its reason.

Such and so would be my record if I wanted to present it at this time and place. I have no such desire, partly because my record has not been kept, at least by me. I did not think I lived in a police state. The somewhat dreary list of organizations which the Board of Education has drawn up is in my own mind, I confess, an unreal and academic thing. The emphasis it places on membership and association seems merely technical, or else fanatical. My interest, as I have said, has never been in organizations as such; my connection with them has usually been short lived; and I am aware at this moment of belonging to none that should cause worry in any mind. The simple fact is that I never did knowingly join any Communist or Communist-front organization.

But I did not come here to say precisely this, and certainly I did not come to minimize my record, such as it is. It is the record of one who never hesitated to agree with others that the good life is worth talking about and fighting for in so far as words can fight. Most of my effort has been spent in the area where artists, intellectuals and teachers have to stand up for their freedom. It is of the utmost importance to me that those whose business it is to use their minds and imaginations should not be paralyzed, either by cynicism or by fear, or by attempts on the part of others to control them, until they lose their function in the world of men. They fared badly in Hitler's Germany, where their books were burned. They fare badly in Stalin's Russia, where musicians and novelists, not to say scientists and philosophers, must work under constant supervision from above. No great work can be done that way, and eventually, perhaps, no work at all. I should hate to see the same blunder made in America, and I shall continue to do whatever I can to prevent it. It was in this spirit that I protested when the Un-American Activities Committee turned its attention to the movie industry as a producing center of art, and when the industry itself made no effort to protect its legitimate interests. The result has been, as many foresaw, a lowering of movie standards and a lessening of the movie audience. This could be an accident, or it could be television; I think it is the chilling and numbing effect of a force felt from the outside, a force that can strangle the imagination even before it is born.

I am opposed to communism, both as a theory and in the form it now takes before the world; but I should like to distinguish between my opposition to it and that of certain anti-Communists who think they need to be nothing else. The good life is both negative and positive; it is against what would hurt it, but at the same time that it makes itself safe it considers what it wants to be safe for, and what it could build if it were free.

The American people may be moving into a period of unprecedented power and responsibility. If this is true, as I think it is, they cannot have too much help from within. They must hold their own, in peace or in war, and toward this end the services of no citizen may be insignificant. The services, or the ideas—or both, for they can be the same thing. The time to recruit these services is now, and the best atmosphere for the purpose is the atmosphere of confidence and faith. If all we have is the fear that communism can destroy us, we are already destroyed; for we have lost our self-respect. Democracy that believes in itself and remembers its great origins need have no fear of competition with any system in the world, least of all a system that distrusts individuals. The true opposite of communism is not anti-communism as it is preached by those in panic; it is democracy, which, when it knows itself, is never afraid. We ought to be not only against communism but above it, as justice is above despair. The Communists are promising to save the world, but we can really do it. Equality is a better thing than uniformity, liberty than the enforced love of law, and fraternity than the domination of one class. The question is how deeply and simply we understand this. If the world is hesitating to follow us away from communism, the reason may be that it sees signs in us of fear and doubt. We cannot convince others if we are not convinced.

My own position would be funny if it were not fairly serious. It is, of course, not unique. I have remained the liberal I was in the beginning, with the result that I have never been in what you would call the fashion. In the 1930's I was unconvinced by communism, and today I am uncontaminated by the fear of it that makes many Americans forget how much they naturally believe in the good heart and the just mind. By never fluctuating in my love of these things I have become, as appearances now go, suspect. But only, I am sure, as appearances go. It cannot be true—most of my friends persuade me of this—that any considerable body of Americans seriously doubts its obligation to be for those better things which Communists only pretend to be for. Communists can say what they do not mean, for purposes of their own; but we must mean, for no purpose beyond our integrity, whatever we say. And we must not stop talking. We may or may not arrive at the truth; but we shall utterly fail if we desist from the attempt.

In Plato's *Republic,* which is a dialogue about justice, there is a speaker named Thrasymachus who suddenly denies that justice exists. It is only the name, he says, we give to the right of the strong.

Last year in New York, lecturing on Karl Marx, I called him the
Thrasymachus of the modern world. He said, as communism still
says, that justice is merely the will of the strongest class. Marx
wanted a new class to prevail, and therefore a new justice. But
justice is neither new or old. It is not one will, whether of a tyrant
or of a class. It is itself, and it is the thing that all men love when
they are serious. That, if you still care to know, is the politics I have.

24
LET THE MOVIES BE NATURAL

Any art is in a perilous position from the moment it begins to be recognized as an art. It is difficult for anything to be natural after its nature is known. And the movies are no exception, as their current situation testifies. From having been merely entertainment they have by no means advanced to a point where they threaten to cease being that; nearly a hundred million Americans pay their way into movie houses weekly and I do not hear that this multitude is less entertained than it formerly was. But talk about "the art" grows louder and louder; a certain percentage of the audience is said to be achieving sophistication with respect to theory and technique; and there are abundant signs that Hollywood itself takes a day off now and then to worry about the seriousness of what it produces. All this can be either fortunate or unfortunate and doubtless it is neither thing very clearly. It is, however, the aspect of the movies that seems most worth discussion at the present juncture.

The peril of which I have spoken is greatest in the case of a popular art which has been satisfying some widespread and scarcely conscious need and for which an enormous audience—virtually the whole population—has rapidly and naturally collected itself. In all such cases it should be plain that what the art was accomplishing before it became known as an art was the thing it could best accomplish—was perhaps the only thing it could accomplish—and that this continues to be true. If the movies were entertaining, for instance, they should still be that. And if they were popular they should by the same token hold on to their vast audience. Furthermore, if the persons responsible for their success—the producers, the directors, the writers, the photographers, the actors—have never quite known the reasons for it they should persist in that same ignorance, at least as long as the success endures.

I am not offering, I hope, a counsel of stupidity. There is plenty of stupidity at Hollywood and elsewhere and some movies are certainly much better than others; nor should any movie-goer pretend to like what he despises. It is particularly important that a movie-goer should not pretend that a dull picture is an interesting one. But this is what a great deal of solemn talk has been forcing him to do in recent years and it is against such talk as well as against such misguided solemnity that I write. The talk is inspired by the belief that the movies, being an art, should be "dignified," "valuable," "true," "improving" and what not. My point is a very simple one. Movies can be most dignified by being most clearly themselves and, since they are after all very truly an art, by being interesting. There is nothing more vicious in criticism than the distinction to which college students, for example, are so prone, the distinction between the interesting and the good in books, painting, or music. The interesting *is* the good and any criticism which serves to submerge the fact is more than wrong; it is harmful, not merely to the art in question but to the people whose pleasure in it is thereby decreased. The movies began by being simply interesting; indeed so much so that an evening in attendance upon them was assumed to be, and still is generally assumed to be, a sure cure for fatigue, boredom and mental or spiritual inanition. I cannot think of such an institution as anything but valuable, which is the reason why I look with some trepidation at many attempts to "dignify" what already filled a profound human need. It may be unfortunate that our society cannot entertain itself with conversation, folk dances, ballads sung to the lyre or the lute and romances recited by minstrels while we sit around on straw-littered floors. But that is another issue, not to be argued here. I am assuming the society which we have and which has its own notions as to the way it prefers to be entertained.

The happiest movie-goer is still, I think, the one who walks more or less regularly around to his neighborhood house and passes in without inquiring what is on the bill or who, if he does inquire with a glance at the posters, remembers that a given movie never perfectly declares itself until it is being seen. The newspaper critic Monday morning may have been wrong or right about it; there is no telling. The neighbors have delivered several verdicts which cancel one another out. The star whose name occupies the prominent space on the poster was acceptable in her last film and indeed she may be our citizen's favorite actress but that does not mean that she will suit the story tonight. The title may be exciting and may call up a subject very prominent just now in the news, but what of that? It may be a sea picture, a Western, a gang film, a society fable, a kid thing, a comedy, or one of those that take place on transcontinental trains, with narrow mahogany doors constantly swinging for shiny black porters to come through; yet experience has taught our friend that none of these categories is safe in itself. There have been poor examples of each, just as there have been good examples, and maybe this next one will prove that the possibilities have at last been exhausted. He will, in other words, refrain from expecting anything in particular from his evening. All he will expect is that he will be absorbed in what he sees. He hopes he will be absorbed and of course he has every right to do so. And we should trust him to be quite frank on this point when he comes out blinking at eleven o'clock.

What he will see if he is fortunate is a story being told by cameras. The movie was invented, I am sure, to tell stories and the one way it can perform this function well is through photography. It is the only way in fact that it has, and the result of forgetting the limitation is always fatal. The history of the art is bound up with no other principle. The great mistakes have consisted in departing from it and the great successes have followed upon its rediscovery. The great directors, from D. W. Griffith to Alfred Hitchcock, have never lost sight of the fact that the art of the movies is not a verbal art. Words have come in with the "talkies" but a decade of effort has so absorbed them into the primary function that they are no longer disturbing as they once were—and indeed the term "talkie" has ceased to be in common use. We still go to "movies" and can take the dialogue in our stride. The gloomy predictions that dialogue would kill the art have only their historical interest, for the art managed not to forget its original function. Like most such innovations this one slowed up its development for a while. A silent picture of 1927 or 1928 was likely to be superior in sophistication to any talkie of 1931. Had not audiences been trained to interpret movement, gesture, change of scene and flutter of symbol—and to interpret these things with the eye alone? Sometimes we had to lean over and talk to our neighbors about what was going on. "He thinks she is behind the door." "That window was not open before; the burglar must have entered while the party was going on downstairs." "This is the girl who fainted at the factory." And so on. We can no longer indulge in such confidences. We must be as silent as the films themselves used to be. But we have regained our visual sophistication, we still have need of a trained eye. The most interesting of current movies still move and could be followed without serious loss by a deaf spectator. Something would of course be missed yet not the main thing, which as always consists of a series of transformations in plastic material.

The movie-goer, then, has gone in to see a story told, not to hear it told or in any other fashion to be talked at. He will not always get what he wanted. And usually when he gets something far off the track of his desires the fault will lie with a director or a producer who has forgotten the movie principle. Of late the radical error of producers has consisted in believing that the art can be elevated above its natural level by the screening of masterpieces from other arts, particularly the arts of the theater and of prose fiction. They have been trying to make movies which seemed less like movies than like plays or, if a famous novel was the source, they have wanted to hear from the public that the movie is good because it is faithful to the novel and in some sense a substitute for it. The error is serious, for it consists in ignoring the limits of the movie art and no art can be elevated by ceasing to be itself. Movies made from classics are by and large inferior in interest to movies made out of the material traditional to them—out of material indeed which has no name and which cannot be recognized until it appears in its proper form. Our movie-goer is, I hope, an honest man. If he is he will admit both to himself and to anyone who asks his opinion that many an unheralded movie was more absorbing while he saw it, was more authentically exciting or amusing, than any heavily advertised classic on which the producing company was known to have spent two million dollars. There is no necessity that this should be the case. A movie made from a novel by Dickens, for instance, could be a very fine movie indeed. But the director should have had his eye on the movie and not on Dickens—which is usually not the case.

Movies should model themselves on their sources not with more respect than they do but with less, and indeed with no respect at all for material in the source which does not permit of translation into the language of movie art. The reason that Shakespeare has so far not been a genuine success at Hollywood is partly at least that Hollywood has been buffaloed by his name—also, of course, by a long tradition in criticism which ridicules movies for changing, cutting, expanding and otherwise transforming their sources. Whereas the truth is that any movie must transform a novel or a play almost out of recognition if it is to make a veritable movie out of it. That was what Shakespeare did to his sources, whether they were sections of Holinshed's *Chronicles* or other men's plays or novels from Italy. Shakespeare never hesitated to suppress an ending which did not suit his purpose, to add one which did, to invent anywhere from one to ten new characters, to change their dispositions and roles in accordance with the theme he had settled upon, to lighten or to deepen the tone of his original. He was particularly brilliant at condensation but he could equally well elaborate the point being that he considered himself free to do what he chose and felt his only duty to be towards his own theater and his own art. Most of his transformations are made in the interests of poetry or poetic effects, of which he is still the world's master. But I suspect that for this very reason he would expect another art to transform him in the interests of its own effects, whatever they might be. He probably would hope that some equivalent might be found for his poetry but he would know better than most people that the equivalent would look, sound and feel very different from the thing itself. He would know, too, how difficult it is to produce such equivalents. He had himself been buffaloed, by Plutarch. The Roman plays lack the naturalness and vivacity of the English and the Italian plays. This was because Shakespeare recognized in Plutarch an excellent artist whom one was reluctant to alter; an artist also who offered few hints for alteration since there were next to no cracks in his surface. Shakespeare would not or could not remold Plutarch completely to his purposes; hence a certain stiffness in the Roman plays. They have the air of being more "important" than interesting. And that is what happens to most movies which are taken too respectfully from the classics by producers who have grown hypersensitive to the charge that the movies change things—that is, are an art in their own right. The spectator is encouraged to tell himself, not what a fine movie this is he is seeing but how great Shakespeare was. Shakespeare was very great but the fact is irrelevant. He can still be read, and for that matter there are theaters which give his plays from time to time.

In the case of a contemporary or recent play the situation is somewhat different though the dangers are just as real. For better or worse the movie camera has become a moving thing; it tilts, turns around, sweeps a scene, advances and retreats, opens and shades its eyes. It achieves the fadeout, the closeup and many other special effects which by now are as much a part of the whole technique of the movie as blank verse was a part of Shakespeare's technique. These effects invariably alter a play—unless to be sure they are not used at all and the movie in question becomes nothing more than a photograph of *Winterset* or *The Plough and the Stars*. We need hardly consider the latter possibility since it no longer exists and since there is no living director who would have so little respect for himself as to come in like the photographer at a wedding. Every director in this situation tries to make a movie, not a play. But there are many qualities of a play that do not come over into the other art directly. The chief difference has to do with the fixed scene. The audience at a play knows how to accept the three walls of a room or a half of a street or a few forest trees as the whole setting of an act whereas the audience at a movie has learned to expect that the point of view and the amount of anything being seen will constantly change. The exits in a play are all visible all of the time; in a movie only one is attracting our attention at any given moment—that through which someone happens to be walking or running. This difference might appear to be slight or "merely technical" but it is really of great significance. The dramatic qualities of a play can easily leak out between the shifts in point of view; and on the other hand some of them can be too much intensified by the closer glance we give them. The movie director, then, will need to know quite precisely what he wants each of his effects to be and if there is nothing in the play to give him this effect he will have to invent something which will, or if there is something in the play which will not count in the movie he must relentlessly suppress it. But the directors have listened too long, or most of them have, to those who say that movies change too much. So they change too little, with the result that we get something not only different from the play, as any movie would have to be, but inferior to it; and certainly we get something far below the level of the average movie conceived and executed in pure studio terms.

Too much respect for a novel, particularly if it is a long one, results either in unintelligibility or in dullness. And this is most true when the director's ambition has been to please the author of the novel or his devotees, to flatter him with a faithful copy. Here again it is perhaps plain that the spectator should be thinking not of the novel but of the movie; if his attention is split between the two it is of course not attention. A novel is usually too long to pass in its entirety into the form of a film. *David Copperfield* should have been five or six movies, not one. The effort to get it all into one two-hour film ruined the latter parts if it did not render them unintelligible. They were intelligible to any spectator who remembered Dickens and supplied what was missing; but as I have suggested, the attention should not have been encouraged to wander in any such fashion. Those who saw the movie will have most clearly in their minds that earlier portion of it in which Mr. Murdstone (Basil Rathbone) played so sinister a part in the young hero's life. That was a movie in itself, the natural end of it being the arrival of David at Betsey Trotwood's house after his walk from London to Canterbury. Betsey Trotwood's house should have been the scene of a second movie, Mr. Wakefield's house the scene of a third, and Peggotty's the scene of still a fourth, not to speak of a fifth with Dora as heroine. These latter movies were as a matter of fact huddled and incomplete as we saw them fragmentarily two years ago; they were true neither to Dickens nor to themselves, and I suspect that a spectator ignorant of the novel must have had much difficulty with them. It is the ignorant spectator who must be the judge in all such cases—which reminds me that I enjoyed *Romeo and Juliet* much more the second time I saw it than the first because I was surrounded the second time by a great many people who seemed to be unaware of the catastrophe that was coming at the close and they communicated to me their special degree of suspense. It was as if I too were unaware that Romeo was destined to drink the poison and that Juliet was bound to stab herself.

The movies that derive most successfully from fiction are taken either from novels which fame has not sanctified *(The Thirty-Nine Steps, The Informer, The Clansman)* and which therefore lay no chilling hand on the director, or from obscure sketches and short stories like those which inspired *Mr. Deeds Goes to Town* and *The Ghost Goes West.* Returning to Dickens for a moment, there is the highly successful film called *Scrooge* which comes to this country every Christmas from England and which is based on the *Christmas Carol.* That is the length which is usable; it allows for development to the full possibilities of the tale and offers a single effect procurable within the time limit at the director's disposal.

Our movie-goer will educate himself in the history and theory of the art at his own risk. If he holds on to the original and fundamental principles there will be no risk and he will enjoy what he sees all the more for having some wisdom about it. He may, for instance, proceed to read the excellent analysis of the movie which Mr. Mortimer Adler has recently provided in the closing section of his long volume, *Art and Prudence,* and thereby enrich his understanding of the processes involved in the collaboration of many experts to produce any film at all, let alone a good one—which, indeed, will then seem even more than before a marvel in his eyes. But if he loses contact with the principle he will go astray as many highbrows do.

He will haunt, for instance, only the little movie houses where foreign films are shown to students of the "cinema." I have not so far mentioned the films of Russia, Germany, France and England, and I certainly do not wish on this late page to suggest that I consider them either uninteresting or unimportant. Indeed the best living director so far as I know is an Englishman, Alfred Hitchcock, and *The Thirty-Nine Steps* is almost a model of what a film should be. But the haunter of foreign or artful films is likely to be a pedant of some sort and by dismissing Hollywood without further thought he is absenting himself from that great audience which is the life as well as the desperation of the art. Much trash comes out of Hollywood but much that is powerful and fascinating comes out of it too. It is still the capital of the art and as such has many valuable secrets in its possession. A true lover of the movies is not committed for or against Hollywood. He goes to see what is around the corner for him to see and he can trust himself to know whether it is really interesting or not.

Nor is he likely to forget that what the movies can do best is to tell stories and that they are the prime medium through which that indispensable function is exercised in modern society. One of the pedantries now current is that movies are more valuable for something else—for the thing we have got into the habit of calling documentary. Newsreels, travelogues, studies of other races and natural backgrounds—these are maintained to be the proper business of the film. I like such things as well as anybody, but I cannot agree. Movies tell stories, and they tell them in a way that no other art can imitate, just as they cannot imitate the ways in which other arts tell them.

25
KNOW WHAT YOU WANT

My brother Carl, the biographer of Benjamin Franklin, was famous for his generosity. Asked for anything, he was likely to give it. And nothing was more valuable than his advice, which he gave freely when asked. He was not one of those men who pull long faces and wonder whether you oughtn't to decide things for yourself. If you wanted his help, and said so, he never doubted that you did; nor did he foolishly assume that you were bound to take it; the final decision would of course be yours, but meanwhile he was happy to throw what light he could upon your problem.

I owe him more than I can say, and not merely in this one department of advice. Here, though, he was better than generous to me; he was prodigal, he gave me every thought he had. Books to read, people to meet, trips to take, restaurants to try—he included me in his world, so that I lived doubly while he lived. He was nine years my senior, and when we were boys in Illinois he did not hesitate to counsel me sometimes as if I were his son. If I didn't know enough to ask, he told me.

But as I grew up, and later when I followed him to New York, this changed. Nothing, I think, interested him more than what I did or did not do, but he was never in my way. He took it for granted now that I knew enough to ask; and when I did, which was often enough, he held back nothing. I was never dependent upon him unless I chose to be. It was always my choice. And the wonder-ful thing—wonderful, I mean, about him, not me—was that when I made it I felt stronger rather than weaker because I did. My prob-lem immediately became his own; it excited him, it aroused him, it aroused his imagination; so that as we talked I could believe the alternatives to be his as well as mine, and the pleasure too of doing whatever thing would eventually be done, even though in the nature of the case I was to do that thing alone. There was the time, for example, when I begged him to tell me what I should write about for my doctor's dissertation at Columbia. He suggested a criticism of John Dryden's poetry; and within a few minutes was racing through the subject with such contagious zest that I caught fire and contributed a few ideas myself—to his work, as it were, though in the end it was entirely mine.

The one great comprehensive piece of advice Carl gave me, however, came later than that, and I am sorry to say I do not pre-cisely remember the occasion that called it forth—perhaps it was a teaching position I had doubts about, or a job of editing I was afraid I should not stop other work to do. But no matter, it was what he said that counted. I have never forgotten it, nor do I expect to while I live. It has made all the difference to me. And I gladly pass it on.

"The real question is," said Carl, "do you *want* to do it?" "Why," I said, "that's what I can't decide." He laughed. "It seems to me you have decided." "What?" "That you don't want to do it." "How can you tell?" "Why, by your doubt. In my own case this would be decisive." "But doubts are not decisions." "Yes, they are. I have made it a rule never to do anything I didn't want to do—immediately, that is, or else without much thought one way or the other. The longer I hesitate the better I know my answer must be negative." "But you do hesitate. You've even come to me and asked me what I thought you ought to decide."

He laughed again. "Well, then, I was weak. I didn't know the strength of my own inclinations—or disinclinations. Believe me, *they* are clear. And the thing to do is to be as clear yourself. Of course things get in the way—duty, obligation, the desire not to disappoint or offend, the wish always to be liked. But in the end, my boy, do only what you want to do. And do nothing you *don't* want to do. Now in this case you surely don't expect me to tell you what your inclination is—or your disinclination. You are the only one in the world that knows. I think I understand you pretty well, but here is private ground. I'm keeping off.''

Now in one sense this was not advice at all. But in the best sense it was the best; and I needed it the most. Not, of course that it was easy to take. For it threw me back upon the question of who and what I was, and whether I had knowledge of this person. How far should I trust my doubts and my desires? How confident could I afford to be that even if I knew my feelings I should let them master me? Who was I to announce that I would never do anything I didn't want to do? It sounded arrogant. It sounded ruthless.

And the queer thing was, Carl qualified in neither of those roles. He was singularly unselfish; everyone said so, and I knew it for a fact. He was generous to a fault; he praised people to their faces and behind their backs; he gave incredible amounts of time and strength to helping others through hard places; he rejoiced in their successes; he was humane to the last ounce. Also, as I told him in our dialogue, he didn't find it easy to follow his own rule. He could be tortured by doubts as to what he should do next, and by misgivings over what he had done last. His large nature was at the same time extremely sensitive; which was why so many loved him, and why there were those who could take advantage of his kindness. I knew these things then, so what should I conclude?

What I concluded at that dramatic moment was less important for me than what I have concluded since. Without reservation, I now think Carl was right. His ideal—difficult for him, to be sure, but all the more an ideal because of that—still makes the clearest sense. Nothing else perhaps makes any sense at all.

Shall we consult the wishes of others? But what others? And if we could pick the right ones—whatever that means—how could we know that we would please them in the end? We would certainly fail in this if what we did was done unwillingly, unnaturally for us, and therefore against the grain. What they want is that we should want the same thing they do. When they invite us to their house they hope that it will give us happiness to come; and we hope they mean the invitation. Unwilling hosts and unwilling guests do not exactly mix; everybody has a poor time. My wife tells me I lean over backward with respect to this; she says I urge people to come only if they want to; she thinks I sound as if I weren't too eager to see them myself. Possibly so, but I defend the principle. There is only one guide through the labyrinth of choice: our own desire, if we know what that is. Sometimes, I grant, it is difficult to know. But I agree with Carl that ignorance is a serious matter. It causes others and ourselves no end of trouble.

The principle was stated recently by a man who I might have supposed was too young to understand it. But he had had, evidently, the necessary experience. He is a producer of plays and I happened to ask him whether the interest he was expressing in a certain play had its origin in the sympathy and affection I knew he felt for the author.

"Are you being kind?" I asked. He looked at me in astonishment—I even thought, with pity. "Good Lord, no! I learned long ago that anything like that simply complicates everybody's life." He meant that false hope can produce more misery than no hope at all, that lack of frankness—about important things at any rate—has finally to be paid for by the innocent as well as by the guilty.

I remember being asked ten years ago whether I would consider accepting the presidency of a college whose aims I admired. The chairman of the trustees called me on the phone and put it to me in terms that were none too easy to ignore: I was the person they wanted, and I could do the college good. If I hesitated for as long as one minute it was because Carl's voice was for that minute farther away than the chairman's. But I heard it in time, and said what I really felt: this was not my kind of work, I would be unhappy with it, I wouldn't do it well, and therefore I would do the college harm.

"Let me come and see you anyway," he said. "But it wouldn't change my mind." "Then it will simply be a visit." "All right. You know I'd like that. But remember what I said. I'll never accept."

He did come—it was a day's train trip to my house in Connecticut where I was spending the winter—and when he left the next morning he assured me that he liked train trips because they gave him time to read. The presidency had been scarcely mentioned, and I still don't know if he was disappointed with respect to it. I do know, however, that his disappointment in me as president, supposing I had been weak enough to argue down my instinct, would have been enormous and woeful; beginning and ending with me, everybody concerned would have had his life complicated for nothing.

Ruthless? No, I am convinced it is the finest form of scruple. I have not been describing a curmudgeon. The curmudgeon wants nothing, whereas the normal thing is to have many desires—and the ideal thing is to know which ones of them are strongest. The curmudgeon, presumably, wants neither work nor a wife, and does without them. The normal thing is to want a wife, and the ideal thing of course is to take (if you can) the one you want the most. What if you consulted her parents and her friends? What if you married her only because you promised to, and meanwhile had changed your mind? This has been done, but neither party could have benefited by the act. The truly ruthless thing is to do what you do because you believe you ought to, and for no gentler reason. That is invoking monsters you have no human right to invoke. It is being, in the crudest possible sense, impersonal. It will not merely complicate life, it will ruin it.

Why is it that we are flattered when an animal likes us—when, for instance, we are in somebody's house and the cat, after staring at us from across the room, comes over and jumps up on our lap? The mistress of the cat can say nothing better at that moment than: "Look! He doesn't do it to everybody." We may pretend otherwise, but we are deeply pleased; and surely the reason is that we know cats—particularly cats—to be devoid of the sense of duty. They do what they want to do, and cannot be forced to do anything else. So in this case the motive is pure. Which is to say, it is purely selfish. Which is to say, it is capable of giving pleasure unmixed with any other thing. The same is true of small children—those who are too small to have compromised with complicaton, the adult vice that will beset them later.

As a vice it has its uses in society, and sometimes its beauty too. But it is a vice. Which is why I have learned, when someone comes to me and asks for counsel, that the most helpful thing to do is let him talk until he has told himself what his own choice is. He probably knew before he came, but doubted that others would approve. Now, though, in an atmosphere free of disapproval, he convinces himself that at last he knows what he wants. He is lucky in the knowledge, and so will those be with whom he is to be concerned.

26

THE KINDS OF KNOWLEDGE

When a university, in the name of that knowledge to which it believes all men as men have right, reviews its own career of learning and of teaching it is bound to ask itself what knowledge really is, and how much of its exists at present or can be imagined as existing in some day to come. Such a university, putting such a question to itself, will be expected to make a modest answer, for in no other place should the limits of the human mind be better known; but it is not required to deny that knowledge exists at all, or to suggest, if knowledge be supposed to exist in several kinds, that these are like the kinds of snakes in Ireland: varieties of nothing in the end.

The university has faith in knowledge. Or to put the case more accurately, it has faith in the possibility of knowledge. The possibility is what matters, plus a method, or a set of methods, whereby the actuality may in ever higher and higher degree be encouraged to exist. Those to whom the problem is not real assume the actuality already to exist: somewhere, somehow, someone knows everything. But to others it is a familiar fact that the true scholar is more interested in what he may know tomorrow than in what he knows today, and is more likely to want to talk about it. The modesty of the true scholar is neither a gesture nor a joke. To him it is quite literally the case that a science of anything presupposes a vast ignorance concerning it: an ignorance, indeed, so vast that even its very nature may never be understood. He as a scientist, in other words, may never become clear as to what it is of which he is ignorant, or ought to consider himself ignorant; he may never learn just what it is that he should seek to know. Meanwhile, however, he has his method; he does know how to proceed within the field of ignorance he has managed to define. And that one field is vast enough; nor will all of it, perhaps, be ever conquered. So he is always busy, with scarcely the time to pause and tell us, should we ask, how much he knows; and more particularly, how much of what he knows.

To the extent that he is a true scholar he will contemplate this question of the what, and seriously ask it of himself. Is he studying the right thing?—which means, for true scholars, the most difficult, the most hidden, the most abstract, the most inaccessible thing. Has he been content thus far with fields of ignorance that others have defined? Has he discovered any for himself? And if he has, is it the farthest field, beyond whose fences, conceivably, the simple truth sits looking at itself: Often this farthest field seems nearest to the uninitiated mind, which asks elementary questions about it: What is it, after all? Why are you studying it? What would it mean to know what you say you want to know? What difference will it make? Or, in a more friendly voice, even an eager one: What is electricity? What is life? What is poetry? Can history be true, and if so, what history is most true? Is there such a thing as human nature, and does it grow? What is government? What is law? What is money? What are the stars, and why is there so much space between them? Where is God? And if men knew everything would they be God?

The truest scholar will be the most tolerant of such questions, for they are like the ones he asks himself when he is simple and serious; and if he is never simple and serious, he is a pedant or a quack, and the long face he wears as he discourses on his method is a sign that he does not know why he has it, or what he will do with the results of it when he gets them. Universities have their share of persons who practice learning without a divine license; who do not know what is important unless someone else tells them; who work in fields of ignorance from which for them there is no escape; who labor in the dark to raise ever higher and higher the heap of little fragments which in their boastful moments they call the sum of human knowledge.

But what is the sum of human knowledge? Or what would it be if it ever were complete? And is it necessarily a future thing, something to be hoped for only, something impossible now? Can one be certain that it does not already exist? If it needs to be the equivalent of God's knowledge, certainly it does not exist; for men are neither more nor less divine than they originally were. But doubtless there is no such need. Men may know merely what men can know. And according to one view they have always known it. Jonathan Swift thought men knew it in his time, two centuries and more ago. But most of them, he concluded, were not aware that they knew it, and so had got lost in mazes of speculation and experiment for which there was no earthly use—nor divine use either, since God does not find it necessary to be a scientist, a philosopher, or a theologian. These are human terms, less admirable for Swift than the monosyllable man. Most men in any time, he said, know all that can be known about how to live and how not to live; it is only sickness, or corruption, or perversity that cuts them off from life itself, which everywhere is simple and makes no mystery of its rules. Liars are liars in any world; and so are hypocrites and thieves, and lazy people; and so are the lovely people—the kind, the just, the generous, the temperate, the courageous, the wise, the strong.

There is validity in such a view. Men's thoughts about themselves are different from one decade to the next, but their virtues and their vices do not seem to change. The very man who tries to prove that there is no longer any distinction between good and bad—that these are words, not things—will in his next breath denounce a neighbor of whose conduct he disapproves. The very man who swears that it is old-fashioned to speak of truth may find himself, before the day is over, calling some other man a falsifier. Most of us, it may be, know more than we admit; we know, as Swift said, how to live; at least we keep on living, as our great-grandfathers did. And this regardless of whether or not we have access to the kinds of knowledge with which universities are concerned.

And properly concerned. For the possibilities of knowledge which haunt and inspire scholars are themselves among the things that prove man human. Not animal, certainly, since animals know perfectly how they should live in order to survive and to repeat themselves. Not godlike, just as certainly; for the possibilities can never be more than possibilities. And if Swift with all his genius could despise them, so we too may remember how they limit us; we too may learn from him and them how not to be too proud.

Yet they are half the truth about mankind. To be a scholar is not to be an unnatural thing. The nature of man is to want more knowledge then he will ever possess, and to work for it as if it still might be possessed. And if in his universities he gives that knowledge a variety of names, if he recognizes it in more than a single form, he does not in so doing deny that the many may be one, or might be if a proper view of them could be obtained. Perhaps in our day he tries less hard than once he did to master the perspectives that would be involved in such a complete and distant view of himself in the act of contemplation. His nature does not, it would seem, permit him to do this; yet he has made the attempt, and he will make it again. At the moment, however, he looks as if he lacked the ambition, not to say the curiosity. We do not hear him asking what it is, if it is anything, that the poet and the mathematician know together, or the historian and the chemist, or the musician and the doctor, or the moral philosopher and the atomic physicist. The sum of human knowledge, were it attainable and stable, might be a single sentence, a single word; or it might be only so clear a view of everything that sound was superogatory, and speech an impertinence. Granted that the sum is inaccessible, man still may speculate as to its parts, and as to the niceties of their relation. Contemporary man, at least in universities, refuses to do so. He lets the study of literature be altogether different from the study of bacteria and the stars. If some resemblance actually is there, he does not know of it because he has never inquired. He assumes a perfect absence of relation; and so if he is a student of poetry he is content with total ignorance of energy, proportion, and equation, though poetry is built of just those things; and if he is a natural scientist he does not stop to wonder whether it is more than a coincidence that art must be natural too, or must seem so if it would exert its utmost force; nor does he ask that force to confess any resemblance it may bear to gravity and whirlwinds, to natural selection and a mushroom cloud.

But even if he did this, and even if the poet were better educated than he is, the answer would never come, we may be sure, in the form of one apocalyptic word. The knowledge of such a word which the theologian has is another kind of knowledge, unsupported by what is ordinarily called evidence, either in universities or in the outer world; but especially in universities, whose scholars are experts in evidence, and grow wary at once if told that something is true although it never can be proved. Yet revelation belongs in their lives too, as it belongs in the career of every healthy intellect, no matter what the training it has had, and whether this be great or small. Any man knows things he has not been told; the good teacher gives forth more than he was taught; sometimes the truth comes easily, as if it said itself. And this can be the case whatever the theory of knowledge one professes—Swift's or that of the most methodical scholar. The knowledge that advances, like the knowledge that stands still, is studded with discoveries which cannot be traced to any source. It is vanity to deny this, and folly to underrate it. Nor is it the same thing as that apocalyptic word which is never to be spoken. It used to be understood that the knowledge of angels came with less difficulty than that of men. It came instantaneously, whereas for men it was the labor of a lifetime to learn the little that they knew. Men still are less than the angels, and what they know is of a lower order; yet any man, on any occasion, may be more wise than he is able to explain. The name for this is brilliance: a sudden light that no one has turned on. And it can come on anywhere: in the laboratory, the recitation hall, the midnight study; in the field, the street, the noisy or the quiet room; in sleep, or at the hour of waking, or halfway through an otherwise eventless day. It too is knowledge, though it never has been earned.

Most human knowledge, nevertheless, comes hard. Either it distills itself painfully out of common experience, or it subjects the scholar, its uncommon devotee, to excruciating efforts of observation and close thought. Seldom if ever does inspiration come without such fiery trials before it, and even then it may not come; but if it does, it has to that extent been earned, and is deserved. The university does not count upon its coming, any more than it lays out work in the expectation that only geniuses will do it. Miracles and geniuses are rare in any world, and it is the part of wisdom not to await them. The academic life is bound to be laborious, however many or few the kinds of knowledge it is lived for. It is not as dull as some men think it, but it is duller than a circus or a battlefield; and so it ought to be, since neither in game nor in earnest is it lived in defiance of death. The definition of all life is rather its province: all life, whose most exciting secrets it has no mandate to unearth. To define a thing is not in so far to possess it. The clearest definition of life would be the completest statement of what it is not. Life itself, the individual thing, prefers to be known for what it is; and those who have known it the most directly may be the least articulate about its essence. Its essence, tragic or comic, the university is under no obligation to reveal.

But to say this is not to justify the vulgar charge that academic life is unreal life. It is as real as definition is; as useful, and as clear. In an ideal world the privilege of experience and the duty of understanding would doubtless not exclude each other. Nor in the world we have do they do so altogether; if they could, neither one of them would then make sense. The pure thing and the pure word are not for men as men are made. So the university continues to be looked to for more than dry information and dead fact; for more, even, than the cold light of clearest comprehension. It is looked to for wisdom, a warmer and wilder thing than any of those. And often enough wisdom is there; nor does it seem too different from the wisdom of the great world, begotten by virtue upon the body of experience. The scholar is not forbidden to have experience; he is a man too, and loves and hates and undergoes ambition. At his worst, if the extreme case be considered, he is unable to make his humanity appear; it was weak to begin with, as could have been true of any man, or else he has darkened it and dampened it with cellar growths which have shut him away at last from the sun and from all things that the sun makes clear to normal men. But in the best cases, and happily these are numerous, he has been rendered more sensible, not less so, by the education he has given himself and others. He has become a man of whom other men will not hesitate to ask advice. In the best world we have any right to expect, the scholar and the citizen will freely converse, will freely compare experience, and will freely tell each other how to live. Not that the distinction between them will have disappeared. It is a rich distinction, not to be minimized in any world that wants to keep on being simple and serious. But talking will take place; and all the kinds of knowledge may then lie down with one another.

27

THE JOY OF BEING SERIOUS

Let me say first of all how much I appreciate the privilege of being present as a new year opens at the University of Illinois, where I myself ceased to be a student fifty years ago. And it is more than a privilege—it is a high honor—to be asked to speak on this occasion.

I have decided to do so in the spirit of one who has been a student and a teacher through his entire adult life, and who has never lost interest in the question what a university is—ideally is, for I propose to be shamelessly ideal as I consider with you what difference is made, or might be made, in anybody who spends four years or more in such a place as this. There is no other kind of place in our world where persons are supposed to change so quickly and so much. But what is this change, and can it be defined? Permit me to assume that it can; and permit me, furthermore, to address myself directly to the students, new or old, before me. For it is they in whom the university chiefly lives; it is they who will undergo the change of which I speak. Indeed, I should like to think I was talking to one student—any student—rather than to many. Education is finally an altogether personal affair. Its result can best be measured in the individual who has received and enjoyed it. There are those, properly enough, who ponder what it does for society; and there are those who tell the young that they should study for the sake of others rather than themselves. But I prefer to emphasize the difference that study makes in every separate person who gives himself to its delights. It is a pleasure, and pleasure is not collective. In the long run, of course, society benefits from the happiness of its members, no matter by what means their happiness has been achieved. So it may make little difference from which end we view the subject. I shall stick, however, to the near end, the end in you; I shall ask you to imagine what education might mean, at the utmost, to yourself. Once in Virginia I heard a man from Alabama—a university man, a dean, even—ask this simple question: "If we are here to help others, what are the others here for?" In the spirit of that man I suggest that you are here to help yourself to the best education you can get.

What would that be if it were really the best, as with your assistance, and by your own demand, it might indeed be? For you too must assist, and you must make demands; you must meet at least halfway the education that is coming here to you. You must not only hope you will be changed; you must insist that it happen, and see to it that it does. Changed, of course, for the better, since no one would willingly be changed for the worse. And I mean by changed for the better, changed into somebody who is more like yourself than you are at present. You are here, shall we agree, because you do not yet know who you are. The purpose of education is to give you this knowledge, in whatever form and to whatever extent it may be available. Perhaps it has never been fully available to any man. Perhaps? No, certainly it has never been. For a man who knew everything about himself would know everything about everything else, and there has been no such man. The limits of human knowledge are nowhere so clearly seen as here: the limits, nor the delights either, for in whatever measure we do know ourselves we are happy. And I take it that happiness is the thing we all most deeply desire.

In what, however, does knowing ourselves consist? What did Socrates mean when he said to those who studied with him: Know thyself? He meant, I suspect, the opposite of what we sometimes think he did. He meant: Know in thyself the person thou hast never discovered was there, the person who is identical with all other persons in the end, the ideal, the perfect person insofar as he is knowable. Granted, he is not fully knowable. But education is never serious except when it is trying to dig him out, to bring him to a second birth, to make him think and speak. This person, this self, is the same in all, though in some he is more deeply buried than he is in others. But to the extent that we are human we are more alike than we are different. Good and reasonable people, Abraham Lincoln once said, are the same everywhere. And if this sounds like a superficial remark, consider the profundity of the man who made it. And consider his uniqueness—in which a paradox resides. He was more like everybody else than anybody else was; hence his mystery, which we shall never fathom any more than we shall fathom the mystery of Shakespeare, who knew what everybody has always known, but knew it better, so that it came all the way to the surface in him. The person we all are somehow exposes itself in his poetry, which is why we call it the greatest. We learn from him what we already know, as in every lineament of Lincoln we recognize the person we would be if only we could—could be, that is, so selfless and so simple. Yet we call him complicated too; and he was. Complicated and selfless; and therefore, in his grand outline, simple. The paradox here has many branches, another of which is this: Those who know best that all men are the same are themselves the most individual, the most personal, the most moving and lovable of men.

If happiness is our deepest desire, then we should be altogether serious in our pursuit of it. Not that it is outside of ourselves, so that we must go somewhere to find it. It is here or nowhere. If all men are the same, it is everywhere; yet the germ of it is hidden in each of our souls, and grows there only if we tend it. We and our teachers. Neither Shakespeare nor Lincoln went to college, but who can doubt that they had teachers: Plutarch, Euclid, with themselves assisting? Each of them made a living, and each of them made a life: a life that was different from other lives only in that it was deeper, more copious, more certain of itself. It is life to which education introduces us: merely introduces us, leaving us to become friends in the best way we can. You may be here to help yourself make a living; but if that is your only expectation, some day you may regret that you did not insist on more. Livings can be lost as well as made. Life, as invisible as air, but also as permanent, is surrendered only with our last breath. And by life I mean once more the thing that all men have in common: the immaterial thing that sets them apart in creation from animals and stones.

The thing that lives uniquely in man is his intellect. No other creature has it, and no other object. It is the one thing that makes us equal, if we are. And the greatest men—Lincoln, for instance—know how to believe that we are. They trust their own intellects, and pay to others the supreme compliment of trusting theirs. They have faith in the only instrument we possess—and who else, or what else possesses it?—by which the truth can be discovered. Not the whole truth, but as much of it as possible; and if at last we have to settle for a small amount, it is this amount that distinguishes us. Without apology for a term which embarrasses some teachers, a term which all Americans have been accused of despising, or any rate of fearing, I urge you to look within you for the intellect that is there. To look, and look hard; for as I have said, it hides itself. It seems reluctant to come forth. Who knows, in fact, that it isn't lazy? It is our will that makes it work: our will, our hope, our faith, our preference for being alive. If some of us are weak of will, it does not follow that the intellect itself is absent from us; it is only, with our permission, slumbering. To the extent that it wakes up in us, however, we are happy men. Not at ease, but happy: a more active thing. Thinking is difficult, and even dangerous; nor does it go on by itself, since it is not a little motor we can wind up when we please. It is our very selves, discovering with great labor who we are.

My hope is that each of you will be ambitious for his intellect: will keep it busy by giving it work to do. Or games to play—perhaps that describes its operation better. But whether it works or plays, its own desire, once it has come awake, is to behold the truth—yes, all of it, though it will never satisfy this desire. Yet what of that? Not to have had the desire at all is never to have lived. To have it is to want to know, to want to understand. And when we really mean this, there is no item of knowledge that we dismiss as not for us. The world has plenty of people in it who think that most knowledge is not for them; they have lost their ambition, they have given up, they have become members of an intellectual proletariat which has no longer the right to call itself human. Beware of such membership. Do not give up. Keep inquiring, and remember what you learn. Be suspicious of specialties—even your own, and indeed that most of all. For the specialist can be ignorant of the very field he claims to master. When he is truly its master, the reason must be that he knows other things as well. Short of this, he qualifies as ignorant, and so is a poor pillar to lean upon. The fairly common assumption that we ourselves can afford to be ignorant because somewhere there is somebody who knows the answer—such an assumption builds ignorance fast, and builds it widely. The rapid growth of knowledge we sometimes boast about, seen in this perspective, looks like its opposite: the rapid growth of ignorance. Unchecked, it could become absolute; and that would be disaster. For no one then would trust himself to speculate about the huge central things that matter most. He would have lost the ambition, and to that extent the power, to do so.

To speculate once meant to see, or try to see: to put on spectacles and peer into the dark. With all our knowledge we are still in darkness about many things. Let me encourage you to cultivate cat's eyes, with which you may at least make out the dim, still forms of truth. As undergraduates you are not too young for this. What better time, indeed, to begin? I hope you will astonish your teachers by asking them the hardest questions you can frame, and by waiting for an answer. The answer may be that no one knows. Well, that is where speculation takes its start; and if some teacher does it before your eyes, so much the better for both him and you. The teacher learns by being asked hard questions, and the student by watching him struggle to do them justice. The whole process yields the richest pleasure possible to man. Nothing is more strenuous, and nothing is more fun.

I am asking you, in brief, not only to be serious but to enjoy being serious. To bring ideas in and entertain them royally, for one of them may be the king. To talk, and listen to yourself while you do so as if you listened to a stranger who might be wrong; who might be right. To talk better the next time, and better still the next. To read books—whole books, not articles, not digests—and live with them as if they were your friends; or, it could be, your enemies who will have to be put down. And finally, to listen, for listening is the final art a student practices. If speculation consists of seeing, the very heart of it may consist of seeing, or trying quietly to see, what others see. There are twice as many eyes as men, and this is not too many for the truth. To talk, then, and listen, listen— not merely, either, to human voices, but quite as much to the speech of the world, the speech of things, of animals, of the sky. To listen, and take into yourself whatever you hear. To listen, and to notice; and last of all, if it is in you to do so, to adore. For the final stage of happiness is joy—joy that the world, imperfect though it may be, is at all. Joy has no aim except to let the world be what it is, for better or for worse. It is feared these days that men will destroy the world. But any man has already destroyed it who has decided that it is not worthy of his full and continuous attention. It is older than man, and doubtless will survive him. Certainly it will if in his arrogance he wants to be the only creature on it. That will be the end of him, but not of the world. It is a vast place, difficult to see into, and nobody yet has found its center. Nevertheless, the good student—the serious one, the humble one, the joyful one—will keep on trying.

28

STATEMENT OF PURPOSE:
ON THE DEATH OF JOHN F. KENNEDY

This is a day of mourning on a scale so wide that the imagination can scarcely take it in. The shot fired on Friday was heard around the world, and it was heard almost immediately. The echo of it has grown louder ever since, so that now, at this very hour when we have been called together here, hundreds of millions of people, thousands of miles away, are doing what we do: assembling to ponder an act which none of them—or of us—can fully understand. Nor can we foresee its consequences. And because we cannot, we are afraid. We may not confess this, but it is true.

It is altogether natural that we should be afraid, nor should we be ashamed to say so. For what we fear is a weakness that has appeared in a world of which we all are parts. If those are right who say that the world is one, that all mankind is one, then the weakness is in us too. Certainly on Friday, and through every hour since then, the people of the world have acted like one person. No deed done in our time has affected so many minds, nor affected them so uniformly. In silence or in speech, we have understood one another as we never did before. We have contemplated the same fact: that a weakness is present among us, a great and terrible weakness, and we do not know how soon it can be cured.

The thing most to be feared by men is something in themselves. Twenty-four hundred years ago Socrates defined courage as the knowledge of what is to be feared and what is not to be feared. He meant by what is not to be feared, anything that others may do to us. He meant by what is to be feared, the worst that we can do unto ourselves. And he meant by the worst that we can do unto ourselves, anything we do when we are lacking in the virtue of which as men we are capable. The virtues he prized most highly were wisdom, temperance, and courage; and he said that each of them depended upon the other two. You cannot be wise without temperance and courage; you cannot be temperate without courage and wisdom; and you cannot be courageous without wisdom and self-control.

Now it could be that some of us would apply all of this to one man alone: the assassin of President Kennedy. And certainly he was unwise to the point of madness; he was intemperate to the point of a brutality almost impossible to conceive; and he was cowardly to the point of doing what he did in secret, with an unseen weapon against which there could be no defense. Yet it is not him, nor even a few other individuals of his kind, that most of us now fear. Or if we do, the reason is that we recognize him to have been one of us. Humanity in him completely failed. But we are human also; we are pieces of the world of which he was a piece; and we can wonder—indeed, we do wonder—whether we too may fail. Or whether we already have.

We have failed, of course, if all of us have not become perfect in wisdom, temperance, and courage. And it goes without saying that none of us is perfect, either in those virtues or in the still greater one, charity, which a teacher who came after Socrates, and who is better known to us than he is, told us was the sum of all virtues, as finally it is. All men will always be imperfect; there is no escape from that. But what a difference would be made if every man tried not to be: tried with all of his strength, and with all of his intelligence. Tried each day, beginning now, to be more thoughtful, more loving, rather than less. To be more aware, not less, that other men have souls. To think before he speaks or acts, and to hesitate before he hates. To comprehend as best he can—and this is difficult—the view of men that God must have: none of them good enough, but all of them forgiven. Forgiven because loved, and loved because they are His children, and His children, equal in His sight: more alike than different, and more one than many.

The oneness of the world is what we now are feeling; and fearing, if we doubt that it can soon enough be good, at least within the limits of mankind's capacity. But there are fears and fears, noble and ignoble; and the noblest fear is that which each of us can have lest he himself fall short of being as sensible, as reasonable, as steadfast, and as loving as he can. It is not for others to be these things to the limit of possibility. It is for ourselves, each one of us, whoever, whatever, and wherever we may be.

Goodness begins at home. If it is not there, it may be nowhere. The clearest sign that it is there, the unmistakable sign, is our fear that we ourselves have not been all that we could be. This is a noble fear, another name for which, when hope and faith come with it, is humility. Hope and faith, and not despair, upon which fear can feed until it fills the world. Hope and faith, the final cure of fear; along with knowledge—all of it that we can possess—and charity: the rarest, the most difficult, and still therefore the greatest of these.

29

ROBERT FROST: 1874-1963

The old poet and the young President who on a cold day not quite three years ago did public honor to each other both are gone. If in this present year our loss is double, theirs is single because it is mutual, though in some dimension beyond our sight. Yet mutual in such a case could not mean equal; for one of them had lived much longer than the other and endured much more, both of grief and of joy; he had grown old in grief as he had grown young with joy; so that his view of what has happened, supposing him to have a view, would be all but impossible for him to state.

Robert Frost, in the memory of most living persons, was always an old poet. Of course he was not always old; he had been a boy in California and he had been a young farmer in New Hampshire. Yet it is true that he did not emerge into fame until he was forty; and after that he was given almost fifty years in which to become the massive, sculptured man we all remember. Nor did we ever begrudge him the name of poet because he looked and talked and wrote like one who had been on the earth since time began. Indeed, that was the chief reason we recognized in him the profession of which he was so proud. Good poets die young, but by and large the best ones live long and die late. It is an ancient tradition, honored in our age by the examples not only of Frost but of Hardy and

Yeats. And we ourselves can be a little proud because, in the face of a thousand temptations to do otherwise, we recognized and accepted the tradition.

Most poets in any age put forth theories about life which life itself will disprove. So they are dismissed at last as foolish men, and their profession is dishonored as one that seeks no serious connection with the truth. Dishonored, that is, in the minds of those who do not know what poetry at its best has always been. Poetry at its best is knowledge of the world; and not of the world as it might be, or ought to be, or in some moonstruck moment *maybe* is, but as it plainly and complexly is, beyond the shadows of doubt and falsehood. And it takes time to learn all this: time, and experience, and a deep respect for both; so that a poet is fortunate whom death does not cut down before he begins to see what life is like. Life is like nothing but itself: a simple statement, but it is not too simple for those like Robert Frost who understand that life is finally more important than the cleverest thing we can say about it.

The knowledge of the world Frost share swith us in his poetry is both intricate and obvious, both subtle and self-evident. He is forever probing for mysteries and coming up with things we have always known. He is tentative, yet terribly certain too. He is humorous at precisely the same moment that he is serious; for he knows how little we can know, yet is anxious lest we shall know nothing at all. These poles in him are firmly fixed, and his gaze goes forever back and forth between them. The contraries of which his thought was composed made him unique in his time—unique without being odd. The word for him, in fact, was always wise.

But enough of his philosophy, if that is what it should be called. It came to us in a man who first and last considered himself to be a poet. If the two identities are in some sense inseparable, he himself was always clear about the difference. He made no secret of his interest in the poet's craft, and of his conviction that within whatever limits fate had imposed upon him he was master of this craft. Nor is anything so plain as that he succeeded in his art to a degree that no contemporary matched. One proof of this is his immense reputation; another proof is the cunning which any study of his work discovers: the conscious cunning, along with a deep, natural knowledge of what words are able at their best to do when musically placed. The music in his case is said by some to be scarcely notice-able; but is everywhere, and it is the ultimate explanation of his power.

As for his power, what better proof of this could be than that he wrote, along with many others, these poems?

The Pasture
Into My Own
Storm Fear
Mowing
Revelation
The Tuft of Flowers
Mending Wall
The Death of the Hired Man
Home Burial
The Wood-Pile
The Road Not Taken
An Old Man's Winter Night
The Telephone
Hyla Brook
The Oven Bird
Birches
The Hill Wife
New Hampshire
Two Witches
Fire and Ice
Nothing Gold Can Stay
The Runaway
Stopping by Woods on a Snowy Evening
To Earthward
Good-by and Keep Cold
Spring Pools
Once by the Pacific
Neither Out Far Nor In Deep
Build Soil
The Silken Tent
I Could Give All to Time
The Gift Outright

The Lesson for Today
Directive
A Masque of Reason
A Masque of Mercy
Away!
A Cabin in the Clearing
One More Brevity
In Winter in the Woods Alone

Long as the list is, to many it would be too short. Which only proves the point. Robert Frost thought as a poet, felt as a poet, labored as a poet and triumphed as one.

30

THE HOUSATONIC I KNOW

Really it is just four miles—the stretch of the river from West Cornwall, Connecticut, down to Cornwall Bridge. And let me emphasize the "down," for although I cannot say precisely how many feet the Housatonic falls from village to village, I am convinced that it hurries all the way, foaming around or over rocks, tossing its head even in the smoother stretches, and rounding several great bends at a rate no less than lordly. I used to watch this descent from the windows of trains; now I watch it from the highway as I drive, and this is actually better, for I am closer to the water, which all but hypnotizes me at times, so that I am in danger of colliding with other cars.

What is there about the river here that fascinates me so? I am well aware that other rivers in the world are wider, deeper, and looked down upon by higher hills—great mountains, in fact, with famous names; I know of certain gorges through which wild water plunges and deafeningly roars. And this is not like that. This is mild by comparison; this is a civilized descent, these rapids know their limits and can be counted on to keep them in mind. Yet the river does hurry—no doubt about that—and is wild enough in its way. The point is, I suppose, that it is our way; for it is our river, and the valley it flows through is our valley, and naturally there is none other like it in the world.

It is beautiful throughout its length, not all of which I know, though many an early evening I have walked along the river's broad mouth near Stratford, and seen white sailboats making for the Sound, silently, as if they understood how important it was not to disturb Shakespeare at his work in the theater named both for him and for his birthplace. The serenity of that scene, the depth of the pleasure it gives, has made me at such moments forget the excitement of the four miles below West Cornwall—or, now that I think my way back up the river, other excitements too. The falls at Bull's Bridge, for instance, and the Ten Mile River tumbling in from the west. The wide expanses between there and Kent, and the smooth stretches where races can be rowed. Or beyond West Cornwall the massive cascades at Falls Village; and further up, in Massachusetts, the narrower Housatonic, the meanderer through meadows, the serpentine stream that idles along in apparent ignorance of the dramatic experiences it is soon to have. Certain dramatic experiences it had in the nineteenth century it doubtless never knew it had: the trips along its banks of Herman Melville and Nathaniel Hawthorne, who lived for a while not far from each other in Western Massachusetts, and went on expeditions together like the one to Monument Mountain above Great Barrington, and like the one to Hancock, near Pittsfield, to see the Shakers there. No record survives of their conversation on these days, but it could not have failed, I think, to be of interest, since both were men of genius and they liked to talk—Melville especially, and even the silences of Hawthorne are said to have been impressive.

To speak of such things is to be reminded that the Housatonic Valley contains more than the river which is its original reason for being. The river is never to be put out of mind, for it is beautiful and permanent, and changes only as men change it, with dams and bridges, and here and there canals, and electric plants whose machinery is turned by portions of the stream that have been impounded for the purpose. Man's hope now is that industry will prove to be something with which the river can live as it was created to live. Industry will continue to be indispensable to human life—but human life itself depends on water, air, and earth, and after those upon ideas and laws, upon science and art, upon memory and dream. So the Valley has more in it than a moving stream; it has the signs of civilization, it has the responsibilities of men to one another. The combination is sobering to consider, and a good place to consider it might be Bartholomew's Cobble, that utterly charming hill at Ashley Falls, Massachusetts, where the Housatonic, not very wide at this point, winds its way towards Connecticut. The little limestone hill which it almost encircles has seats upon it where one can sit and realize how ancient the earth is; for the Cobble itself has never changed, it is what it always was, it nourishes the same ferns and mosses that were there not only centuries but millenniums before history began.

Most of the Valley has seen, of course, more changes than the Cobble has. And more changes still are certain to be coming. But there was one great change that never happened. Salisbury, Connecticut, which might have become a Pittsburgh, did not do so because Alexander Lyman Holley, the leading metallurgist of his time, brought the Bessemer process for making steel not to Salisbury, his home town, but to St. Louis, Harrisburg, North Chicago, and— yes, to Pittsburgh itself. Holley never explained this, but legend has it that he loved the Valley too much to blacken it as he knew it would be blackened if the superior ore of Salisbury and its environs were developed to capacity. A worthy legend, deserving to be remembered and repeated. Few persons will ever be in a position to make such a decision as Holley made—assuming that he did make it—but the legend has great value nevertheless. For all of us make decisions sooner or later, and none of us knows for sure that he will never be called upon to make one for the good of all the world.

31

THE NAMES OF GREECE

The glory that was Greece survives, we said, in its place names. The
Orient Express had toiled all night, all day, through Yugoslavia
where no shape or label was familiar, and where the inhabitants,
stolid at best, looked even more so beneath the burden, borne to be
sure with impressive patience, of an anonymity as blank as that of
the muddy slopes over which they drove their spotted cows, sub-
stitutes for oxen.

Then suddenly, on Thursday evening, the train stopped at a little
station in front of which men sat at tables, smiling and talking
while waiters brought them thimblefuls of coffee and towering
glasses of clear water. There were no guards with pistols, and somewhere music played. At last we were in Greece; and there was
brightness in the air. These men knew where they lived, and who
they were; and obviously they liked it, as by instinct we did too.

If we had leaned out to ask them whether we would see Olympus
as we passed they would certainly have known that we would not;
nor Pieria, nor the Vale of Tempe, nor the nearby peninsula where
golden apples still are grown and still are called Hesperides. No,
we were not to see daylight until the plains of Thessaly were behind
us. But after breakfast a high, handsome mountain rose on the
right, and as I stood in the corridor admiring it the porter came

softly to my side and said: "Parnassus," and when I showed my
pleasure showed his pride. Nor had many minutes gone before the
train slowed down for a village and I made out of the letters on
the station sign no less luminous a word than Helicon.

Parnassus, Helicon; and in another hour or so there would be
Thebes. The names said themselves over and over in my ears: a
marvelous music, suitable somehow to a swiftly unfolding landscape brilliant everywhere with its own natural sculpture, and to a
race of women on the hills—slender women, conscious of their
grace—who rode small donkeys debonairly, their feet swinging,
their red blouses and white kerchiefs blowing as they descended to
pick cotton in miniature fields where their dark husbands already
stood, waving at the train as if it were something that did not pass
them every morning.

So here we were. And every day after this, for the more than two
weeks that we had in Greece, I repeated my discovery: its glory is its
names—of places and of persons, on earth or in the sky. For the
incomparable people who once lived here had a myth-making
power, which is to say a poetic power, such as no other people has
ever had, unless indeed the ancient Hebrews, with their Hebron
and their Jordan, their Moses and their David, had as much. But
surely even then it cannot be true, I thought, that any other country,
big or little, has given the world so many magic words to say, so
many actions to remember. The words and the actions, the names
and the legends, went together in the great Greece that has disappeared; they danced as one in a deeply colored world shot through
with mind that penetrated everywhere, delighting in all forms of
thought and feeling.

And yet great Greece has never disappeared, since if nothing else
the names it lived with have survived. Hephaestus, for example,
my favorite among its gods, who limped at his forge because Zeus
in a fit of anger once threw him down from Olympus and he broke
his left leg falling "on Lemnos, the Aegean isle," has not been
forgotten. I have two evidences for this. One afternoon in Athens
we were walking through a narrow street which all at once grew
narrower still, and we became aware of blacksmith shops on both
sides of us: dark caves of stone in which hammers rang and white
fire blazed in forges kept alive by huge hand-operated bellows.

Iron and bronze were being worked by men in leather aprons, and I thought of sundry gold objects that the lame smith-god had fashioned for the heroes and gods: Achilles' shield, for instance, and the cups from which the Olympians drank their nectar. The companions of the divine artificer laughed at his lameness, Homer tells us; probably they despised him because he worked with his hands, or because he worked at all. And to be sure he was swarthy as well as lame, and closer to the ground than beautiful cruel Apollo or the implacable Aphrodite with her snow-white arms and shoulders (his own wife, in fact, and she was untrue to him with Ares, god of war; but that is another story). Well, I glanced up to see where we were so that we could come this way again, and the sign said, of all things, "Hephaestus Street." I learned the next day that we had been at the bottom of the north slope of the hill on which the temple of Hephaestus stands overlooking the Agora—and so has stood for two millenniums; an archaeologist assured me that the name was no coincidence.

Then in Arcadia, when our driver was crossing a dizzy range of mountains and the radiator sprang a serious leak, we found it necessary to stop in a village where the blacksmith was reputed to be skillful with solder. He was indeed, and we worked the bellows for him while the entire population gathered to watch both him and us—us, certainly, for we were strangers and their curiosity about us was at least as strong as the sense of hospitality which moved them to bring us chairs and a little table to eat our lunch on in the street. The smith, who would not proceed with the mending until he had shared his own lunch with the driver, at last got down to work; and he did it so well that in admiration I said to him the one word I considered relevant: "Hephaestus." His teeth gleamed as he tapped his chest, nodding energetically, and corrected my accent: "Eéphestos!" This was as good as being in Arcadia, not many miles north of Sparta where Helen lived (except for ten years) with Menelaus; or northwest of sandy Pylos, where young Telemachus came in his chariot to ask what Nestor knew of his father Odysseus; or southwest of Mycenae where Agamemnon once was king of men. As good, I say, as being in Arcadia, though I saw nothing of its most famous inhabitant, goat-foot Pan.

Pan is not there, and of course in Sparta there is no visible suggestions of Leda whose experience with an immortal swan produced Helen, the most beautiful of women. Even no trace is there of the dour folk whose only god was discipline, and who won their fatal war with Athens. Thucydides' prediction about them has long since come true; possessing no ideas and no art, they have utterly disappeared; so the Athenians with their intellectual goddess and their innumerable poets and philosophers have at last the perfect revenge: their city is the metropolis and capital of living Greece.

Athens itself is certainly alive. In fact we sometimes thought it too much so; it seemed feverish and intense, with dust blowing in the streets and a thousand drivers doing their demon best to run us down. Doubtless it was thus when Socrates stood calmly in the Stoa of Zeus and infuriated the sophists who were no cleverer than he and infinitely less serious. It is always dangerous to be serious in the pursuit of truth, and most men then as well as now avoided the kind of death their master died. Most men in Athens now are talkers. And what talkers! Constitution Square boils and buzzes with them every evening before the late dinner the Athenians like. So far as I know it is the biggest area on earth devoted entirely to coffee and conversation, and tonguewise it is the busiest. Politics or love, money or religion—no matter what the theme, the eloquence (with gestures) is enormous. Perhaps they never truly argue, meeting point with point; I have read somewhere that each of them desires only to erect a taller column of words than his neighbor can, and as such more admirable; and if like children's blocks they all topple at last, no one especially cares, for bright new piles, false at the worst, specious at the best, can easily rise again.

Athens is not so much a city as a vast, overgrown town. I was told in the Chamber of Commerce that every Greek now wants to live there, and that too many have come. Certainly the view from Lycabettus or the Acropolis is of white buildings flowing as far as one can see like foam among the hills. But nowhere is there the appearance of power, of sumptuous majesty, such as even the meaner streets of Rome somehow support. The greatness of this Greece was long ago; it departed in the Dark and Middle Ages either east to Constantinople or west to the city of the seven hills.

Athens degenerated into a village at the feet of the Acropolis; and if it is large again, it is still a village. Only monuments—the Parthenon on high, the temples of Olympian Zeus and Hephaestus lower down—remain to prove how measureless the might of Athens was in its own bit of time. Its wealth then, and its profundity of wit—its prowess in myth, in idea, in the bestowing of imperishable names—the mystery of these is deeper than any ever guarded at Eleusis, today a suburb surrounded by soap factories. To go there by the Sacred Way is to end up among ruins—scattered fragments of columns such as at last become routine for tourists in Greece. The rubble is convincing, but it is also heartbreaking. So much glory, so utterly gone.

The mountains and the plains are as stunning as ever; but at Delphi, say, where are the votaries for whom the Castalian Spring is an effective rite before they proceed to the oracle? Where is the Pythoness, and where is the gold that once lay heaped in the treasuries? Where is the slave who struggles to arrive and touch this holy ground so that henceforth he may be forever free? Where is the sense that Delphi keeps the secret, unknown to even the wisest city-states, of permanent peace? Eagles still soar between the summit of Parnassus and the Corinthian Gulf, but they look down upon a desert of human history. So at Olympia, across the Gulf: cyclopean drums of fallen columns lie everywhere among huge trees, but where are the brilliant athletes who for a thousand years competed here for laurel and the praise of poets? The river whose floods have carved away the stadium— "Return, Alpheus, the dread voice is past that shrunk thy streams"—meanders through gravel with no memory of the shouts and prayers it used to overhear. At Mycenae the tombs of Agamemnon and Clytemnestra—or, some say, of Perseus and Andromeda—are beehive holes in little hills from those tops there is nothing to see but the burnt tops of bigger mountains, or in one direction the Argive plain where it is quite impossible even to imagine the chariot of Agamemnon bearing him to his bloody death at the hands of Clytemnestra and her paramour. How can Cassandra, princess and prophetess, be ever so faintly made out as she stands behind her new master, shrieking because she knows he will be murdered? And where is Pelops' line for whom the peninsula is named—Atreus and Thyestes, barbarous brothers whose sons still hate each other?

Orestes went wandering from here pursued by the Furies because he had killed his mother; but we did not see him at Delphi, clinging to the base of Apollo's statue, nor in Athens was it thinkable that the Areopagus ever witnessed the trial by which at last he was acquitted. So up in Thebes, the town we passed through on the train, there was no feeblest vestige of the place where Oedipus discovered his guilt and Jocasta hanged herself; of the gates—there are no gates—beyond which Polyneices and Eteocles slew each other, and Antigone was forbidden to bury her brother's body; or of the still older city built by Cadmus, where Zeus visited Semele in a bolt of lightning and Pentheus was torn to pieces by Agave, who thought him a beast and herself inspired. Outside the city Cithaeron still heaves its slopes on one of which the infant Oedipus was exposed to die, and on toward Delphi there is the place in the mountains where three roads meet and Laius, angrily contesting the right of way, was killed by his accursed son. But whether here or off in rocky Ithaca which once awaited its returning lord, or north by Olympus, or east among the shining Cyclades that still appear to revolve about Delos, their sacred center, the glory lives only in the sound of syllables a modern Greek, it sometimes seems, outrageously mispronounces.

Not that the modern Greek is unworthy of full praise. For one thing he has kept the names, and is proud to note that we come five thousand miles to hear them spoken. But better yet, he is hospitable and kind, and his ever-present smile is as sweet as it could be if he were richer than he is. He is certainly poor; yet among the valleys of Arcadia—much deeper and grander than I had thought—he looks at you as you pass and returns your greeting in triple measure. So does his wife—often she is beautiful, with serious dark eyes—as she jogs home at sunset on her donkey from the fields. And so do his children, who may bring you flowers to smell (perhaps also to buy), but who in any case will stare at you with a solemn consuming curiosity, as if it still were true that you could be a god come through their village in disguise. All of them are courteous, and concerned about your comfort. I shall not forget the little boy in Heraklion, chief port of Crete, who as I stood wearily in front of our hotel, waiting for the bags to come down, tapped me on the shoulder and showed me a rickety chair he had dragged from some doorway for my use. Neither shall I forget the mistake I made in offering him a drachma. He shook his head and grinned. It had been a ritual, not a transaction.

We had gone to Crete, of course, to see the palace at Cnossus. Yet, splendid as it is (or was), I shall keep uppermost in mind not only this boy but an ancient couple further inland at whose tavern our driver stopped so that we could drink country wine. I say tavern; it was only their small house, by a bridge that crossed a dry stream under a gigantic plane tree which our host assured us was five hundred years old. He had lost one eye, and so had his yellow cat; and his wife hobbled on feet that evidently hurt her as she set out, in addition to the wine, cups of bitter coffee and the inevitable tumblers of water, then after that a plate of veal deliciously soaked in the juices of onions and red peppers. The two of them stood and watched us enjoy what may in fact have been their lunch. And they did accept some drachmas in return. But we could not have paid for their beaming faces as they bowed us out to the car, whose driver stopped twice on the way back to Heraklion, once to pick a bunch of grapes from a vineyard he heard us praising, and again to tell us (in terrible English) how he had been a captain of Partisans resisting the Germans between 1941 and 1945, and how on this very bridge—he got out to show us, pointing down, an enemy general had been thrown into the river. He was happy to conduct us to the Labyrinth of Minos, but he insisted too that we see how the Greeks of his time had made history. So they had, and so they will forever, those charming people with the white teeth who know so well the names of their predecessors.

32

HOW PRAISE A WORLD
THAT WILL NOT LAST?

Governor King, President Weigle, members and friends of this College, I consider it a great honor to have been asked to speak on the occasion of the 275th anniversary of the College. Two-hundred-and-seventy-five years is a long time to survive. St. John's College more than survives, it flourishes. That I think is all that needs to be said about the College as of this moment; it flourishes and the evidence is everywhere.

When I was asked by Dean Darkey to come today and address you, I wrote him as an old friend as well as a dean whom I respected and asked him if he had any suggestions about what I should talk about. Being a true dean, he answered my question seriously. He didn't say, "oh, anything you like." He said, "I've often heard you talk about the act and the art of praise. I think I agree with you," he said, "that praise is the noblest act of man, and if you have anything that you want to praise, or any person you want to praise, this might be a time to do it." I said yes, of course, I would come and talk about praise. And I would even do some praising. I would praise everything and everybody. I would have the nerve to praise the world.

For the world we live in must be praised; or its maker must, for it is he that we praise when we are serious. The greatest of all songs are the Psalms, which are songs of praise.

> The heavens declare the glory of God; and the
> firmament sheweth his handywork.

They are songs in praise of things—of stars, mountains, trees—
but only as these things testify to the power and beauty of their
creator's mind, than which there is nothing more lovable or fearful
in the universe we think we know. It is the presence among us of
this mind that causes us to tremble, now in terror, now with joy.
The Psalmist cried over and over: Praise ye the Lord, and never
tired of doing so, as witness the song he numbered 148, which still
was not the last one that he sang:

> Praise ye the Lord. Praise the Lord from the heavens:
>   praise him in the heights.
> Praise ye him, all his angels; praise ye him, all his hosts.
> Praise ye him, sun and moon; praise him, all ye stars of
>   light.
> Praise him, ye heavens of heavens, and ye waters that be
>   above the heavens.
> Let them praise the name of the Lord; for he commanded,
>   and they were created.
> He hath also stablished them for ever and ever; he hath
>   made a decree which shall not pass.
> Praise the Lord from the earth, ye dragons, and all deeps;
> Fire, and hail; snow, and vapour; stormy wind fulfilling
>   his word;
> Mountains, and all hills; fruitful trees, and all cedars;
> Beasts, and all cattle; creeping things, and flying fowls;
> Kings of the earth, and all people; princes and all judges
>   of the earth;
> Both young men, and maidens; old men, and children;
> Let them praise the name of the Lord; for his name alone
>   is excellent; his glory is above the earth and heaven.
> Praise ye the Lord.

The things he made, the Psalmist sings, he made for ever and
ever. The world he fashioned was, is, and will be a world without
end. Unthinkable that it should cease. Not only the power and

beauty of the Lord, but his lastingness—perhaps that was his most stunning attribute, since it assured us that the world we walk on is lasting too. We shall not last, for we are grass, we wither and blow away; but the world itself—how can that ever be a thing, a place, that is not?

For centuries, for millenniums, we did not ask this question; or if we did, we thought we knew the answer. We kept on praising as best we could the universe and him who made it. Our poetry when it was serious had no other subject, though often enough the subject was not named as I am naming it now. It had its variations, its disguises; truth at times delights in indirection and even dares at special moments to be difficult. Yet there was never a time when we knew how to imagine the world's coming to an end—literally that, with no trace of it left anywhere. Whereas we now are haunted by this thought; as I was, for example, a few years ago when I wrote a poem called "So Fair A World It Was":

> So fair a world it was,
> So far away in the dark, the dark,
> Yet lighted, oh, so well, so well:
> Water and land,
> So clear, so sweet;
> So fair, it should have been forever.

> And would have been, and would have been,
> If—what?
> Be still. But what?
> Keep quiet, child. So fair it was
> The memory is like a death
> That dies again; that dies again.

The dialogue may be understood as taking place between two intelligences so far removed from Earth that the rumor of its extinction comes faintly yet clearly, as echoes travel; but those intelligences are near enough to have witnessed the beauty that is gone. The suggestion is of physical catastrophe; nothing less than the total disappearance of a planet. The fear does not always take this form. It is more likely to be the fear that life and thought will cease, so that no mind will exist to know the world that still is there—an equivalent catastrophe, perhaps, but at least a different one, though in fact it might be the more ghastly of the two.

The strange thing is that at the same time with this poem, or very near the same time, I was writing a psalm of my own which contained no hint of catastrophe.

> Praise Orion and the Great Bear,
> Praise icy Sirius so burning blue,
> Praise the slow dawn, but then the razor rim
> Of sun that in another hour
> Cannot be looked at lest it blind you; praise
> Mountain tops, praise valleys, praise the silver
> Streams that circle towns; praise people's houses;
> Praise sitting cats that wait for doors to open;
> Praise running dogs; praise women, men;
> Praise little boys who think their fathers perfect;
> Praise fathers who believe their Father perfect;
> Praise him because he is, because he has
> His being where no eye, no ear can follow,
> No mind say whence or whither,
> Yet he is, and nothing else is
> Save as witness to his wonder,
> Save as hungering to praise him—
> Let all things, then, great or little,
> Praise him, praise him
> Without end.

How explain this inconsistency in me, except by saying that it is in others too: in all of us, no matter who we are or what we think we know? Or am I correct in saying all of us? Quite possibly the young are altogether singleminded here: the young, whose generation is the first one born into a world that wonders whether it will endure. Earlier generations had no such problem. Their members knew that the world was here to stay—nothing more simple, nothing more certain. Regardless of what they felt or did, the earth and the heavens above it would survive them. To the extent that no one can wholly believe this any more, those of us who can remember having believed it once are likely to find our minds curiously mixed: at one moment yes, at another no. But with the young this may not be true; and so their minds are single; they do not look ahead because there is nothing to see, and they do not look behind because only ruins—ghosts of worlds—are there; they look at the present moment, and have their own secret way of penetrating its mysteries, which seem to be for them alone.

If, however, we are mixed of mind we oscillate between belief and despair: more often than not, I suspect, believing as we did before that the foundations of being are somehow firm. And better yet, bound to remain so. For there is something in the mind that cannot be satisfied with less than the prospect of infinite duration, whether it be of life, or the earth, or the stars, or simply everything. Let me confess at any rate that this is true for me. I hear that the earth is six billion years old, and that is not enough for me. I hear that it has a few billion years ahead of it, and I shudder at the thought that they are not innumerable. There was a queer comfort for me in a chance remark I once heard Harlow Shapley make—a parenthetical remark, for he was really interested in something else—concerning the age of the earth. He said it was roughly as old as the great stars in Orion, compared to which I had always assumed that our planet was a newcomer in the universe. Childishly I was proud and pleased, though I did not risk my happiness by asking him how long he thought either we or Orion would last: I was afraid he knew, and could name the term.

The terror of being lost in the ocean of time is something like another terror to which many of us have grown accustomed. The size of the universe has become so unimaginable, what with the discovery of galaxies too distant and too numerous even to count, that space can be a terror too, particularly if we hold on to the notion that what is there was once created, and still is kept in view by an intelligence whose location it is no longer possible to have sensible ideas about. Yet how to abandon all thought of that intelligence, even though we cannot even frame questions of who, and what, and where? So I said once in a poem I called "The God of Galaxies."

> The god of galaxies has more to govern
> Than the first men imagined, when one mountain
> Trumpeted his anger, and one rainbow,
> Red in the east, restored them to his love.

One earth it was, with big and lesser torches,
And stars by night for candles. And he spoke
To single persons, sitting in their tents.

Now streams of worlds, now powdery great whirlwinds
Of universes far enough away
To seem but fog-wisps in a bank of night
So measureless the mind can sicken, trying—
Now seas of darkness, shoreless, on and on
Encircled by themselves, yet washing farther
Than the last triple sun, revolving, shows.

The god of galaxies—how shall we praise him?
For so we must, or wither. Yet that word
Of words? And where to send it, on which night
Of winter stars, of summer, or by autumn
In the first evening of the Pleiades?
The god of galaxies, of burning gases,
May have forgotten Leo and the Bull.

But God remembers, and is everywhere.
He even is the void, where nothing shines.
He is the absence of his own reflection
In the deep gulf; he is the dusky cinder
Of pure fire in its prime; he is the place
Prepared for hugest planets; black idea,
Brooding between fierce poles he keeps apart.

Those altitudes and oceans, though, with islands
Drifting, blown immense as by a wind,
And yet no wind; and not one blazing coast
Where thought could live, could listen—of, what word
Of words? Let us consider it in terror,
And say it without voice. Praise universes
Numberless. Praise all of them. Praise Him.

The two terrors differ in one important respect: if there is too much space, there is too little time, and the second terror is probably worse than the first. But both are at times intolerable to any mind (always excepting the young), and both of them therefore breed inconsistencies in us. In spite of what we think we know we go on assuming an intelligible cosmos, just as we go on assuming that there is all the time in the world—an ancient phrase that comes in patly here. In other words, we go on writing psalms, and in some of them we betray our faith that the world will last indefinitely long; will forever and ever be there for minds to measure and for souls to love. At least there are moments when we do this, in between moments when we listen to the prophets and accept their words of doom. For the time being—another ancient phrase—this is our predicament. And, it may be, this is our distinction.

How then shall we praise a world that may not last? What would be praiseworthy about it if it were unable to endure? But say it may last. What then? Shall we have been silent on the entire subject? With half our minds could we not have speculated upon the possibility that the world is durable after all, and infinitely so? My final poem, written incidentally for this occasion, commences there.

> How praise a world that will not be
> Forever? Stillness then. Time
> Sleeping, never to wake. No prince's
> Kiss. No prince. Praise? Even
> The echo of it dies, even
> Memory, in the last brain
> That loved it, withers away, and mind
> Not even dozes, being done
> With work that mattered not at all.
> How then praise nothing?
>   Yet that day
> Has never dawned. Here is the world
> So beautiful, being old, so
> Mindful of its maker—what
> Of him when that day comes—you say
> It must—what then of him, and of this
> Place so crowded with his creatures—
> With us all—oh, praise the time
> That's left, praise here and now, praise
> Him that by his own sweet will
> May suddenly remake the world
> Forever, ever, ever, ever.

PRINCIPAL PROSE WORKS BY MARK VAN DOREN: A CHECKLIST

Henry David Thoreau. Boston: Houghton Mifflin Company, 1916; New York: Russell-Russell, 1961.

The Poetry of John Dryden. New York: Harcourt, Brace & Howe, 1920; Cambridge: The Minority Press, 1931; New York: H. Holt & Co., 1946; also various paperback editions.

Edwin Arlington Robinson. New York: The Literary Guild of America, 1927.

Shakespeare. New York: H. Holt & Co., 1939; Anchor Paperback, various editions.

The Private Reader. New York: H. Holt & Co., 1942; reprint ed. by Kraus, 1968.

Liberal Education. New York: H. Holt & Co., 1943; many reprintings.

The Noble Voice: A Study of Ten Great Poems. New York: H. Holt & Co., 1946; various paperback editions.

Nathaniel Hawthorne. American Men of Letters Series. New York: W. Sloan Associates, 1949; reprinted frequently in Morrow Paperback.

Don Quixote's Profession. Drawings by Joseph Low, The Walter Turner Candler Lectures for 1956-1957 at Emory University. New York: Columbia University Press, 1958.

The Autobiography of Mark Van Doren. New York: Harcourt, Brace and Co., 1958; reprint ed. Westport, Conn.: Greenwood Press, 1968.

The Happy Critic. New York: Hill & Wang, 1961; reprinted in paperback in U.S. and England.

The Dialogues of Archibald MacLeish and Mark Van Doren, edited by Warren Bush. New York: E. P. Dutton, 1964.

The Book of Praise: Dialogues between Mark Van Doren & Maurice Samuel. In the Beginning, Love: Dialogues on the Bible, edited by Edith Samuel. New York: John Day Company, 1973. Also, by the same authors, **The Book of Psalms.**

A BIBLIOGRAPHIC CHECKLIST OF SELECTED INTRODUCTIONS, PREFACES, AND MISCELLANEOUS BOOKS EDITED OR WITH PROSE CONTRIBUTIONS BY MARK VAN DOREN

Samuel Sewall's Diary. Edited with preface by Mark Van Doren. New York: Mary, Masius, 1927.

Journey to the Land of Eden and Other Papers by William Byrd. Edited with preface by Mark Van Doren. New York: Macy, Masius, 1928.

Travels of William Bartram. Edited by Mark Van Doren. New York: Macy, Masius, 1928.

Correspondence of Aaron Burr and His Daughter Theodosia. Edited by Mark Van Doren. New York: Covici, Friede, 1929.

Faust—A Tragedy by W. von Goethe. Translated by Alice Raphael. Introduction by Mark Van Doren. New York: Cape and Smith, 1930.

The Oregon Trail by Francis Parkman. Introduction by Mark Van Doren. New York: Rhinehard and Co., 1931.

The Oxford Book of American Prose. Chosen and edited with a preface by Mark Van Doren. London: Oxford University Press, 1932.

Letters of Emily Dickinson. Edited by Mabel Loomis Todd. With an introduction by Mark Van Doren. Cleveland: World Publishing Co., 1943.

Invitation to Learning. Notes to the Books. A pamphlet by Mark Van Doren. 1940-1942. New York: Columbia Broadcasting System, 1940-1944.

New Invitation to Learning (1942-1944). Edited by Mark Van Doren. New York: Columbia Broadcasting System, 1940-1944.

Night of the Summer Solstice. Russian Short Stores. Selected, with preface by Mark Van Doren. New York: Henry Holt, 1943.

Walt Whitman—Poems and Prose. The Portable Whitman. Edited with essay by Mark Van Doren. New York: Viking, 1945.

The Portable Emerson. Edited with Introduction by Mark Van Doren. New York: Viking, 1946.

Letters of Ezra Pound. Edited by D. D. Paige. With preface by Mark Van Doren. New York: Harcourt Brace and Co., 1950.

William Wordsworth: Selected Poetry. Edited and introduction by Mark Van Doren. New York: Modern Library, 1950.

The Best of Hawthorne. Edited by Mark Van Doren. New York: Ronald Press, 1951.

Selected Letters of William Cowper. Edited and introduction by Mark Van Doren. New York: Farrar, Straus, and Young, 1951.

Return to Ithaca: The Odyssey Retold as Modern Novel by Eyvind Johnson. Preface by Mark Van Doren. London: Thames and Hudson, 1957.

Man's Right to Knowledge and the Free Use Thereof. Collected Aphorisms and Quotations by Mark Van Doren. New York: Columbia University Press, 1954.

The World of Odysseus by M. I. Einlay. With preface by Mark Van Doren. New York: Viking, 1954.

Dictionary of Early English. Edited by Joseph T. Shipley. With short foreword by Mark Van Doren. New York: The Philosophical Library of New York, 1955.

Dictionary of American Proverbs. Edited by David Kim. With preface by Mark Van Doren. New York: Philosophical Library of New York, 1955.

Two Years Before the Mast by Richard Henry Dana. Introduction by Mark Van Doren. New York: Bantam Books, 1959.

Selected Poems of Thomas Merton. Introduction by Mark Van Doren. New York: New Directions, 1959.

Washington Square, by Henry James. Introduction by Mark Van Doren. New York: Bantam Books, 1959.

Four Poets. Edited by Cameron Allen. Essay by Mark Van Doren on Thomas Hardy. Baltimore, Md.: Johns Hopkins University Press, 1959.

Adventures of the Mind, by Richard Thruelson and John Kobler. Preface by Mark Van Doren. New York: Knopf, 1959.

William Barnes by William Turner Levy. Short foreword by Mark Van Doren. London: Longmans (Dorchester) Ltd., 1960.

Carl Sandburg—Harvest Poems, 1910-1960. With an introduction by Mark Van Doren. New York: Harcourt, Brace and World, 1960.

What's a College For? Essay on Liberal Education by Mark Van Doren. Washington, D.C.: Public Affairs Press, 1961.

Personal Integrity. Edited by William M. Schutte and Erwin R. Steinberg. With essay "Know What You Want" by Mark Van Doren. New York: W. W. Norton and Co., 1961.

A Portion of That Field. Essay on Poems of Civil War by Mark Van Doren and others. Centennial of the Burial of Lincoln. Urbana, Ill.: University of Illinois Press, 1967.

INDEX

About the Editor

WILLIAM CLAIRE was the founding editor and publisher of *Voyages* and is currently the director of the Washington D.C. office of the State Universities of New York. His previous books include *Publishing in the West: Allan Swallow* and a collection of poems, *Strange Coherence of Our Dreams.*

Recent Titles in
Contributions in American Studies
Series Editor: *Robert H. Walker*

Hemispheric Perspectives on the United States: Papers from the New World Conference
Joseph S. Tulchin, editor, with the assistance of Maria A. Leal

"Ezra Pound Speaking": Radio Speeches of World War II
Leonard W. Doob, editor

The Supreme Court: Myth and Reality
Arthur Selwyn Miller

Television Fraud: The History and Implications of the Quiz Show Scandals
Kent Anderson

Menace in the West: The Rise of French Anti-Americanism in Modern Times
David Strauss

Social Change and Fundamental Law: America's Evolving Constitution
Arthur Selwyn Miller

American Character and Culture in a Changing World: Some Twentieth-Century Perspectives
John A. Hague, editor

Olmsted South: Old South Critic/New South Planner
Dana F. White and Victor A. Kramer, editors

In the Trough of the Sea: Selected American Sea-Deliverance Narratives, 1610-1766
Donald P. Wharton, editor

Aaron Burr and the American Literary Imagination
Charles J. Nolan, Jr.

The Popular Mood of Pre-Civil War America
Lewis O. Saum